# Hope

# Hope

## *Promise, Possibility, and Fulfillment*

Edited by RICHARD LENNAN and
NANCY PINEDA-MADRID

Paulist Press
New York / Mahwah, NJ

Unless otherwise noted, Scripture quotations contained herein are from the *New Revised Standard Version: Catholic Edition* (Copyright 1989 and 1993, Division of Christian Education of the National Council of the Churches of Christ in the United States of America). Used by permission. All rights reserved.

Unless otherwise noted, all references to the documents of the Second Vatican Council are taken from Austin P. Flannery (ed.), *The Documents of Vatican II*, new rev. ed. (Northport NY: Costello Publishing Company, 1996).

Cover image by marekuliasz/Shutterstock.com
Cover design by Sharyn Banks
Book design by Lynn Else

Library of Congress Cataloging-in-Publication Data

Hope : promise, possibility, and fulfillment / edited by Richard Lennan and Nancy Pineda-Madrid.
    pages cm
Includes bibliographical references and indexes.
ISBN 978-0-8091-4777-9 (alk. paper) — ISBN 978-1-58768-295-7
    1. Hope—Religious aspects—Catholic Church. I. Lennan, Richard, editor of compilation.
BV4638.H68 2013
234`.25—dc23

2013022736

ISBN 978-0-8091-4777-9 (paperback)
ISBN 978-1-58768-295-7 (e-book)

Published by Paulist Press
997 Macarthur Boulevard
Mahwah, New Jersey 07430

www.paulistpress.com

Printed and bound in the
United States of America

*To the students of the School of Theology and Ministry at Boston College—past, present, and future.*

# Contents

# Contents

## III. Sustaining Hope

## IV. Living Hope

# Acknowledgments

The editors would like to thank our colleagues in the School of Theology and Ministry at Boston College, the contributors to this volume, for their enthusiastic participation in the development of this book: their willingness to be a part of the project and the wisdom displayed in their chapters have encouraged our hope.

Particular thanks is due to Kevin Dowd, a doctoral student at Boston College, who acted as assistant to the editors; the final form of the book has benefited immeasurably from Kevin's skills. Kevin's painstaking care in reviewing drafts of the chapters, no less than the constancy of his commitment to the project, is much appreciated.

The progress of the book to its final form was enhanced greatly by the insights of a number of generous reviewers, who read the entire manuscript and came together with the editors to offer suggestions for its refinement. The editors are most grateful to these readers: Sarah Attwood, Gustavo Morello, SJ, Rev. Jack O'Brien, Marina Pastrana, Jacqueline Regan, and Jean Ponder Soto.

The editors are also most appreciative of the support for the book that has come from Paulist Press, especially Mark-David Janus, CSP, and Donna Crilly.

# Introduction

Every age bears experiences that spotlight hope. Ours is no different. Thus, hope played a starring role in the U.S. presidential election in 2008. Barack Obama's choice of hope as a central motif for his campaign became emblematic in the well-known poster featuring his image underscored simply by "Hope," and emblematic in his political autobiography, *The Audacity of Hope* (2006). This campaign came to express the promise and excitement that the election of the first African American president generated. His election invited U.S. citizens to see themselves differently, as a people more willing to recognize and place our trust in a person of color. For some voters, the Obama campaign captured a sense of dissatisfaction with the prevailing models of leadership and style of politics. For others, it promoted the desire for a future rich with a sense of possibility, for a society transformed for the benefit of more than a select few. Hope, in short, crystallized a longing for life-giving change.

In 2010, hope brought the longest underground nightmare in history to an end when thirty-three Chilean miners, trapped for more than two months, were rescued. Some 700,000 tons of rock collapsed above them and seventeen days passed before anyone knew whether they were still alive. Their survival and rescue depended upon the hope they placed in their shift foreman, Luis Urzua, who kept their spirits up and strictly rationed food and supplies so as to increase the possibility of their rescue. He cultivated hope in the miners by encouraging their endurance and unity. After sixty-nine days, rescuers raised up the miners through a small shaft plunging over 2,000 feet below the earth's surface. Hope guided the imagination of the miners themselves, the rescuers on the surface, and the many others who offered prayers. Without a strong sense of hope this nightmare could have ended very differently.

If these great events gave witness to the prevalence and power of hope, there are counter-witnesses as well. Many challenges we face at the dawn of the twenty-first century take us once again to the precipice of despair, where hope is our greatest ally but is often difficult to find and maintain. We have witnessed the horror of the 9/11 attacks, the rise of mass killings in schools and other public places, the calamity of Hurricane Katrina, the worst economic downturn since the great 1929 stock market crash, the horrific earthquake in Haiti, and many other disasters that stemmed either from nature, human actions, or a combination of both. Each of these pushes us to ask: Is there hope for our world? In whom do we place our hope?

This book addresses both the possibility that hope offers and the capacity of hope to respond to the challenges that life presents to us all. What is particular to this book is that it presents a theology of hope. This means that this book defines hope in relation to the revelation of God in Jesus Christ and the Holy Spirit. It locates *hope* in relation to *faith* and *love*, thus deepening our understanding of the three great pillars of the Christian life. It also establishes a dialogue between the Christian tradition and the concrete circumstances of contemporary society in order to show the difference that hope can make.

Each of the authors represented in this book is a member of the faculty of the School of Theology and Ministry at Boston College. As part of the faculty, the authors contribute to the preparation of women and men for pastoral ministry in the church, including the service of working as theologians, who help others to reflect on the implications of faith. The authors of the essays in this book encompass the full range of theological disciplines: biblical studies, practical theology, liturgical theology, moral theology, historical theology, and systematic theology. As working theologians, the authors bring to this book a rich experience of involvement in the life of the church in the present-day world, as well as a deep familiarity with contemporary theology. The essays in this book distill those resources into accessible reflections on the myriad dimensions of hope. The authors conferred together to plan their chapters, review drafts of each other's work, and highlight connections among the various chapters in order to construct from their different disciplines an integrated theology of hope.

Each section of the book draws out the implications of a particular aspect of hope. The first section, Grounding Hope, explores two notions that form the subtitle of Colleen Griffith's essay, "Christian Hope: A Grace and a Choice." In speaking of hope as a grace/gift, Griffith highlights the connection between hope and faith in the God revealed in Jesus Christ and the Holy Spirit, the God who enables more than we could even dare to imagine. In speaking of hope as a choice, Griffith reminds us that, unlike machines, we do not operate according to a program: we are free to choose how we will respond to life, including life's difficulties. The Spirit, however, draws us to hope, to be people engaged with God and with the world as it is. In detailing the implications of viewing hope as gift and choice, Griffith also sketches the contours of a spirituality of hope. Dominic Doyle's essay, "'A Future, Difficult, Yet Possible Good': Defining Christian Hope," extends Griffith's framework by taking up a notion from the great medieval theologian, St. Thomas Aquinas: hope as the choice to pursue a good that is difficult to attain. Doyle asks why we would embrace such a challenge: the answer lies in understanding hope in relation to faith and love, which also helps to distinguish hope from both presumption and despair.

The next two essays in the opening set explore hope in relation to the life of the church. First, Thomas Stegman's "'That You May Abound in Hope': St. Paul and Hope" reviews how St. Paul talked about hope to the earliest Christian communities. Here, the emphasis is again on both the gift—what God has enabled through Jesus Christ, in whom we are called to a life of discipleship—as well as the choice—how are we to live in response to what God has begun in us through Christ. Richard Lennan's "The Church: Got Hope?" looks at how we can construe the relationship between the church and hope by understanding the church as a theological reality, at the heart of which is the life of the Spirit. Lennan acknowledges, however, the ways in which the church can represent an obstacle to hope, a circumstance that looms large in the wake of the tragedy that is clerical sexual abuse. He suggests that we might reclaim the connection between the church and hope by a fresh retrieval of the ancient marks of the church: the church as one, holy, catholic, and apostolic.

The second section of this book, Nurturing Hope, begins with the disciples on the road to Emmaus in Christopher Matthews' essay, "'We

Had Hoped…': The Fragility of Hope in Luke-Acts." As well we know, these disciples, like so many of us, attempt to come to terms with their hope that feels shattered by Jesus' crucifixion. They had hoped that Jesus was the one who would redeem Israel. This essay invites us to see that the author of Luke-Acts understands that hope for the salvation of Israel is integral to hope for the salvation of us all. Luke-Acts takes us on a journey to discover this truth. Our journey with hope is always deeply personal as Philip Browning Helsel illustrates in his essay, "Imagining Hope: Insights from Pastoral Care and Counseling." We have to become skilled at identifying our hopes and using our imaginations to see a more life-giving future for ourselves. As we clarify our particular hopes, we also take the first steps toward transforming our future. When we pursue our hopes in Christ, we begin to see how the future that God promises breaks into our present.

Along our journey, Thomas Groome's "Is There Hope for Faith?" suggests, there are times when it is not faith that precedes and grounds our hope, but rather hope that precedes our faith. For example, during times of anguish and suffering we hope that we have the strength to maintain our faith. A more Christ-centered emphasis in Catholic cate-chesis offers the best promise for cultivating hope for faith. This empha-sis is reflected in a pedagogy that journeys from life to faith to life-in-faith. Hosffman Ospino's essay, "Glimpses of Christian Hope along the Migrant Journey," examines the experience of Latin American migrants who travel to the United States in search of work so that they and those they left behind might have a chance of surviving. Their journey—that is, preparation, travel, and arrival—serves as a lens by which we may come to see hope anew. Their hope invites us to consider the kind of community of faith of which we are all a part.

Sustaining Hope, this book's third section, considers the ways in which hope is challenged and sustained. Perhaps nothing hurls a sharper threat to hope than tragedy, which Nancy Pineda-Madrid examines in her essay, "Hope and Salvation in the Shadow of Tragedy." If we fail to come to terms with tragedy, then our capacity for hope is diminished. However, when we resist the evil of tragedy and pursue a greater good, our practice of resistance gives an account of our hope. Our resistance can make present the ways God's saving grace transforms the world. In his "'Happy Are Those Who Fear the LORD': Hope, Desire, and Transformative Worship," Christopher Frechette shows us how the biblical concept of fearing God calls us to draw closer to God in worship. We cultivate a more intimate relationship with God through our emotional investment in this relationship. Yet our own emotional attachments to other objects of desire can impede our intimacy with God. Hope helps us to continuously turn toward God and away from other desires that limit us. John Baldovin, in his "*Pignus Futurae Gloriae*: Liturgy, Eschatology, and Hope," makes clear that worship lifts up for us the coming reign of God in which God is victorious over evil, sin, and death. Liturgy invites us in the here-and-now to be present to God's reign and to recommit ourselves to the work of divine justice in our world. Our liturgies of the Eucharist, the rite of the anointing of the sick, and the rite of Christian funerals—each not only celebrates the past and present, but also extends a pledge of the future glory in which we will participate.

We long for justice in our world, a longing examined in the last two essays of this section. Thomas Massaro's "Hope for a More Just Future: Wisdom from Catholic Social Teaching" considers how this body of teaching encourages us, in cooperation with the promptings of the Holy Spirit, to create institutions and policies that further a more equitable distribution of resources. Social justice, an integral part of our faith, means ongoing attention to our public and common life. While there are many examples of the failure of human society, we must nonetheless be faithful to forging a more just world. In his essay, "Hope Springs: Shaping the Moral Life," Andrea Vicini looks at how hope, while both gift and choice, also moves us to action in our world. We may receive the gift of hope and choose to work toward its integration into our lives, but there is another distinct moment in which a creative insight "springs" within us. Taking environmental sustainability as his focus, Vicini reflects on the life work of Kenyan activist Wangari Maathai as an example of how such a creative moment became a commitment to the well-being of humankind and the earth, and a source of hope to others.

The concluding quartet of essays, Living Hope, develops in a concentrated way a theme that occurs often in the book: that hope connects us to the present, not simply the future. Daniel Harrington, in his "The Future Is Now: Eternal Life and Hope in John's Gospel," leads this section with his analysis of John's Gospel, which hope pervades even though John does not mention it directly. Harrington explains this paradox by focusing on John's emphasis on the presence of Christ as the means of present, not merely future, encounter with God's saving love, which is the source of hope. From a very different perspective, Ernesto Valiente's essay, "From Utopia to *Eu-topia*: Christian Hope in History," applies the insights of contemporary theologies of liberation to indicate how hope can shape our response to those situations in the world where injustice and oppression seem to reign unchallenged. Valiente highlights the implications of the terms utopia and *eu-topia* to indicate how hope, understood in relation to God's kingdom inaugurated in Jesus Christ, can guide the ongoing struggle for justice.

John Sachs ("Hope for Creation") then takes up the same interplay between the future fullness of God's reign and its present manifestations. Drawing on the work of the great twentieth-century theologian Karl Rahner, Sachs demonstrates how our commitment to the well-being of God's created world can express our hope that God's vision for "a new heaven and a new earth" entails the fullness of what we experience here-and-how, rather than a reality without connection to the present. Finally, Francine Cardman, in her "History and Hope: Retrieving *Gaudium et Spes* for the Church and the World," proposes a positive retrieval of the Second Vatican Council's great document on the relationship between the church and the modern world. Cardman illustrates how the hope that guided the writing of that document, the hope that the document itself embodies, can still encourage today's church to engage with the world in ways that promote hope, that remind the world—and remind the church itself—that hope for history is inseparable from the God who chose to become part of that history.

# I

## GROUNDING HOPE

# Christian Hope:
# A Grace and a Choice

## *Colleen M. Griffith*

This essay explores hope as a grace *and* a choice, something to be received and responded to in freedom. The possibility of hope is an aspect of God's self-communication to be cherished. The choice of hope involves regular turning to the God of hope, keen attentiveness to the inbreaking of God's Spirit in specific contexts, and active response to the summons of God as it becomes apparent.

She is the lithe figure in the shadows of the Good Friday experiences of our lives, the one who speaks in low tones in the darkness, reiterating the promise of accompaniment. In the Holy Saturday spaces of life, where we anxiously rummage through the rubble of difficult aftermaths looking for signs of life, she points to the "more" in the immediately real, urging attentiveness to the *inbreaking* of God. Easter Sunday moments dawn, and she moves in the current of resurrection life, praising the One who has drawn near, inviting others into a joy that renews. In the paschal reality in which Christian discipleship unfolds, hope is a most welcome companion.

Never a mere emergency friend that shows up in crisis, hope is a quotidian comrade, and as such, a lasting resource upon which a vibrant Christian spirituality depends. In the process of coming to spiritual maturity as persons, we grow into wider and steadier familiarity with the figure of hope, as she is bodily incorporated and manifest in the world. This hope defies abstraction. It is spoken about most adequately in concrete, incarnate terms, because hope is a fleshly virtue. Its presence is locally perceived; its inherent grace comes to the forefront in memorable words, images, places, stories, and bodies. Lived Christian faith is impossible without it.

Christian spirituality recognizes hope to be a powerful resource, something that is both *gift* and *choice*. This essay explores the double dynamism of Christian hope as grace and choice and considers what it means to "live by hope" in accord with the Spirit. As the gift of a generous God, hope stirs within the human to be received and tended. As a choice made in the context of human freedom, hope remains something ultimately to be embodied and practiced.

## HOPE AS GIFT

"For as the heavens are high above the earth, so great is his stead-fast love…" sings the psalmist in Psalm 103:11. The largesse of God, portrayed biblically as *hesed*, an expression of loving kindness and mercy, stands as the foundation of Christian hope. Hope remains an ever renewable resource because of the Givenness of God speaking pronouncement on the present as Promise.[1] In the human reception of Godself as given, hope becomes a stirring in the human that is positively grace. Hope is born of a gift, and as the theologian Anthony Kelly notes, "that gift is precisely the energies of God-given love."[2]

For Christians, the Pauline conviction that nothing "will be able to separate us from the love of God in Christ Jesus our Lord" (Rom 8:39) is the foundation of a courageous hope. In Jesus, the "parable of God"[3] unfolds, and hope is unleashed in bodily terms, carrying the promissory pledge of a new creation. Invited into the resurrection life of the one Christ by the "circumambient Spirit,"[4] Christians, called to live by hope, seek to act in collaboration with the creative Spirit of God, who prods our immediate contexts, and us with them, toward a breaking dawn. In the words of David Kelsey, hope emerges as "the *way* in which the tri-une God goes about drawing us to eschatological blessing."[5]

The God-given character of hope corresponds with a God-created capacity in the human to receive it. Karl Rahner writes about the eschatological horizon etched into human existence. He describes the human as "a being who is open to the future of God,"[6] a being who exists from out of a present "now," toward a future. The human ability to hope is there all along in the circumstances of our lives, in accord with our nature, and yet it is unsuspected more often than not. It remains grace to be chosen rather than squandered. The "Givenness" of God, or what Rahner calls the self-communication of God, has "'divinizing' effects in the finite existent in whom this self-communication takes place."[7] The possibility of hope is a cherished effect of God's self-communication.

## A Vision of Hope

The twentieth-century spiritual giant Pierre Teilhard de Chardin (1881–1955) writes with confident hope about this earthly existence as a "divine milieu" in which the emergent face of God can be found in both what we do and what we undergo. Identifying these realms as the "activities" and "passivities" of human existence, Teilhard looks upon each as a horizon burgeoning with the possibility of collaboration with the Christ who is to come. He proclaims his hope actively in the God awaiting us with love in the realms of our activities and passivities.[8]

Teilhard is not Pollyannaish about the impact of the forces of diminishment that humans experience as "passivities," those things we undergo:

> We have only to look back on our lives to see them spring-
> ing up on all sides: The barrier which blocks our way, the
> wall that hems us in, the stone which throws us from our
> path, the obstacle that breaks us, the invisible microbe that
> kills the body, the little word that infects the mind, all the
> incidents and accidents of varying importance and varying
> kinds, the tragic interferences (upsets, shocks, severances,
> deaths) which come between the world of 'other' things and
> the world that radiates from us.[9]

Yet Teilhard points consistently to the God who is bigger than the diminishments that threaten us, reminding his readers that Christ has con-quered death, not only overturning its effect, but reversing its sting.

Teilhard seeks to give articulation to a strong hope, so as to surrender to it all the more completely. He is ardent in his desire to cooperate with the creative initiative of God, desiring to coincide with it, "becoming not only its instrument but its living extension."[10] He also urges his readers to do the same. The liberating possibility of cleaving to God in hope comes into view. For it is God who awaits us in our action, in the work of the moment, and God whose two hands stretch across to us in our struggles, in ways more active and penetrating than the diminishments we undergo.

# HOPE AS CHOICE

Hope is the gift of God offered for human receiving in freedom. The choice of hope stands in direct response to the initiative of a God who is always bigger than our ideas about God. Yet the option of hope as one's choice arises in specific socio-cultural historical circumstances. Christian spirituality highlights the *choice* of hope as involving (1) a regular turning to the God of hope, (2) an attentiveness to the inbreaking of God's Spirit in specific contexts, and (3) active response to the summons of God as it becomes apparent.

## A Turning to the God of Hope

In Christian spirituality, the practice of prayer becomes an opportunity to yield to the God of hope. In prayer, persons are steadied and renewed, and readied to trust in God's commitment as revealed in the life, death, and resurrection of Jesus. Trust in God is born of prayer, and, as Richard Lennan notes, it is trust that "frees us to risk involvement with the world we cannot control."[11] The Spirit of Promise in prayer leads us to engage in the chancy business of life more courageously and effectively. In prayer, we are turned toward the future with our senses awakened to the drawing near of the God who is to come, and this happens in our specific life contexts. Bringing heightened sensitivity to Christ as the Coming One, we are able to acquire a taste for hopefulness, and with it we can move past any inhibitions we might have that are linked to an over-concern for success versus failure.

*Waiting with expectancy* is one central aspect of Christian prayer, and it indeed is a stance to be cultivated in the practice of hope. William Lynch, in his classic text *Images of Hope* asserts: "If hope directs itself toward good things that belong to the future and that are often difficult to achieve, then it must know how to wait."[12] The form that one's waiting in prayer might take may include silence, discourse, lament, and longing. The waiting involved is neither passive nor disengaged. It is open-eyed and expectant, the kind of "wide-awakeness" that, as Thomas Stegman reminds us in this volume, Paul urged the Thessalonians to assume (1 Thess 1:3) in order to persevere. Many Christian mystics understood it as attentiveness to the movement of God, both within and beyond us.

## Attentiveness to the Inbreaking of God's Spirit

To listen, observes the French philosopher Jean-Luc Nancy, is *tendre l'oreille*, a reference that indicates the movement and stretch of the pinna of the human ear, and a reference that literally means "to incline the ear." In the sensory function of hearing, sounds travel to the ear as vibrations, traveling along the ear canal to the eardrum in the middle ear. Vibrations sent to the inner ear change into electrical signals that are carried to the brain to be interpreted. The pinna, the outer segment of the ear that "collects" and "filters" sounds, acts as a funnel, amplifying and ushering sound to the auditory canal.[13]

The process by which humans hear becomes a rich organic metaphor for the kind of listening with the heart required when attending in hope to the inbreaking Spirit of God in specific localities and life contexts. In the physical act of listening, *hearing* becomes a matter of grasping the sense of things. Jean-Luc Nancy states that to be really listening means being "inclined toward the opening of meaning."[14] When attending to the inbreaking of the Spirit, persons incline the ear of the heart in order to notice vibrations of the inbreaking Spirit, and to allow these vibrations to resound within. The vibrations of God's Spirit reverberate and expand, highlighting interconnections that are relevant for human ways of thinking and acting. Through grace, we come to sense the "summons" in sound drawing near from the future.

That which resounds within the body in our attending to the Spirit has the potential to expand our immediate reality. It can emit an existential call through which we are edged forward in the direction of God's reign. For attending to the Spirit involves more than being *inclined toward* meaning: it entails being stretched and fashioned *by* meaning, and summoned in accord *with* it.

Christian spirituality understands the practice of discernment to be an essential element in attending to the inbreaking of the Spirit. The purpose of discernment, within the context of a lively relationship with God, is to reflect critically on personal and communal life experiences, and to do so in the context of prayer, in order to adjudicate wisely between choices of possible action. The need for discernment in lives of hope is of paramount significance, as ambiguities are so frequently apparent in our readings of present reality and our senses of what the "more" is in the real.[15] We are not adept at catching sight of operative assumptions that affect our sensing, interpreting, and responding to the God who is yet to come. Good discernment makes it possible to move past limiting and illusory assumptions that bind us, and toward the creation of new moments that will often include the fashioning of something *in common* rather than the familiar protection of our individual turf.

Discernment enables people to recognize not only *what is* but what *could be* with some vision and agency. Through the practice of discernment, we are able to bring clear eyes and more attuned ears to what is of right concern in present reality and to witness to what is inbreaking. Being able to use our imaginations by looking forward to possibilities is a central aspect of a discernment process. As Phil Browning Helsel demonstrates in his essay in this collection, flexing our imaginations has a way of pushing us beyond feelings of isolation and magnification of our problems; it turns us instead in the direction of other dimensions of present reality. In Christian hope, the human imagination finds inspiration in Jesus' parables of the reign of God. In these exemplary stories, one gains access to "the mind of Christ" (1 Cor 2:16). The vision of the reign of God reflected in the parables of Jesus stimulates a looking forward to the possibilities at hand.

The practice of celebration is a further component of attending to the inbreaking of the Spirit with hope. The promises of God, recalled and remembered in such a way that makes them present, are rich causes for celebration, as are the glimpses of *not-yet* realities, visible in penultimate ways now. The God of the future comes, *ever comes*, so that our joy may be complete. The promise and the vision both are extraordinary reasons for celebration; it is difficult to imagine "accounting for the hope that is in [us]" (1 Pet 3:15) without referencing them. Acts of celebration in the practice of hope include both a return to the promises of God, and a catching sight of the vision of the *not-yet*. These function to alert us to alternatives in present reality, and they affirm our agency and freedom to participate in the creation of something new.

## Active Response to the Summons of the Spirit

Attentiveness to the inbreaking of the Spirit leaves discerners poised for active response. What is it that enables people to hasten toward that for which they have waited and longed? The theologian Jürgen Moltmann responds, "Hope!" Moltmann maintains that ethical action is impelled by hope and that "we become active insofar as we hope."[16] In accord with its character, Christian hope—in its specific, local, and contextualized manner—intends action. In the words of Andrea Vicini in this anthology, "hope springs." It becomes action in motion that affects existential environments. Hope, after all, is a virtue, "a *virtus*, an ability to act well."[17] Anthony Kelly describes this virtue: "It gives vigor and buoyancy to intelligence. It engenders a deep moral sense and points in the direction of a more passionate self-involvement in the making of a world."[18] People of hope move toward and act on behalf of a life-giving future in ways that help bring it to birth.

Hope's disposition to act is what distinguishes it from mere wishing or fantasy. The person who hopes opts to start acting as if that which is longed for will come to fruition. She/he leans forward with hands ready, perceives possibilities, and steps into what is anticipated. In this way the choice of hope enlivens the present because it hastens toward a future that has not fully arrived yet.

In acting, people of hope will also want to pray and keep discerning. Addressing the God who is Future is already an *act* of hope.

Thanksgiving for what is dawning is part of the "action" of hope too, as is petition for endurance to undergo what is necessary for the sake of what has yet to be born. Stewards of hope maintain conscious connection with the Source of hope, and in a Christian spirituality of hope, prayer and action are inextricably linked.

## A Practical Mystical Hope

In the early twentieth century, few voices in Christian spirituality witnessed to the union of prayer and action more insightfully and practically than that of the English-born spiritual writer Evelyn Underhill (1875–1941). Underhill, a married laywoman, was the first woman invited to give theological lectures at Oxford, and the first woman to direct clergy retreats. In her writings, she underscores the natural and unforced character of life with God in quotidian worlds. She encourages people of hope to develop a *practical mysticism*, something she views to be accessible to all persons, in accord with each one's uniqueness. For her, the term practical mysticism refers to that union of prayer and action that makes possible "a life soaked through and through by a sense of God's reality and God's claim."[19] Practical mysticism points to "the art of union with Reality,"[20] in which persons move toward an ever deepening and realistic adoration of God and are turned simultaneously to new levels of the world. Hope, for Underhill, emanates from a practical mysticism lived from a singular center, where we are anchored in God.

Practical mysticism always grows out of the life process itself, causing persons to feel less and less distinction between their spiritual practices and their living, and more linkage between contemplative awareness and the furthering of God's creative Spirit in transformative action. For Underhill, the "invisible attachment," the leaven of one's hoping, is, in fact, a person's life of prayer, which inherently turns us with interest toward the flourishing of others. She writes: "…our deepest life consists in a willed correspondence with the world of the Spirit, and this willed correspondence which is prayer, is destined to fulfill itself along two main channels; in love towards God and in love towards humanity—two loves which at last at their highest become one love."[21] Practical mystics like Underhill cannot conceive of life in God without concern for

God's world. The prospect of education into this kind of life in God instills a resolute hope. Underhill's practical mysticism has unmistakably active propulsion. Reflecting on the Lord's Prayer with public life very much in view, she asserts:

> Thy Kingdom *COME!* There is energy, drive, purpose in these words; an intensity of desire for the coming of perfection into life. Not the limp resignation that lies devoutly in the road and waits for the steamroller, but a total concentration on the interests of God which must be expressed as action.[22]

Hope grounded in practical mysticism as described by Underhill is what will allow us to assume our small part in the vast operations of God's Spirit. It will serve as a formative and truthful way of proceeding, particularly in times of struggle that require backbone and long effort.

## TO LIVE BY HOPE

Living by hope is not a choice made once and for all for a lifetime, but an ongoing one decided in freedom, many times over. Human beings are forever orienting to "the next thing" in the contexts of their living, and daily worlds evolve over time. As a result, the decision to hope is never static, but something that presents itself anew as circumstances of life change.

Furthermore, it is foolhardy to think that living by hope in shifting existential contexts is the interior achievement of a single individual alone. While it remains the nature of hope to nourish a personal sense of calling, hope both requires and includes a larger sense of community. There are, after all, no lone Olympians of hope. We neither hope simply for ourselves nor hope on our own. In the words of the great existentialist philosopher of hope, Gabriel Marcel, "there can be no hope which does not constitute itself through a *we* and for a *we*....all hope is at bottom choral."[23]

As Christians, we meet one another in the body of Christ, our Hope, and this meeting shapes our consciousness and commitment to gospel values of truth, justice, and dignity. What may begin as hope for oneself, therefore, necessarily expands to hope for others. Richard Lennan observes: "Hope expresses the recognition that we depend on one another, that we are called to solidarity with one another. Hope, then, underpins human communion."[24] Just as hope counts on history being something open rather than predetermined, it assumes that human agency, in its collaboration with the inbreaking Spirit, is communal.

Living by hope corresponds with our highest calling as human beings, and yet we fail at it over and again. It is, after all, difficult to look beyond self-regard alone, to welcome the inbreaking of the new when the old suits us well, to break with illusions and the kinds of false attachments written about by Christopher Frechette in this collection, in order to hear the summons of hope. For these many reasons, hope points in the direction of continuing conversion, the kind that "affects mind, heart, and imagination in the effort to understand what we are hoping for and on whom we rely."[25] One major aspect of the conversion demanded by hope is a fuller realization of our interdependence, or what the theologian Johann Baptist Metz calls our "poverty of spirit."

Assent to God, claims the political theologian Metz, begins with genuine assent to ourselves as created. In contrast, retreat from God involves flight from ourselves. And what does assent to becoming human entail? It implies saying yes to being limited selves, something Metz identifies as the "categorical imperative" of Christian faith, and something we might consider to be the "categorical imperative" of Christian hope as well. Metz exclaims: "You shall lovingly accept the humanity entrusted to you! You shall be obedient to your destiny! You shall not continually try to escape it! You shall be true to yourself!"[26] In Metz's understanding, the embrace of our poverty of spirit implies facing the human situation squarely as it is, and knowing full well our incompleteness. Metz observes:

> We are all members of a species that is insufficient unto itself.
> We are all creatures plagued by unending doubts and restless,
> unsatisfied hearts....In the elements and experiences of our
> lives, we do not find satisfying light and protective security.
> We only find these in the intangible mystery that overshad-

ows our heart from the first day of our lives, awakening questions and wonderment and luring us beyond ourselves.[27]

God's fidelity is what empowers us to stay true to our humanness, and Jesus models what this looks like in concrete terms. Poverty of spirit involves recognition of our neediness as humans and, at the same time, acknowledgement of how we have been endowed richly with God's life. It implies accepting ourselves "as beings who do not belong to ourselves"[28] realizing that what completes us springs not from us but from the mystery of God, others, and the created order. The matter of *this fact* is what Metz identifies as "our only innate treasure."[29]

Hope raises her head eagerly in response to a more thoroughgoing embrace of our poverty of spirit as creatures and clearer recognition that the ultimate word and judgment regarding the future is not ours. William Lynch notes: "If the last word were ours, we would indeed be badly off. It is imagination and hope, even when they look at their worst, that leave room for another and a better world."[30] There is something unmistakably salvific about hope's interdependent character. It remains ever *gift*, extended in grace by a generous hand, and *choice* in freedom, to be received and embodied with courage in the face of God's promised eschatological blessing.

To live by hope is to *practice hope* in the concrete and in the everyday, as a particular way of intending the future. We do not travel the way of hope alone, and the situations calling for our practice of it will vary vastly. But there are recognizable constants that are helpful to remember when seeking to practice hope in the places where we do our living. For example, we can count on hope being renewed and deepened through a regular turning to the God of hope in prayer. This will entail a waiting with expectancy at many points in which the goal becomes to seek, with God's help, to stay clear-eyed and attuned, positive and creative. The practice of hope further will require intentional discernment of the inbreaking of the Spirit in present reality, something that will be aided greatly by remembering the specific promises of God in salvation history, and imagining a future that is aligned with the reign of God as described in the parables of Jesus. Most of all, practicing hope in the concrete will take will, grit, and determination to step into what discernment has caused us to anticipate, to celebrate existing signs of the more in the real, and to act in whatever small or large ways manifest themselves in creative collaboration with the Spirit of God.

The lithe figure of hope keeps appearing in the shadows of our daily lives, edging us forward toward the God drawing near. Leaning in hard on the inbreaking Spirit, we hasten to greet the dawn.

## Notes

1. For this notion of the "Givenness" of God, I am indebted to Evelyn Underhill, a spiritual writer of the early twentieth century. Underhill exclaims, "Your whole life hangs on a great Givenness." See "The Spiritual Life of the Teacher," in *Life as Prayer and Other Writings of Evelyn Underhill*, ed. Lucy Menzies (Harrisburg, PA: Morehouse Publishers, 1946), 174.

2. Anthony Kelly, *Eschatology and Hope* (Maryknoll, NY: Orbis Books, 2006), 205.

3. David Tracy, "Approaching the Christian Understanding of God," in *Systematic Theology: Roman Catholic Perspectives*, 2nd edition, eds. Francis Schussler Fiorenza and John P. Galvin (Minneapolis: Fortress Press, 2011), 113.

4. David H. Kelsey, *Eccentric Existence: A Theological Anthropology*, vol. I (Louisville: Westminster John Knox Press, 2009), 501.

5. Ibid.

6. Karl Rahner, *Foundations of Christian Faith: And Introduction to the Idea of Christianity*, trans. William V. Dych (New York: Seabury Press, 1978), 431.

7. Ibid., 120.

8. See Pierre Teilhard de Chardin, *The Divine Milieu* (New York: Harper and Row, Publishers, 1960).

9. Ibid., 81.

10. Ibid., 62.

11. Richard Lennan, "The Church as a Sacrament of Hope," *Theological Studies* 72 (2011), 253.

12. William F. Lynch, *Images of Hope: Imagination as Healer of the Hopeless* (Baltimore: Helicon, 1965), 177.

13. See Jean-Luc Nancy, *Listening*, trans. Charlotte Manell (New York: Fordham University Press, 2007).

14. Ibid., 27. What Nancy describes here receives distinctly theological expression from Karl Rahner in his classic work *Hearer of the Word*. See Rahner, *Hearer of the Word: Laying the Foundation for a Philosophy of Religion* (New York: Continuum, 1994).

15. For this notion of the "more" in the real, see Jon Sobrino's "Presuppositions and Foundations of Spirituality," in Sobrino, *Spirituality of Liberation: Toward Political Holiness* (Maryknoll, NY: Orbis Books, 1985), 13–22.

16. Jürgen Moltmann, *Ethics of Hope* (Minneapolis: Fortress Press, 2012), 3.

17. Kelly, *Eschatology and Hope*, 6.

18. Ibid.

19. Evelyn Underhill, *The Spiritual Life* (Harrisburg, PA: Morehouse Publishing, 1937), 32.

20. Evelyn Underhill, *Practical Mysticism* (Guildford, Surrey: Eagle, 1991), 2.

21. Evelyn Underhill, *Concerning the Inner Life* (Oxford: Oneworld, 1995), 94.

22. Underhill, *The Spiritual Life*, 77.

23. Gabriel Marcel, "The Encounter with Evil," in *Tragic Wisdom and Beyond*, trans. Peter McCormick and Stephen Jolin (Evanston, IL: Northwestern University Press, 1973), 143.

24. Lennan, "The Church as a Sacrament of Hope," 258.

25. Kelly, *Eschatology and Hope*, 209. For an excellent discussion of various types of conversion apparent in the choice of hope, see pp. 209–18.

26. Johann Baptist Metz, *Poverty of Spirit* (New York: Paulist Press, 1998), 5.

27. Ibid., 25.

28. Ibid., 31.

29. Ibid., 26.

30. Lynch, *Images of Hope*, 256.

2

# "A Future, Difficult, Yet Possible Good": Defining Christian Hope

## *Dominic Doyle*

This essay explores an expanded definition of Thomas Aquinas' definition of hope as the desire for the future, difficult, yet possible good of eternal life through the coming of the kingdom. It explores the relationship of hope to its accompanying theological virtues of faith and charity, and contrasts it with the flanking vices of despair and presumption.

There is nothing timid about the hope that Christians bear in their hearts. It wishes for eternal union with God through the coming of a kingdom that will remove all suffering and injustice. As a result, hope not only sustains believers as they go through the bitter valley but also enables them to make it a place of springs (Ps 84).

The goal of this essay is to define Christian hope and thereby show how it enables us to share in God's redemptive action that brings good out of evil. I will begin by defining hope in very basic terms and then explore how these general features receive specific content in the Christian tradition. After this introductory section, I will elaborate the meaning of hope by comparing it to the accompanying theological virtues of faith and charity, and then contrasting it with the opposing vices of presumption and despair. This exploration of the precise meaning of hope will bring out what it means for Christians to make their own Vaclav Havel's striking words: "Hope is not the expectation that

16

things will turn out successfully, but the conviction that something is worth working for, however it turns out."[1]

# THE SHAPE OF CHRISTIAN HOPE

Hope is the desire for a future, difficult, yet possible good, as Thomas Aquinas' classic definition makes clear.[2] If the good we wanted were already present, we would rejoice in it, not hope for it. If the good we desired were easy to attain, we would simply say that we *want* it, not that we *hope* for it. And if the good we sought were impossible to reach, we would despair of attaining it. Hope, then, is the movement toward something we long for but do not yet possess—something that is hard to get, but not impossible.

For believers, hope is the desire for unending union with God. It moves the person to seek a happiness that will last forever, that is set free from all the sadness and injustice that so often mark this life. The goal of religious hope is thus called *eternal happiness*. This hope supports believers through the difficulties they wish had not happened. As Pope Benedict XVI taught in his 2007 encyclical on hope, *Spe Salvi* ("Saved by Hope," a reference to Rom 8:24), hope is the disposition "by which we can face our present, [since] the present, even if it is arduous, can be lived and accepted if it leads towards a goal" (no. 1).[3] And so this same hope that faces suffering also causes joy, for its goal is nothing less than the unending presence of God's love. It is the greatness of this goal that supports the pilgrim through the hardness of the journey. It relativizes, but does not trivialize, the difficulty along the way (see 2 Cor 12:10). Hope, after all, is not just about something that is arduous, but also about something that is good. It thus savors present but transient happiness as a foretaste of future, unending joy.

Christians base their understanding of hope on the story of God's loving mercy that is told in the Bible. While other essays in this book will explore in more detail the biblical treatment of hope, it is worth sketching some basic elements up front. The Hebrew Scriptures describe Israel's reliance on God in numerous ways. The covenant, in particular, shows Yahweh as the powerful and loving patron guiding

Israel's destiny: Yahweh is the proper source and goal of Israel's hope. The promises of land and offspring are rewards for Israel's fidelity. The psalms constantly exhort the people of Israel to put their trust in Yahweh (Ps 33:18; 130:5–7). Hope (v. *yāhal*; n. *tiqwāh*) becomes acutely important in times of destruction and exile, when consolation and liberation are found solely in God (Lam 3:21). The opposite of this trusting expectation in the fulfillment of Yahweh's promises is the condition of hopelessness that results from rejecting God and turning to idols (Hos 2:10). But even then, Yahweh wishes to forgive (Ezek 18:23).

Although the word *hope* (*elpis*) is little used in the Gospels, elsewhere in the New Testament it conveys the confident trust in God's redemption won through the life, death, and resurrection of Jesus Christ (Rom 5:5; 2 Cor 3:12), whom 1 Timothy simply calls "our hope" (1:1). On the basis of what God's power wrought in Jesus after his death— "the pioneer of salvation made perfect through sufferings" (Heb 2:10)— believers hope for the resurrection of the dead (1 Cor 15:12–28). The complete reliance on God, with its present assurance of future salvation, transforms the believer and so liberates from false hopes and causes joy (Rom 12:12). In such a way is the kingdom said to be already present (Luke 17:21). Indeed, the desire for the coming of the kingdom is at the heart of Christian hope. One cannot inherit eternal life unless one's heart is set on the values and right relations that make up the kingdom (Matt 25:31–46). To long for eternal life with God, then, is to long for a world made new, in which God's presence removes all suffering and death (Rev 21:3–5). And as John R. Sachs' essay in this volume shows, there is a biblical warrant for the cosmic dimensions of hope. From this brief sketch of the biblical elements of hope, it is clear that although hope reaches out toward a transcendent future, it is very much an experience that is felt now. What one wishes for in the future has profound consequences for how one acts now. For this reason, Pope Benedict insists that even though hope is "certainly directed beyond the present world, as such it also has to do with the building up of this world" (no. 15). More precisely, it draws the person into Christ's self-giving love for humanity (no. 28) and into union with others who have likewise felt this love.

Therefore, Christian hope is not irresponsible flight from the world. On the contrary, it is the basis on which one can realistically and honestly face the world's shortcomings. More positively, hope grounds an authentic commitment to the world that seeks to increase its joy and relieve its suffering, not least by "keep[ing] the world open to God" (no. 34). And so, in Benedict XVI's terms, the "great hope" for a future with God sustains all the "greater or lesser hopes" for human flourishing now. Christian hope thus envelops all ordinary hopes within a transcendent horizon of meaning and dignity. It keeps alive the noble yet fragile wish for peace and justice by connecting the person to the deepest moral Source, a point examined in Thomas Massaro's essay elsewhere in this collection. This attitude of hope therefore grounds any genuine discipleship that at once wishes for eternal life in the future and works for the human good now.

Such are the basic features of theological hope. Clearly, it is a fundamental aspect of the Christian experience of human life. For that reason, it is often grouped with the two other great markers of Christian identity: faith and charity. Together, these three dispositions are known as the theological virtues. Since the goal of this chapter is to define hope, and since a definition becomes clearer when it is set alongside closely related ideas, I will now set hope alongside its flanking virtues of faith and charity. This approach will allow me to bring out in more detail this virtue's distinctive nature, for Christian hope only makes sense within the context of faith and love.

## COMPARISONS: FAITH, HOPE, AND CHARITY

In the following discussion of the differences between faith, hope, and love, it should be remembered that all three virtues form a unity within the person. It is only in the process of reflection that we may neatly distinguish them. The reason for making these distinctions is simply to better understand the whole experience of living in faith, hope, and love, and for those of a more reflective bent of mind, to bring into sharper relief the distinctive nature of hope.

Benedict XVI poetically describes the relationship between the theological virtues through the following image of light, way, and goal:

> Hope is the fruit of faith…; in it our life stretches itself out towards the totality of all that is real, toward a boundless future that becomes accessible to us in faith. This fulfilled totality of being to which faith provides the key is a love without reserve….Christian hope approaches [this divine love] in the light of faith.[4]

In this account, faith lights up the way upon which we travel by hope toward the final goal of love. Because these virtues are so integrated, they cannot be separated. "Hope and love therefore belong immediately to each other, just as faith and hope are not to be separated from each other."[5] In a more prosaic fashion, Thomas Aquinas summarizes the relationship between the three theological virtues as follows: "Faith shows the goal, hope moves towards the goal, charity unites with the goal."[6] With these clear statements of the unity of the theological virtues, we can now explore the distinctive nature of each.

Faith is "the assurance of things hoped for, the conviction of things not seen" (Heb 11:1). It involves the personal response to God's self-revelation in the person of Jesus Christ. It is the basic acceptance of the offer to share in God's own life by following Jesus as his disciple. As such, it involves assent to certain truths, although Aquinas is quick to point out that faith does not culminate in propositions but in the reality to which those propositions refer and thus ultimately in the mind's union with God.[7] Aquinas argues that these truths, contained in the Bible, are summarized in the creed. Furthermore, those creedal truths themselves distill down to two fundamental truths: (1) God is and (2) God cares. At the heart of Christian faith, then, lies the affirmation of the existence and providence of God, a providence most clearly shown in the incarnation of the Word and the gift of the Spirit.

Hope is similarly twofold. It (1) seeks to be united with God's eternal existence and (2) relies on God's providential help to reach that goal. It therefore relates to God as both goal and helper. Critically, hope becomes a theological virtue precisely when it relies on God's help here and now to reach that future goal. It is the attitude of trusting expectation that moves the person toward the goal that faith has revealed. Hope, therefore, is the point at which the believer becomes a pilgrim.

Charity is the culmination of the theological virtues since it unites the person to God and to neighbor in friendship. What were previously separated—person from person and humanity from God—now share in overlapping pools of consciousness.[8] Through that relationship, made possible by God's sharing of divine happiness, the pilgrim can rest with God in mutual and benevolent friendship. In this union, the person is, in a way, transformed to the goal that was revealed in faith and approached in hope. In this way, pilgrims become "participants in the divine nature" (2 Pet 1:4).

This brief snapshot of the distinct role of each theological virtue allows us to see the different ways they relate to God. Faith encounters God in the primal terms of *truth*. This aspect of the relationship to God is not meant in terms of proof or certainty. Faith, for Aquinas, lies midway between knowledge and opinion, since it has all the conviction of knowledge but only the evidence of opinion. Thus, if you try to prove faith you will make it look as weak as the arguments that purport to demonstrate it. Rather, faith concerns God's truthfulness or reliability. We can quickly recognize the importance of truth by recalling the last time someone lied to us, or withheld or evaded the truth. You cannot have a serious relationship without truthful communication, and faith is the acceptance of the self-communication of God as the ultimate truth. That is why Aquinas considers faith the first of the theological virtues, for it establishes the meaningful awareness of God's purposes for humanity.

If faith encounters God as truth, hope approaches God in terms of *mercy* and *power*, for one needs a compassionate and powerful helper to reach a difficult and distant goal, as both Nancy Pineda-Madrid's and Hosffman Ospino's essays in this collection make clear. In hope, one realizes that God has the motive and the means to save. Once again, it is critical to note that what makes hope a theological virtue is that it relies on divine power, not human achievement, to reach its goal. Clearly, eternal life and the coming of the kingdom are beyond unaided human reach. Similarly, just as hope relies on God's power, so too it is awakened by God's mercy, a sense that God is intimately present to human misery. Mercy is the heartfelt sorrow at another's suffering and the desire to remove that suffering. This loving kindness of God (*hesed*) is recounted again and again in the Hebrew Scriptures, and is embodied in the person of Jesus Christ. Hope, then, involves encountering God's power and mercy simultaneously, a sense at once of God's exalted transcendence from, and intimate presence in, creation. Perhaps the tradition connects mercy and power in the experience of hope because effective compassion not only suffers alongside the person in need, but, crucially, it is not overwhelmed by that suffering. On the contrary, it transcends the suffering it truly co-experiences and therefore can remain powerful enough to overcome it.[9]

Finally, since charity unites the person to God as friend, it relates to God in terms of God's *goodness*, not just self-referentially in terms of the good for me (as my hoped-for salvation brought about by God's omnipotent mercy). The person with charitable friendship loves God not just for what God has done for him or her, but simply on account of God's goodness itself. Charity does not seek something else from God; it simply rests in the divine embrace. God is no longer a means to an end, something useful to me. God is now the end itself, intrinsically good. As such, charity "makes us tend to God by uniting the longing of the person to God, so that we live, not for ourselves, but for God."[10] Charity, then, is the form of the virtues, since it unites the person to God and thus gives shape and purpose to all of human life. It gathers the whole person into God's enveloping love, and so makes the person a transparent agent of God's love in the world, "an instrument of Your peace," in the words attributed to St. Francis of Assisi.

Such are the basic elements of the three theological virtues. With these elements in place, we can now lay out more fully the logic of their interrelation. Aquinas summarized that interrelation as follows: faith shows the goal, hope moves toward it, and charity unites with it. The theological virtues follow this order because some knowledge (faith) must precede meaningful desire (hope), since you cannot want something unless you first have some notion of what it is you want. Hope, after all, is for what is possible, and one cannot hope for eternal life unless one first believes it is possible. Likewise, the movement of desire (hope) in turn precedes union (charity), since you cannot unite with something unless you first move toward it.

Faith is therefore foundational to Christian life because of its critical assent to God's existence and providence, especially as revealed in the person of Christ. Arising from this personal assent is hope, the providential movement toward the future, difficult, yet possible goal of eternal life with God, a journey already "pioneered" by Christ. Finally, charity unites the person to God, a union modeled on Christ, through which the pilgrim can experience, even now, the peace and joy that will come with the journey's end.

These key dispositions of Christian life are called *theological* virtues because they are infused by God's grace, not achieved by human effort. But they are called theological *virtues* because they transform the human person, healing and elevating human knowing and loving so that the person can cooperate with God's grace to build the kingdom. And so, as theological virtues, they are divinely infused, yet humanly possessed. They lead the person to God, and thus perfect the human. Collectively, these three key markers of Christian identity answer the three great questions of a Christian virtue ethics as follows: Who are we? A people of faith. Who do we want to become? A people of love. How do we get there? By hope.[11]

## CONTRASTS: DESPAIR AND PRESUMPTION

Definitions become clearer not just by comparison with related ideas, but by contrast with divergent ideas. The nature of hope can thus be further clarified by contrasting it with its opposing vices, despair and presumption.

Virtues lie in the mean between two extremes. Courage, for example, falls between cowardice and rashness. It overcomes the inclination to flee harm, but with due reflection instead of hasty impulsiveness. In the vices that flank any virtue, it often happens that one vice clearly contrasts with the virtue, while the other resembles it by way of a false likeness. Thus, in the case of soldierly courage, cowardice clearly opposes it (since the soldier is running in the other direction), whereas rashness is a counterfeit (since the person is charging ahead, but without deliberation or waiting for orders). In the case of hope, the mean lies between despair (which clearly contrasts with hope by giving up the expectation of reaching the goal) and presumption (which resembles hope, but lacks the proper grounds to reach the goal). I will deal first with despair before treating presumption, since the latter, as a simulacrum, is more subtly contrasted with hope.

To despair, literally, is to be without hope (Latin: *desperare* [*sperare* = to hope]). It is to act on the conviction that God will not pardon the sinner who repents, or bring him or her to eternal life.[12] In effect, despair says that human sin exceeds God's mercy. It thus opposes hope, which acts on the conviction that God graciously forgives and unrestrictedly wills the salvation of humanity (1 Tim 2:4). It differs from depression, in that it is a deliberate choice of the will based on a false conviction about reality, not an unbidden lowness of mood based on a complex set of psychological factors.

Despair is a sin because it destroys the movement to share in God's goodness. The person who despairs categorically rejects the possibility that he or she can participate in divine life. This rejection of the theological understanding of human dignity often leads to a fixation on finite goods (Eph 4:19). But finite things, as their name suggests, come to an end, or at least sooner or later they reveal themselves to be inadequate to the human longing for the infinite. Therefore, this fixation, or idolatry, leads to sorrow, or if one doesn't want to face the truth just yet, to dissipation, the restless substitution of now this good, now that good, as each in turn fails to satisfy.

The net result of this process is that as despair snuffs out the promise of eternal life, it removes joy from the present life. It is therefore closely linked to sloth, the spiritual sadness that refuses the greatness to which God beckons humanity, in part because it wishes to evade the obligations that come with that vocation.[13] Those obligations involve letting God transform the person's life in such a way that he or she is worthy of union with God. They involve actively cooperating with divine grace in the exercise of one's freedom, in the cumulative acts that, over time and through conscious repetition, make up a person's character. At this point, we are already starting to describe the other vice that opposes hope and so to that vice we now turn.

Presumption is the expectation of reaching the goal without letting God change one's life in the process. (It is because of this appearance of movement toward God that presumption bears a false resemblance to hope.) Presumption demands pardon without repentance. It expects eternal life without ongoing conversion. If despair ignored divine mercy and so turned away from God, then presumption overlooks divine justice and so approaches God inappropriately. Presumption tries to move toward God while still clinging to sin. It wants everlasting union with infinite love while inordinately grasping to finite goods. It is the futile attempt to serve two masters (Matt 6:24). But, as stated, one can only become worthy of union with God by cooperating in divine grace. To presume is to reject that grace.

Such are the two vices that flank the theological virtue of hope. Each destroys the dynamism that is at the heart of hope, but in different ways. To see how, we must recall that hope involves the recognition of a fundamental *not yet* in its awareness that the kingdom is clearly a long way off but has already begun. This tension generates movement toward what is possible but distant. In the vices that oppose hope, that tension is either wound down into the still *never* of despair, or artificially cut through with the *already now* of presumption. Either way, the end result is the same: the loss of the sense of life as a deepening conversion and pilgrimage through time to eternal love. These vices destroy this fundamental Christian attitude to life because, as Josef Pieper puts it, they "block the approach to true prayer"—prayer being "nothing other than the voicing of hope."[14] In despair, one assumes that what one prays for will not be granted. In presumption, one expects that it is already a done deal. In both cases, there is no point in praying. But true prayer—what Aquinas calls "the interpretation of hope"—finds the path between despair and presumption.[15]

Hope is the pivotal trait at the heart of any Christian understanding of human life. To experience hope is to experience a sense of movement or development in one's identity as a Christian. That development is intimately related to the experience of faith and charity. If faith gives the person conviction about central Christian beliefs, then hope convinces others that the person really believes those claims, because they are held despite the cost they entail. Likewise, if through hope the person receives God's power and mercy in his or her own difficulties, then as hope develops into love for this divine helper, that love empowers the person to become an agent of God's mercy to others, in their difficulties. Hope, then, plays a pivotal role in the growth of Christian life, the sharing in God's redemptive activity that brings good out of evil. Over time and through difficulties, hope moves the believer into an ever-closer union with God that is modeled on Christ, the "pioneer" (Heb 12:2) of the journey to eternal life.

## Notes

1. Quoted in Donald Kerwin, "Honoring the Rights of Migrants: A Catholic Approach to Migration and National Security" online at http://nccbuscc.org/mrs/kerwin.shtml.

2. This definition, along with many ideas in this article, is drawn from Thomas Aquinas' theology of hope, which can be found in his major work, *Summa theologica* (hereafter *ST*), translated by the Fathers of the English Dominican Province, 5 vols. (Allen, TX: Christian Classics, 1981), at II-II, qq. 17–22. I have also drawn on my book length reflection on Aquinas' theology of hope in the context of Christian humanism: Dominic Doyle, *The Promise of Christian Humanism: Thomas Aquinas on Hope* (New York: Crossroad, 2012).

3. Pope Benedict XVI, Encyclical Letter, *Spe Salvi*, Accessed online at http://www.vatican.va/holy_father/benedict_xvi/encyclicals/documents/hf_ben-xvi_enc_20071130_spe-salvi_en.html.

4. Joseph Ratzinger, *Aus Christus Schauen: Einübung in Glaube, Hoffnung, Liebe* (Freiburg in Breisgau: Herder, 1989); English translation, *To Look on Christ*, trans. Robert Nowell (New York: Crossroad, 1991); republished as *The Yes of Jesus Christ: Spiritual Exercises in Faith, Hope, and Love* (New York: Crossroad, 2005), 69. References here are to the 2005 English-language edition.

5. Ratzinger, *The Yes of Jesus Christ*, 70.

6. "Fides autem ostendit [finem], spes facit tendere in eum, caritas unit." Aquinas, *In Epistolam I ad Timotheum*, cap. 1, lect. 2, in *Opera Omnia*, Parma ed. (New York: Musurgia, 1949), 13:587.

7. Aquinas, *ST*, II–II, q. 1, art. 2, ad 2.

8. The phrase "overlapping pools of consciousness" is, I believe, from Virginia Woolf, but it is recalled from memory and I cannot find the reference.

9. On this notion of empathy, see Don Browning, *Recovering Christian Humanism: The New Conversation on Spirituality, Theology, and Psychology* (Minneapolis, MN: Fortress Press, 2010), 35.

10. Aquinas, *ST*, II–II, q. 17, art. 6, ad 3.

11. Daniel Harrington and James Keenan, *Paul and Virtue Ethics* (Lanham, MD: Rowman & Littlefield, 2010), 3–27.

12. Aquinas, *ST*, II–II, q. 20, art. 1.

13. See Josef Pieper, *On Hope*, trans. Mary Frances McCarthy (San Francisco: Ignatius, 1986), 55–57.

14. Ibid., 70.

15. Aquinas, *ST*, II–II, q. 17, art. 2, obj. 2.

# 3

# "That You May Abound in Hope": St. Paul and Hope

## *Thomas D. Stegman, SJ*

This essay sets forth Paul's teaching about hope by focusing on three letters: 1 Thessalonians, 2 Corinthians, and Romans. According to Paul,
hope is grounded in the resurrection of Jesus and is confirmed by the
gift of the Holy Spirit. Hope transforms grief in the face of death,
empowers perseverance in the context of suffering, and works synergis-
tically with faith and love.

Paul's magisterial Letter to the Romans contains his most systematic
presentation of the gospel he proclaims. In the body of this letter,
Paul first sets forth a sustained exposition of the revelation of God's
righteousness through the death and resurrection of Jesus the Messiah
and the sending of the Holy Spirit (1:18—11:36). He then issues a series
of exhortations that call the members of the house churches in Rome
to live out the implications of the gospel, exhortations whose focus is
the mutual welcoming, through Christ, of Jewish and Gentile believers
into the family of faith (12:1—15:13). At the very conclusion of his
lengthy teaching and impassioned encouragement, Paul offers a prayer:
"May the God of hope fill you with all joy and peace in being faithful,
in order that you may abound in hope by the power of the Holy Spirit"
(15:13).[1]

The fact that Paul, at the climax of his argument and exhortation
in Romans, refers to God as the source of hope and prays that the
Roman Christians "abound in hope" is significant. These references sug-

gest the importance of the theme of hope for Paul, an intimation that is reinforced when one looks at his undisputed letters.[2] In what follows, I present his teaching on hope under four headings. First, Paul's earliest extant letter focuses on resurrection hope in the face of death. Second, hope is the necessary horizon against which he defends and expounds his understanding of cruciform ministry.[3] Third, hope is, more broadly speaking, an essential aspect of Christian existence. Fourth, hope for Paul operates dynamically in relationship with faith and love. I conclude with some brief reflections on the relevance of his insights today.

## HOPE IN THE FACE OF DEATH (1 THESSALONIANS)

First Thessalonians is the earliest writing we have from Paul, likely written in AD 50, a few months after he founded a community in Thessalonika, the capital of the Roman province of Macedonia (northern Greece). Because of opposition to his message, Paul had been forced to depart hastily from Thessalonika. Moreover, circumstances prevented him from returning shortly thereafter, so he dispatched his co-worker Timothy to see how the fledgling community was doing and to offer them encouragement. Paul later wrote 1 Thessalonians in response to what Timothy reported back to him.

Paul typically foreshadows key themes in his greeting and thanksgiving prayer at the beginning of letters. In 1 Thessalonians 1:3, he gives thanks to God for the Thessalonians' "work of faith and labor of love and endurance of hope." As the contents of the letter unfold, we learn that the Thessalonian Christians have persevered in the face of opposition and afflictions from their fellow countrymen. Paul rejoices in Timothy's report that they have grown in faith and love (3:6). Conspicuously absent here is a reference to their hope. While Timothy's report seems to have been positive for the most part, a problem had arisen since Paul's departure. Some members of the community had died (whether these deaths were caused by persecution or not is not clear). Their deaths left (at least some of) the Thessalonians in grief, as they worried that their deceased loved ones would be left out when

Jesus returned again in glory. Such grief and worry were symptoms, for Paul, of a crisis of hope.

Paul responds to this situation in 1 Thessalonians 4:13–18. In the first place, he does not want the community to grieve as those do "who have no hope" (4:13).[4] Paul's point is not that grief over the death of loved ones is inappropriate; rather, he insists that "lamentation born of fatalism is incompatible with the hope which undergirds Christian belief and commitment."[5] That is, Paul's position is that the death of Christians is no cause for despair. Christian hope is grounded in the belief that, just as Jesus died and has been raised from the dead, so through him "God will gather with him [that is, Jesus] those who have fallen asleep" (4:14).[6] The foundation of Christian hope thus has a bifocal quality. On the one hand, it looks to the past, to the eschatological events of Jesus' death and resurrection. On the other hand, as the following verses make clear, it looks to the future "coming" (*parousia*; 4:15) of Jesus in glory, the consummation of the age to come. We can discover this same quality of hope in our own lives as Philip Browning Helsel's essay in this collection argues.

Paul goes on to reveal to the Thessalonians "a message of the Lord" (*logos kyriou*), most likely a prophetic revelation given to him by the risen Christ (4:15–17). Paul employs dramatic apocalyptic language and imagery, much of it traditional (for example, the archangel's call; the sound of a trumpet). His basic message is that, when Jesus comes again in glory, "the dead in Christ"—referring to the baptized who have died—will be raised first. Then, and only then, will those in Christ who are still living be caught up with them to meet the risen and glorified Lord. Paul's meaning is that the Thessalonians' deceased loved ones will not be disadvantaged in any way at the consummation of eschatological events. He wants the community to "console" or "comfort" (*parakaleō*) one another with this message of hope (4:18).

At the most fundamental level, then, Paul's teaching on hope in 1 Thessalonians pertains to hope in the resurrection from the dead, especially hope on behalf of those who have died in Christ.[7] But there is more. Recall the phrase "*endurance* of hope" (*hypomonē tēs elpidos*; 1:3) from the opening lines of the letter. Hope in the resurrection is not intended to induce passivity or idle speculation about when Christ's *parousia* will occur. Rather, in 5:1–11 Paul admonishes the Thessalonians to keep awake and to stay sober; in other words, to appreciate that hopeful living requires perseverance in growing in the ways of holiness. Endurance of this type is difficult, as Paul suggests by his use of military imagery. The Thessalonians are to put on "a breastplate of faith and love, and hope of salvation as a helmet" (5:8). Once again we see the triad faith-love-hope (see 1:3), a phenomenon to which we will return (see my fourth section below). What is pertinent to notice here is that Paul's military imagery gives prominence to hope, the hope that looks forward to the resurrection by persevering in faith and love.[8]

## HOPE AS THE HORIZON OF CRUCIFORM MINISTRY (2 CORINTHIANS)

The linkage between hope and perseverance becomes clearer when one turns to Paul's *apologia* for his ministry in 2 Corinthians. He founded the church in Corinth, the capital of the Roman province of Achaia (southern Greece), months after founding churches in Philippi and Thessalonika. Paul's founding visit lasted roughly a year and a half, and in subsequent years he engaged in extensive correspondence with the community. Second Corinthians, written ca. AD 55, represents the culmination of that correspondence.

Relations between Paul and the Corinthians were at times contentious, no more so than in the months preceding the writing of 2 Corinthians. The critical issues that lie behind this text are complex.[9] Relevant to the present task is that Paul's apostolic authority and his way of exercising apostolic ministry had been called into question by some members of the community and by a group of rival missionaries whom he sarcastically dubs "superlative apostles" (11:5; 12:11). In particular, Paul seems to have been criticized on a number of points: he lacked letters of recommendation; his bodily appearance was unimpressive and his speaking lacked rhetorical polish; he refused direct remuneration for his ministry (which was interpreted as declining the offer of friendship from potential benefactors), and instead chose to do menial work with his hands to support himself. His ministry was marked more by servility and suffering than by manifesting Spirit-empowered "mighty works" (12:12).

Much of 2 Corinthians is Paul's defense and explanation of his way of being an apostle (see especially 2:14—7:4). The opening blessing prayer (1:3–11) sets forth a number of key themes he later develops. There he refers to sharing in "the sufferings of Christ" as well as to being the constant recipient of God's encouragement and consolation (1:3–7). To illustrate the point, Paul alludes to a recent traumatic event that left him despairing of his life. But this event, which his opaque description prevents from identifying with certitude, has led him to place his trust even more in "God who raises the dead" (1:9). Paul expresses his deepened reliance on God thus: "he delivered us from such terrible dangers of death and will deliver [us]; in him we have placed our hope that he will deliver us yet again" (1:10).[10] The verb tense of *ēlpika-men* ("we have placed our hope") is significant. Paul employs the perfect tense, which signifies an action in the past that has ongoing ramifications. That is, his renewed hope in God is an enduring characteristic of his ministry.

Paul makes clear in the course of the letter that authentic ministry entails sharing in Christ's sufferings. He uses the metaphor of being "the aroma of Christ" (2:15) to convey that his ministry embodies the self-giving love of Jesus (2:15–16). He proclaims the gospel most eloquently through his humble servant ministry patterned after Jesus (4:5). Paul's ministry leads to his being opposed and persecuted in many ways (for example, beatings and imprisonments); it also involves his making a number of sacrifices (for example, toiling with his hands so as not to be a burden on those to whom he ministers).[11] Paul encapsulates this way of ministering by aligning himself with the story of Jesus: he always carries in his body the "putting to death of Jesus" (*nekrōsis tou Iēsou*; 4:10) and is constantly being handed over on account of Jesus (4:11). His ministry is thus marked by "death, " that is, self-giving in love, so that others might have "life"—through receiving the gospel to which his ministry invites them (4:12).

This brief description of Paul's cruciform ministry makes his expression of hope in 2 Corinthians 1:10 all the more remarkable and impressive. How is he able to persevere faithfully in such a difficult and challenging ministry? Paul professes he has knowledge that "the one who raised the Lord Jesus will raise us [that is, ministers][12] also with Jesus" (4:14). Just as Jesus' suffering and death led to his being raised in glory, so will Paul's suffering and "dying" lead to his being raised in glory. But Paul's hope does not rely solely on his knowledge of the God who raises the dead; it also rests on his lived experience of God's bestowal of the Spirit as *arrabōn*, that is, as "guarantee" or "down payment,"[13] of the life to come when "what is mortal may be swallowed up by life" (5:4–5). In short, resurrection hope functions as the constant horizon of Paul's ministry.

This same Spirit, moreover, is the very source of Paul's empowerment for engaging and persevering in cruciform ministry. It is surely no accident, therefore, that Paul's expressions of hope vis-à-vis his cruciform ministry follow upon references to the Spirit. First, his statement in 2 Corinthians 3:12 that his hope undergirds his boldness in ministry comes on the heels of his reference to the "ministry of the Spirit" (3:8), the new covenant ministry empowered by God's Spirit residing in human hearts (3:3–6). Second, Paul's declaration in 4:1 that he does not lose heart comes immediately after his description of the transforming power of the Spirit (3:17–18). Third, his repeated declaration in 4:16 about not losing heart follows his confession that he has the "Spirit of faith" or "faithfulness" (4:13).[14] Faithfulness to the Spirit's movement must undergird our ministry today, a claim that Thomas Groome's essay elsewhere in this book advances.

# HOPE AS AN ESSENTIAL ASPECT OF CHRISTIAN EXISTENCE (ROMANS)

The relationship between the gift of the Spirit and hope is also a key theme in Paul's Letter to the Romans. Here, his focus is more broadly on the role of hope in the lives of all those whom God has reconciled through Christ. This letter was written shortly after 2 Corinthians, likely in the early months of AD 56. It is unique among the undisputed letters in that Paul writes to a community he did not found.[15] One reason for writing was that he sought their financial and logistical support for a mission to Spain. Part of his strategy in writing Romans was to set forth his understanding of the gospel and its implications. As noted at the beginning of the essay, this letter is Paul's most systematic presentation of the gospel.

Following his famous statement about how God's righteousness has been definitively revealed through the faithfulness of Jesus,[16] whose death on the cross has brought about the forgiveness of sins and redemption from sin's enslaving power (3:21–26), Paul turns to the story and figure of Abraham in 4:1–25. This section serves a number of purposes, one of which is to demonstrate the importance of faithfulness in God's plan of salvation. Another is to offer Abraham as an example of proper response to God's grace. While the accent of Paul's portrait rests on Abraham's faith, he also highlights the quality of the latter's hope: "In hope he believed against hope" (4:18). Abraham lived his life, obeying the commandments of God, in hopeful trust that God's promises to him would be fulfilled. These promises were that Abraham would have numerous descendants and that they would inherit the world. Abraham maintained hope, all appearances to the contrary (for example, his advanced age and Sarah's barrenness), and trusted in God "who gives life to the dead and calls into being the things that do not exist" (4:17). Once again, Paul grounds hope—which is to characterize *all* those who have responded to God in faith—in God as the one who gives life.[17]

Paul picks up the theme of hope in the following passage, at the outset of Romans 5, which begins a lengthy section wherein he "turns his attention to the community of those who have embraced this [that is, God's] saving righteousness and describes the experience of salvation that the justified already enjoy in Christ (5:1—8:39)."[18] It is significant that Paul brackets this entire section with teaching about hope. After referring to the reconciliation and peace God has brought about in Christ, Paul proclaims that "we rejoice in our hope of sharing the glory of God" (5:2). But then he adds something that, at first glance, is surprising: "More than that, but we rejoice in our afflictions" (5:3). Observe that it is not only ministers (like Paul) who suffer "afflictions"; commitment to the gospel inevitably brings opposition from various cultural forces. What makes Paul rejoice in afflictions is that, through God's grace, they produce "endurance," which in turn produces "character," which in turn produces hope (5:3–4). The culmination of this *sorites*, or chain-like sequence, underscores that hope is an essential quality of Christian life. A Christian's "proven character" (*dokimē*), honed through the endurance of suffering, is manifested by a disposition of hope—a hope, to be sure, that rests on God's faithfulness. Such hope, Paul goes on to say, does not disappoint because God's love has already been poured into the hearts of Christians through the gift of the Holy Spirit (5:5). This recalls the description of the Spirit as *arrabōn* ("down payment"; 2 Cor 5:5).

Near the end of Romans 5:1—8:39, Paul returns to the gift of the Spirit in connection with hope. He refers to the "first fruits of the Spirit" (8:23), which functions as a synonym of *arrabōn*. Throughout chapter 8 Paul explains the present working of the Spirit in the lives of Christians. The indwelling Spirit empowers them to fulfill the just requirement of the Jewish Law (8:4), that is, to carry out its essential core, "a righteous life before God";[19] bears witness that they are adopted children of God, enabled to be fellow heirs with Christ and to call out to God as *Abba* (8:14–17); helps them in their weakness and intercedes to God on their behalf (8:26–27); and conforms them more and more into the image of Jesus (8:29), "who is the template of a new humanity" marked by self-giving love.[20] These "first fruits" of the Spirit give ample reason for Christians to wait in hope for the glory to be revealed to them, the redemption of their bodies (that is, the fullness of resurrection life). Paul proclaims that "in this hope we were saved" (8:24). While the very nature of hope is that its object is unseen, here he insists that Christian hope has a strong experiential basis in the present.

We have seen that Paul names this experiential basis as God's love poured into human hearts in the Spirit (5:5). He returns to the topic of God's love in 8:31–39, a lyrical passage in which he proclaims that nothing can separate Christians from God's love because God is "for us." The extent of God's love has been revealed in that God "did not spare his own Son but gave him up for us all" (8:32). Moreover, Christ revealed the divine love by giving his life on the cross and, having been raised from the dead, by interceding for his people (8:33–34). It is little wonder that, at the very end of the body of the letter, Paul prays to God as the source of all hope to fill the Roman Christians with joy and peace, that they may "abound in hope" (15:13) by the power of the Spirit. Abounding in hope is an essential mark of Christian existence.

# HOPE'S DYNAMIC RELATIONSHIP WITH FAITH AND LOVE

Thus far we have seen that, according to Paul, hope is connected to God's power to bring the dead to life, manifested in the first place in the resurrection of Jesus. Hope in the resurrection can—and should—transform grief in the face of human mortality: those who die in Christ will be raised from the dead. In addition, Paul links hope with perseverance, especially perseverance in the face of suffering and affliction. He is able to engage in cruciform ministry—to proclaim the gospel through humble love and service; to withstand opposition and persecution—because of his hope that, just as God raised Jesus from the dead, so too will God raise those who proclaim the gospel by following Christ's pattern of self-giving love. Moreover, Paul insists that everyone who belongs to Christ is to abound in hope, trusting that (and especially when), all appearances to the contrary, God's promises of the fullness of redemption will be fulfilled. Such promises can be trusted because God has already poured God's love into the hearts of Christians through the gift of the Holy Spirit, the first fruits of God's love and life.

To abound in hope, for Paul, also involves abounding in faith and love. The triad faith-love-hope, what has come to be called the theological virtues, in all likelihood originated with him. Earlier we saw that he brackets 1 Thessalonians with references to this triad: "work of faith and labor of love and endurance of hope" (1:3) and "a breastplate of faith and love, and hope of salvation as a helmet" (5:8). The triad is not unique to 1 Thessalonians. In 1 Corinthians 13, Paul's famous encomium on love, he writes, "Love bears all things, believes[21] all things, hopes all things, endures all things" (13:7). The encomium concludes,

"Now faith, hope, love abide, these three; and the greatest of these is love" (13:13). Another example is Galatians 5:5–6, where Paul asserts, "For through the Spirit, on the basis of faith, we eagerly await the hope of righteousness. For in Christ Jesus neither circumcision nor uncircumcision avails, but rather faith working through love."[22]

The crucial point to appreciate is that faith, love, and hope are tightly interconnected for Paul. They are not three separate silos. The relationship between faith (or faithfulness) and love is best illustrated by Paul's understanding of Jesus. Jesus' faithfulness to God (for example, Rom 3:22)[23] was shown in his obedience unto death (Phil 2:8), which was also an expression of his love for humanity (Gal 2:20). In short, Jesus enacted the vertical and horizontal dimensions of proper covenant relationship (see Mark 12:28–34), which is beautifully summarized by Ephesians 5:2: "Christ loved us and gave himself up for us, a fragrant offering and sacrifice to God." The death-and-resurrection of Jesus has created a new possibility for being in right relationship with God and with one's fellow humans (granted that one accepts the proclamation of the gospel and receives the empowering gift of the Spirit in baptism). As Michael J. Gorman explains, "To respond to and participate in the cross of Christ is...to enter into a covenantal relationship with both God and humans in which there can be no vertical relationship (what Paul usually calls 'faith') without a corollary horizontal relationship (what Paul normally calls 'love')."[24] This dynamic is captured well by the expression "faith working through love" (Gal 5:6). Hope can then be described as "the future tense of faith."[25] That is, one *continues* to abide in "faith working through love"—even in the face of opposition, suffering, and various other difficulties—because of the assurance that the redemption and salvation God accomplished through Christ will be brought to completion in the life to come (see 1 Cor 15:20–28).

Paul's earliest reference to the triad makes clear that faith, love, and hope are not just interrelated; they are interrelated *dynamically* (1 Thess 1:3). When he prays in thanksgiving for the Thessalonians' "work of faith and labor of love and endurance of hope," the accent is on the actions that proceed from the triad. The terms "work" and "labor" signify strenuous toil and exertion. Authentic faith and love, made possible by God's grace, are expressed through the "total disposition of one's life that involves deliberate choices and determined effort."[26] The "endurance" of hope, as we have seen, includes the notion of perseverance in the face of suffering. Even more basically, it denotes the determination to remain faithful to all one's commitments and responsibilities.[27] Thus, while it is fruitful to analyze Paul's references to hope in their own right, they are more completely understood in light of their dynamic relationship with faith and love.

## RELEVANCE OF PAUL'S TEACHING ABOUT HOPE

What does Paul's teaching about hope say to people today? What relevance does it have for theological reflection and for practical application in the lives of Christians? I suggest five points of relevance.

First, Paul's teaching about hope rests on a profound *theology*. God is the "God of hope" (Rom 15:13), the source of hope, because God is the giver of life. God's life-giving power is preeminently manifested in God's raising Jesus from the dead. God is also the source of hope because God's faithfulness can be trusted. God is faithful to God's promises, including the promise to bring to completion the work of the "new creation" (2 Cor 5:17; Gal 6:15), when God will be "all in all" (1 Cor 15:28).

Second, the resurrection from the dead—a cornerstone of Paul's hope—bears witness to the ultimate sanctity of life in the face of cultural forces that consider the lives of many to be expendable. Paul's confidence about the resurrection also challenges the mindset that the present life is "all there is," a view that is manifested in the expenditure of vast resources in attempts to perpetuate youthful appearance and to prolong life through extraordinary means. Paul's hope in the resurrection is aptly echoed in the church's liturgy: "Indeed, for your faithful, Lord, life is changed, not ended" (*New Roman Missal*, Preface I for the Dead).

Third, the hope that undergirds cruciform ministry speaks to the ongoing work of the Paschal Mystery. That is, Christians can have confidence of entering into the pattern of Jesus' self-giving love for others, trusting that God brings life out of the various sacrifices and "dyings" they endure in bearing witness to the gospel.

Fourth, Paul's teaching that hope is to be an essential characteristic of all Christians can serve as a helpful point of self-reflection for individuals and communities: Do I (or we) bear authentic witness to hope by my attitudes, dispositions, and actions? Am I able to give an account of my hope to others (see 1 Pet 3:15)? Paul's sanguine conviction about the "first fruits" of the Spirit is a valuable reminder of the present working of the Spirit in our lives.

Lastly, Paul's appreciation of the dynamic relationship of hope to faith and love challenges any tendency that regards hope as a stance of passivity. Authentic hope entails an active determination not only to persevere in the face of difficulties but also to remain faithful to the ways of love in the quotidian affairs of life.

# Notes

1. The translations of Scripture are my own.

2. Seven of Paul's letters are almost universally regarded as authentic, that is, deriving from Paul and the context of his life and ministry: Romans, 1 and 2 Corinthians, Galatians, Philippians, 1 Thessalonians, and Philemon. References to the so-called "Deutero-Paulines" (Ephesians, Colossians, and 2 Thessalonians) and the "Pastoral Epistles" (1 and 2 Timothy and Titus) in this essay will function to reinforce points derived from the undisputed letters.

3. The term *cruciform* (or "cross-shaped") points to the cross as the revelation of God's love and as the manifestation of divine power through weakness. See Michael J. Gorman, *Cruciformity: Paul's Narrative Spirituality of the Cross* (Grand Rapids, MI: Eerdmans, 2001).

4. See Eph 2:12.

5. Earl J. Richard, *First and Second Thessalonians*, Sacra Pagina, 11 (Collegeville, MN: The Liturgical Press, 1995), 234.

6. See Victor Paul Furnish, *1 Thessalonians, 2 Thessalonians*, Abingdon New Testament Commentaries (Nashville: Abingdon, 2007), 101, for evidence that 1 Thess 4:14 is a "traditional declaration of faith."

7. See 1 Cor 15:19.

8. In addition to placement at the end position of a series, a placement that functions rhetorically to give emphasis, Abraham J. Malherbe lists three other characteristics that indicate the prominence of hope in 1 Thess 5:8. See Malherbe, *The Letters to the Thessalonians: A*

*New Translation with Introduction and Commentary*, Anchor Bible, 32B (New York: Doubleday, 2000), 298.

9. The main issues are the literary integrity of 2 Corinthians (that is, whether it is a single letter or a compilation of two or more letters) and the identity and teaching of the rival missionaries who came to Corinth after Paul. See, for example, Thomas D. Stegman, *The Character of Jesus: The Linchpin to Paul's Argument in Second Corinthians*, Analecta Biblica, 158 (Rome: Pontificio Istituto Biblico, 2005), 5–42.

10. Tracking the referent of first person plural pronouns in 2 Corinthians is notoriously difficult. Here, Paul is likely talking about himself, or perhaps himself and Timothy, the co-sender of the letter (2 Cor 1:1).

11. See 2 Cor 4:8–9; 6:4–10; and 11:23–33 for more on Paul's apostolic hardships.

12. See note 10.

13. See 2 Cor 1:22; Eph 1:14.

14. For reading the phrase *pneuma tēs pisteōs* as referring to the Holy Spirit of faith, see, for example, Victor Paul Furnish, *II Corinthians: A New Translation with Introduction and Commentary*, Anchor Bible, 32A (New York: Doubleday, 1986), 258, 286.

15. Most scholars see in Paul's greetings to various Christians in Rome evidence that there were several house and tenement churches there (see Rom 16:3–16).

16. I render the controverted phrase *pistis Iēsou Christou* as referring to Jesus' own faithfulness, not to a believer's faith in Christ.

17. See 1 Tim 4:10; 6:17.

18. Frank J. Matera, *Romans*, Paideia Commentaries on the New Testament (Grand Rapids, MI: Baker Academic, 2010), 121 (brackets added).

19. See Brendan Byrne, *Romans*, Sacra Pagina, 6 (Collegeville, MN: The Liturgical Press, 1996), 244.

20. The quoted relative clause is from Luke Timothy Johnson, *Reading Romans: A Literary and Theological Commentary*, Reading the New Testament Series (New York: Crossroad, 1997), 133. While the agency of the Spirit in Rom 8:29 is implicit, Johnson rightly notes that 2 Cor 3:18 makes explicit that it is the Spirit who transforms into the likeness of Christ.

21. The word translated "believe" is *pisteuō*, the verbal form of the substantive *pistis*, usually rendered as "faith."

22. See Col 1:4–5.

23. See note 16. Other instances of Paul's using the phrase *pistis Iēsou Christou* or a variation thereof are Rom 3:26; Gal 2:16 (twice); 2:20; 3:22; Phil 3:9; see Eph 3:12. See Rom 5:19 for another reference to Christ's obedience.

24. Michael J. Gorman, *Apostle of the Crucified Lord: A Theological Introduction to Paul & His Letters* (Grand Rapids, MI: Eerdmans, 2004), 584.

25. Ibid., 585.

26. Furnish, *1 Thessalonians, 2 Thessalonians*, 42.

27. Ibid., 42.

4

# The Church: Got Hope?

## *Richard Lennan*

The church's relationship to hope, especially to its communal dimension, derives from the fact that Christ and the Spirit, the sources of
hope, are the foundations of the church. The church, however, can be
an obstacle to hope, as the sexual abuse crisis has shown so tragically.
This chapter explores how the implication of the church being "one,
holy, catholic, and apostolic" might help us to live hopefully, even within
our flawed church.

Hope, like all virtues, prompts us to engage life in positive ways.
Indeed, the connotations of hope might be uniquely positive
since, as numerous essays in this book illustrate, the impact of hope is
most evident in situations where despair is an option. The generative
dimension of hope becomes even more apparent when we consider that
hope is a risk, that it commits us to a path whose contours we cannot
know in advance.

What, then, enables us to choose hope, to surrender to what we
cannot control, and to sustain the implications of being people of hope?
Answered briefly, hope arises from trust that life is stronger than death.
Hope, therefore, is inseparable from faith. Hope gives expression to our
faith, even if that faith is inchoate and its object largely unarticulated.
When we hope, we claim freedom from both the tyranny of fear and
the obsession with self-protection that fear nurtures. Consequently,
hope is a building block of love: hope frees us to give ourselves to others in love, even to put ourselves at risk for others. For Christians, faith,
hope, and love have both their source and goal in the God whom we

know in Jesus Christ through the Holy Spirit. Consequently, the relationship between the church and hope must have its foundation in the relationship between the God of Jesus Christ and the church: this is a key theme of the chapter.

At issue in this chapter is not whether individual members of the church can be examples of Christ-centered hope or inspire it in others—both history and the present amply affirm this possibility. Rather, the essay asks whether *the church*, taken as whole, has hope as an element of its DNA. In other words, if the church lived without hope in its inner life, if it failed to promote hope in the world, could it be *the church*? That question makes urgent the need to elucidate this essay's definition of *the church*.

## DEFINING *THE CHURCH*

*The church* is a slippery term. That quality is evident in the questions that Joseph Komonchak raises about the term: "Of whom is one speaking when one speaks of the Church? To whom does the word refer? Of whom is it true? *In* whom is it true?"[1] In addition to those fundamental inquiries, Komonchak also asks questions of the titles People of God, Body of Christ, and Temple of the Spirit, all of which appear routinely as synonyms for *the church*:

> What must be true of you if these terms are true of the Church? If these terms are not true of you, are they true of anyone else in the Church? After all, if they are not true of anyone in the Church, what can it mean to say that they are true of the Church?[2]

Underpinning Komonchak's questions is the fact that, in our everyday usage, *the church* has multiple applications: it refers to a building, an object of faith, a people, an institution, and a variety of other possibilities. Further complicating the picture, *the church* exists as *churches*, divided by belief and history, while also struggling for unity. Consequently, rather than seek a single category that is the proper referent of *the church*, we must conclude that *the church* encompasses "all of the above." Although that answer may engender some frustration, it reinforces an inescapable truth: the church is other than a one-dimensional reality.

To be satisfying, therefore, any ecclesiology (the theology of the church) must reflect the "big tent" that is the church. A comprehensive ecclesiology will recognize the church's manifold aspects as assets, not deficits, as possible ways to convey how the church can be symbolic of the richness of God's own life. Such an ecclesiology will also resist the temptation to equate *the church* with, for example, "the pope and the bishops." Although that equation is common, it cannot be valid if it implies that "the pope and the bishops" are an autonomous unit, one whose identity and purpose are unaffected by being part of a church that includes the parish R.C.I.A. program or social advocacy group to which we belong. The opposite, of course, is also true.

Accordingly, when this chapter refers to the relationship between hope and *the church*, it understands *the church* as conveying "all of the above." Every aspect of the church, therefore, must embody a relationship to hope if the church, taken as a whole, is to be an expression of hope. Thus, even the buildings that represent *the church* are relevant to the link between the church and hope: both the architecture of those sacred spaces and the liturgical life of the church that takes place in such spaces can engender hope by inviting us to open our hearts and minds to the God who exceeds our grasp.

A key element of this chapter's effort to portray the church in its richness and complexity is its focus on the historical reality of the church: the church is neither a timeless ideal nor a theoretical construct, but rather a people linked, inextricably, to history. That fact does not separate the church from God or from the future fullness of God's kingdom, but it underscores that the church can express hope only within the concrete circumstances of history. Nonetheless, the church's historical reality is the source of profound challenges to hope. That challenge arises each time we confront the sinfulness inseparable from both individual members of the church and the communal life of the church.

Since the opening years of the twenty-first century, a primary obstacle to the affirmation of a link between the church and hope, and indeed between the church and any other virtue, arises from an especially dark aspect of the church's reality: the sexual abuse of children and teenagers by priests. The failure of a number of bishops to embody the gospel mandate of compassion for the victims of injustice has deepened suspicion toward the church. Reflection on the tragedy of abuse has shown that the bishops who failed to protect victims did so, often, because they privileged an ideal image of the church above the demands of justice and their ministry as leaders in pastoral care. That choice has done incalculable damage to the possibility that people will link *the church* and *hope*.

As the church as a whole encounters the challenge of sustaining hope in the face of such a failure and contradiction, an insight from the German theologian Johann Baptist Metz can be helpful. Metz argues that in the wake of the Second World War, Christians could never again talk about God with their backs turned to Auschwitz.[3] Metz's reasoning runs thus: so devastating was the effect of Auschwitz on our easy assumptions of human progress, and of a God who presided benignly over that progress, that it must change how we speak of God. To speak authentically of God, therefore, requires us to remember purposefully that God is not an idol of our construction, but rather a challenge to our words and actions, including our words and actions related to God. While any analogy to Auschwitz runs the risk of domesticating its unique horror, the devastation wrought by sexual abuse could justify adapting Metz's dictum to the church's present circumstances. Thus, in the wake of clerical sexual abuse, there can be no discussion of hope and the church with our back turned either to the victims of that abuse or to the profound capacity for exploitation and deception that the abuse manifests.

The grim truth of clerical sexual abuse might lead us to abandon any attempt to connect the church and hope. On the other hand, hope, born of faith in the crucified and risen Christ, enables us to face the darkness of our past and present without fearing either that the darkness will consume us or that it alone defines us. Certainly, hope cannot be a ruse to escape the reality of the present, especially a present in which failure or suffering loom large. But trust in God as the object of our faith, which is the foundation of hope, can enable us to retain hope even as we acknowledge our need for conversion.

Past and present failures, then, do not disqualify the church from being a beacon of hope. Those failures, however, signal clearly that the church, in all its expressions, must continually clarify and reclaim the basis of its hope, a process that includes addressing the implications of its failures. As a prelude to examining specific ways in which even the flawed and fallible church might embody hope, the next section of the chapter will discuss God's self-communication in history as the foundation of the church's hope.

## HOPE AND THE IDENTITY OF THE CHURCH

God is the source of the church's hope. That declaration highlights the right relationship between the church and God: the church is not a substitute for God, but depends absolutely on God. For this reason, the primary act of faith for the members of the church is in God, not the church.[4] Although it is vital to maintain the distinction between God and the church, the church exists only because of God. Indeed, it is the relationship between God and the church that establishes the role that the church can play with regard to hope. Those dynamics take us to the heart of the Christian story: God's self-revelation in Jesus Christ.

In Christ, through the Holy Spirit, God "from the fullness of love addresses humankind as friends and moves among them, in order to invite and receive them into his own company."[5] For this reason, the Christian tradition speaks of Christ as the one who inaugurates the kingdom or reign of God. The words and actions of Christ, which heal, forgive, and establish possibility where none was taken to exist, make tangible in our history the reconciling and creative love of God. Christ does not simply do things for people, does not promote a consumerist approach to what God offers, but as Thomas Groome's chapter in this collection illustrates, Christ calls people to new ways of living with one another, ways that embody what God enables, ways that mark the intersection of faith, hope, and love.

The capacity of our hope to be generous, to be resilient, and to allow us to face our failures without despair, all have their origin in Christ. Here, "in Christ" refers to the consequences of his death and resurrection, no less than to his preaching and healing. In Christ's self-surrender on the cross and God's response in raising Christ from death, we see God's unequivocal faithfulness and creative love, which alone can give life in the face of the eclipse of all human potentiality. Because the hope of Christians depends on the God for whom death can never be the final word, the risen Christ is foundational to our hope.

The resurrection identifies and guarantees life in the risen Christ as the fulfillment of our hope. While the resurrection orients that hope to the future, it also frees us to be people of hope in the present:

> Christ is now at work in human hearts by the power of his
> Spirit, not only does he arouse in them a desire for the world
> to come but he quickens, purifies, and strengthens the gen-
> erous aspirations of humankind to make life more humane
> and to conquer the earth for this purpose.[6]

With its basis in the risen Christ, hope prompts us to persevere in love even in the face of death, sin, and failure—including our own. As both Thomas Stegman's and Daniel Harrington's chapters in this text illustrate, hope acts on the conviction that nothing can overcome what God has made possible in Christ.

The vocation to be people of hope in the present, no less than being people oriented to the future fullness of God's kingdom, is the immediate context for considering the role of the church in relation to hope. That role, in turn, has its grounding in the mission of the Holy Spirit.

The Spirit completes the revelation of God as trinity and ensures that the new life of the risen Christ remains available for all times and peoples.[7] The Spirit, however, unlike Christ, does not become incarnate in a single human life. Rather, the Spirit builds on what was begun through the preaching and action of Jesus Christ: the Spirit forms the church as the Body of Christ, the communion of faith centered on Christ.[8] Through the Spirit, the church exists "in the nature of a sacrament, a sign and instrument, that is, of communion with God and of unity among all people."[9]

As sacrament, as the work of Christ and the Spirit, the church is the guarantee of God's saving commitment to creation. The church gives historical form to God's promise that the time will come when Christ will be "all and in all" (Eph 1:23). The church, therefore, is a symbol, a sacrament, of the hope born from God's self-revelation in Christ through the Holy Spirit.[10] Within the church, the Spirit nurtures hope through the scriptures, the sacraments, and the multiple aspects of the church's communal life, through all of which we encounter God's reconciling love. Believing in and with the church underscores that hope is not the product of rugged individualism; rather, it depends on Spirit-formed community, on the gift of others, who provide what we cannot provide for ourselves. As sacrament, then, the church also expresses the human dynamics of hope, through which the Spirit works.

As sacrament, the church is not a magical object that we possess as a way to ensure God's protection in our lives. Rather, the church, through the Spirit, is activity, is mission. The church "receives the mission of proclaiming and establishing among all peoples the kingdom of Christ and of God, and she is, on earth, the seed and beginning of that kingdom."[11] The fulfillment of that mission promotes hope in the world. That promotion comes about, as a number of the other essays in this book show, when the church is an agent of the justice and love that reveal God's reign in the midst of our present circumstances.

Although the case for the church as a sacrament of hope is a strong one, it is important to allay any fears that *sacrament* ignores the limits and failings of the church. This requires, for example, the recognition that the church as the sacrament of Christ is not a second incarnation: as noted, there is always a gap between the church and God. That gap explains why the church, as the Second Vatican Council stressed, remains always "in need of purification."[12] It explains too why the church, to employ another formulation of the council, lives in history as "the pilgrim church," rather than dwelling in heavenly glory.[13]

As a result of the complexity and flaws of the church, to say nothing of its unfinished state, a "Yes" to the church is anything but a self-evident necessity. Indeed, such a "Yes" is itself an expression of hope, a hoping-against-hope in the face of the church's failures. For this reason, it can only be a "Yes" enabled by the Spirit. Through the Spirit, we do not simply tolerate the church as a necessary evil, but draw hope from what our membership of the church offers us. Furthermore, we become able to connect the church, and our life in it, with the pilgrimage to the fullness of God's kingdom. Such an attitude to the church, which the Irish theologian Gerard Mannion characterizes as "aspirational," a word that itself is centered on hope, conveys our conviction that ecclesial faith is "bound-up with trying to build that ideal community of justice and righteousness which Christians refer to as the Kingdom of God."[14]

An aspirational attitude to the church prompts us to more faithful discipleship of Christ, to living more authentically the faith we profess. Through our discipleship, we are able not only to strengthen the hope of others, but also to appropriate our own hope more deeply. An aspirational approach to the church helps us to persevere in the ecclesial community without denying those aspects of the church that contradict the hope that the Spirit enables. In short, a genuinely aspirational approach to the church, as distinct from wishful thinking, enables to confront whatever warps the mission of the church, even the distortions that emanate from *us*, not just from *them*.

## TESTING HOPE: THE CHURCH AS ONE, HOLY, CATHOLIC, AND APOSTOLIC

To test both our hope and our creativity in regard to the church, we can consider how we respond to the creedal affirmations about the church: that the church is one, holy, catholic, and apostolic. At first glance, the use of those four *marks* may seem to be an odd instrument for such a task. Surely, so the objection would go, the marks imply an impossibly perfect church, one less likely to be a source of hope than an object of disdain for its pretensions, especially when the reality of failure reveals the hollowness of those pretensions. For that reason, it is important to begin this section by clarifying what the creedal profession does, and does not, claim about the church.

Because the creed as a whole is a statement of faith in God, the self-revealing trinity, an accurate reading of the sections regarding the church depends on locating them in relation to that God—a method that echoes the argument at the heart of the previous section of this essay. Consequently, our profession of faith in the four marks of the church is not an assertion of the church's perfection or self-sufficiency, but an acknowledgment of the God who, through Christ and the Spirit, is the source of the church. Thus, if the church is one, it is because God is one; if the church is holy, it is because God is holy; if the church is catholic, able to view the whole of reality in its interconnectedness, it is because God's vision is catholic; and if the church is apostolic, dependent on grace for its beginning, present, and fulfillment, it is because God's grace is at the heart of our past, present, and future.

The proclamation of the church as one, holy, catholic, and apostolic, therefore, affirms our faith in God as the enduring source of the church, as the foundation of its hope, no less than its fulfillment. On the one hand, the marks underscore that the church is a future-oriented body, rather than one whose mythic *golden age* resides in our past. As is clear in John Baldovin's chapter on the eschatological orientation of the church's liturgy, our hope draws us forward to the fullness of life in Christ. On the other hand, the marks map out the tasks of the church in the present. As such, they remind us that God's grace is a present reality. The marks underscore that although the church is the product of grace, an aspect of God's self-revelation, that grace is to be embodied: it calls us to become what we proclaim. We believe in a church that, through grace, is one, holy, catholic, and apostolic, but our hope commits us, in response to grace, to working toward the ever-greater realization of a church that is one, holy, catholic, and apostolic. The marks, then, are not simply a gift of the Spirit, they are also a project of the Spirit, working in and through us. As the following paragraphs will indicate, that project unfolds via the particular ways in which each of the marks expresses the hope of the church.

The hope for unity alive in even the divided church of our experience manifests itself in the commitment not to accept division as the norm. Although the churches do not always pursue reconciliation between themselves with the full measure of enthusiasm that the Spirit surely facilitates, the conviction that God enables us to be one fuels the ecumenical imperative, which the Second Vatican Council endorsed resoundingly. Whatever the churches do, therefore, to broaden and deepen the existing, but still-imperfect, communion between them expresses the hope that the Spirit animates.

Similarly, whenever the sinful church professes belief in the holiness that God enables, it also acknowledges its need for a more thoroughgoing conversion to God. As a church, we hear the holy word of God and share in the holy sacraments: through these experiences, we are invited to a deeper trust in God, who is the source of mercy and forgiveness, who enables us to move toward greater integrity. Paradoxically, then, the holiness of the church, no less than its hope, can shine most brightly when we acknowledge our failings and our need for the love of God that is always greater than those failings. Such an acknowledgement is the product of grace-formed humility and the equally grace-formed surrender to God in hope. Both of these attitudes are far removed from the bumper-sticker smugness evident in "Christians aren't perfect, just forgiven."

Holiness, as the expression of the self-communicating God, is anything but ethereal. In fact, genuine holiness underpins both the preferential option for the poor and a commitment to reform in the church. The call to holiness, then, requires that we confront our lack of zeal for mission, as well the continuing prevalence in the church of sexism and the clericalism—"the conviction that ordination to the priesthood confers a special and privileged status that places the priest above the non-ordained baptized by virtue of the sacrament itself"—that undermines the shared mission of all the baptized[15]

The catholic dimension of the church is not always prominent in our thinking, but is no less important or demanding than the other marks.[16] Catholicity tests our vision, challenges us to be as expansive as the God who regards the whole of creation as "very good" (Gen 1:31). For the members of the church, this challenge applies not simply to how we relate to the plethora of faiths and philosophies in the wider world, but increasingly how we deal with difference within the church and with the relationship between office-holders and the rest of the faithful. Here, there are no simple answers, but the willingness to be alert for signs of the Spirit, to attribute good will and to remain open to dialogue with *the other* can express our hope. Conversely, hope, no less than faith and love, suffers when the limits of our personal preferences determine how we measure God's capacity to invite, forgive, and accept.

Our efforts to discern what is authentically catholic are inseparable from the appropriation of the apostolic aspect of the church. Apostolicity reminds us that the church, as the product of God's self-communication in history, rather than our own creation, is not fully at our disposal. Faithfulness to the grace operative through the history of the church means that we are not free to construct the church from scratch in each new generation.[17] Faithfulness, however, also requires that we seek the best ways to continue and develop in the present what God in Christ began with the apostles. Apostolicity, therefore, plunges us into the paradox of discerning, through the Spirit of Christ, how to build a future that springs from our grounding in the history of faith, no less than from our response to the exigencies of the present. Hope triumphs when we accept the challenge of faithfulness to the Spirit-formed unity of past, present, and future, when we struggle to discern, individually and communally, how the Spirit might be speaking to us in the events of our own time.

Taken together, the marks of the church invite us to an ever-deeper engagement with God's Spirit, with our present moment of history, including its diverse cultures, with one another, and with the complexity of the structure and decision-making of the Christian community. For those reasons, the marks speak to the indispensable need for hope in the life of the church. Lived courageously, the marks also manifest and deepen our hope.

Each section of this essay argues that hope is central to the identity of the church. Hope is intimately connected to the faith of the church that is a response to God's self-revelation and to the practice of genuine love that the church is to embody. In particular, hope is always the product of grace, of the Spirit at the heart of the church. Without hope, the church would be the church in name only. With hope, the church can be a symbol of God's kingdom that is the promise of our future, as well as the heart of our present.

## Notes

1. Joseph Komonchak, *Who Are the Church?* (Milwaukee, WI: Marquette University Press, 2008), 10; original emphasis.

2. Ibid.

3. Johann Baptist Metz, *A Passion for God: The Mystical-Political Dimension of Christianity*, trans. J. M. Ashley (Mahwah, NJ: Paulist Press, 1998), 40.

4. On the relationship between faith in God and faith in the church, see Karl Rahner, "Dogmatic Notes on 'Ecclesiological Piety,'" *Theological Investigations* (vol. 5), trans. K.-H. Kruger (New York: Crossroad, 1983), 349–53.

5. Vatican II, *Dei Verbum*, "Dogmatic Constitution on Divine Revelation," art. 2.

6. Vatican II, *Gaudium et Spes*, "Pastoral Constitution on the Church in the Modern World," art. 38.

7. *Catechism of the Catholic Church* (New York: Catholic Book Publishing Company, 1994), 732.

8. For a fuller discussion of the church as the product of both Christ and the Spirit, see Ormond Rush, *The Eyes of Faith: The Sense of the Faithful and the Church's Reception of Revelation* (Washington, DC: The Catholic University of America Press, 2009), 37–62.

9. Vatican II, *Lumen Gentium* (LG), "Dogmatic Constitution on the Church," art. 1.

10. For a fuller discussion of the link between hope and the church's sacramentality, see Richard Lennan, "The Church as a Sacrament of Hope," *Theological Studies*, 72 (2011): 247–74.

11. LG, art. 5.

12. LG, art. 8.

13. LG, art. 48.

14. For the term "aspirational," see Gerard Mannion, "Ecclesiology and Postmodernity: A New Paradigm for the Roman Catholic Church?" *New Blackfriars*, 85 (2004): 305.

15. Scott Appleby, "Clericalism and Sex Abuse," *U.S. Catholic*, 77 (October 2012): 13. For a fuller discussion of clericalism, see George

Wilson, *Clericalism: The Death of Priesthood* (Collegeville, MN: Liturgical Press, 2008).

16. For a discussion of the dimensions of catholicity see Richard Lennan, "Catholicity: Its Challenges for the Church," *New Theology Review*, 24 (2011): 36–48.

17. On this point see Karl Rahner, "Courage for an Ecclesial Christianity," *Theological Investigations* (vol. 20), trans. E. Quinn (New York: Crossroad, 1986), 3–12.

II

---

# NURTURING HOPE

## 5

# "We Had Hoped That He Was the One to Redeem Israel": The Fragility of Hope in Luke-Acts

## *Christopher R. Matthews*

While some Christian interpreters identify Luke-Acts as supersessionistic (that is, that the church replaces Israel as God's people), this essay contends that such a perception runs counter to key indications built into the narrative. It shows that Luke's view is that the hope for the redemption of Israel is an integral part of the hope for the redemption of all, and that this stance reflects the social reality of Luke's early Christian group.

The story of the two disciples on the road to Emmaus on the first resurrection Sunday (Luke 24:13–35) is a pivotal scene in Luke's Gospel for a variety of reasons. Here, I will focus on the expectation of the redemption of Israel voiced by these characters in Luke 24:21, and the implications of this particular hope for the plot of Luke's Gospel and its sequel, the Acts of the Apostles. Speaking for his unidentified companion, Cleopas laments to the incognito Jesus: "we had hoped that he was the one to redeem Israel." The balance of the story aims to show that this expectation had in fact been fulfilled, though in a manner not anticipated by Jesus' adherents. My suggestion in this essay is that the specific "hope" under view in this scene is also an implicit component of the entire story line that stretches from Luke 1 to Acts 28, and that it represents a major impetus to Luke's formulation of his account of the events "accomplished among us" (Luke 1:1) to communicate an essential message to his Christian audience.

In line with Richard Lennan's observation that the church can express hope only within the concrete circumstances of history and Thomas Massaro's analysis of the nature of hope in the context of social relations, both in this volume, my contention is that Luke focuses on precisely this dynamic: an exhortation to hope in the concrete circumstances of an early Christian social body at the end of the first century.

# HOPE FORGONE?

One of the major puzzles confronting interpreters of the narrative action spanning Luke and Acts is how to explain the transition from the hopeful expectation for the salvation of Israel voiced by the Jewish characters in Luke 1—2 to the seeming blanket dismissal of the Jews by Paul in Acts 28. What went wrong? For most Christian interpreters through the ages, Luke's narrative simply presents the basic facts about how the church emerged from Judaism. Thus, Luke's Gospel shows that scribes, Pharisees, chief priests, and even the people of Jesus' hometown rejected both him and his message. And Acts displays more of the same, only now various Jewish authority figures or "the Jews" in general offer the same derisive treatment to the followers of Jesus. Various modern scholars also assert that Luke has "written off the Jews" or even that the origins of anti-Semitism can be traced to Luke himself! In my view, as I attempt to show in what follows, such conclusions ignore significant counter-indications throughout the text of Luke and Acts that call into question Luke's intent to offer a straightforward story of the replacement of Israel/Judaism by the church/Christianity.[1]

# OVERLOOKED RESULTS

Consider some information related by the narrator of Acts and found upon the lips of James and the elders of the Jerusalem church. In the first instance, at Acts 6:7, the narrator informs us, just prior to the long segment ending with Stephen's martyrdom, that "the number of the disciples increased greatly in Jerusalem, and a great many of the priests became obedient to the faith." In the second case, at Acts 21:20, James and the Jerusalem elders stress for Paul "how many thousands of believers there are among the Jews." Both notices occur right in the midst of reported obstacles to the growth of the church. In Stephen's case the threat is from Jewish authorities and a mob, while Paul is harried by "the Jews" numerous times prior to his arrival in Jerusalem, where he also faces serious opposition. What is striking is that juxtaposed to the elements in the narrative that exemplify resistance are Luke's reassurances that the gospel continued to have a substantial impact among Jews, especially among priests! What is going on here? Luke, I suggest, has constructed the text in a way that forces readers to reflect on this very question.

It is reasonable to suppose that Luke formulated the two verses just highlighted (Acts 6:7 and 21:20) to draw attention to an issue of great concern to him, namely, the response of Jews to the gospel message and their inclusion in the church. It should not be overlooked that Luke himself functions as the narrator who explicitly guides readers through the text at various points. This means that the information presented in Acts 6:7 about the continuing influx of believing priests into the Jerusalem church, whether or not it is based on a source, reveals something important about Luke's own convictions. Similarly, as was true of any ancient writer undertaking the composition of a historical account, Luke was obligated to furnish dialogue for his characters consistent with the situations in which they are presented. Thus, when the comment about "thousands" of Jewish believers appears on the lips of James and the elders, this too provides us with knowledge about Luke's own concerns. In strictly historical terms, both of these claims, especially the latter, appear to be rather hyperbolic. Yet whatever one might conclude about their worth as historical data, this in no way detracts from their value as rhetorical constructions that serve to clarify Luke's understanding of what the church should be in both theological and sociological terms.

## THE FRAGILITY OF HOPE

A case can be made, particularly from the infancy narrative in Luke 1—2, that for Luke salvation is a participation in the hope that the God of Israel will redeem his people. A God who promised salvation to Israel but then turned away from this people to offer salvation instead to non-Jews would contradict scriptural promises. A God who goes back on his word would spell the end of hope. It seems that Luke was faced with a monumental theological problem. In the face of what was likely widespread Jewish rejection of, or indifference to, the gospel, the question arose: How is God's faithfulness to Israel to be upheld and Gentile belief legitimated? For Luke the solution to this conundrum seems to involve the formation of a group that includes both Jews and Gentiles (that is, Luke's community/church). But the practical difficulties that must be negotiated to sustain such a complex social situation highlight its fragile nature. Luke addresses this issue by composing a narrative that points the way forward for this new, ethnically diverse social reality. This strategy appears to account for some of the surprising things we learn in Luke and Acts, be it the presence of thousands of Jewish believers in the Jerusalem church (Acts 21:20) or the seemingly impossible benefaction of a Roman centurion who demonstrates his love for the Jewish people by building a synagogue at Capernaum (Luke 7:5).

## ROMANS AND JEWS TOGETHER

The episode of the healing of the centurion's servant is particularly instructive for what it tells us about the focus of Luke's concerns. The account comes from a written source independently available to Matthew and Luke, a source that scholars refer to as the Sayings Source or "Q"; there is a similar story at John 4:46–53 whose relation to the synoptic versions is unclear. When the Matthean (Matt 8:5–13) and

Lukan (Luke 7:1–10) renditions of this episode are compared side by side, several striking differences emerge. There are no Jewish elders in Matthew's story, nor is any reference made to a synagogue. These elements appear to have been added by Luke and, as with the verses from Acts examined above, they appear to tell us something about the concerns that were uppermost in Luke's mind as he composed his Gospel. What is it that we learn here?

The scene in Luke 7:1–10 augments in a significant way our initial observations regarding Luke's focus on Jewish belief in Christ from the texts in Acts. It contributes not only the explicit references to Jewish elders and a synagogue, but also a Roman centurion curiously enamored with the Jewish people and their worship. In simple historical terms, this conjunction of a Roman centurion with Jewish elders in first-century Galilee appears implausible. But the clue to making sense of this scene may lie not in the realm of historical analysis, but rather in the narrative analysis of Luke's broader account and its rhetorical aims. In the ancient world, common convention permitted historians to elaborate their narratives in ways that would be unacceptable to modern practice. Thus, in Luke's day writing history (and it is by no means clear that this is the precise genre that Luke emulates in either of his works) frequently included the rhetorical contribution of the author. We may surely stipulate that Luke's intent is not to deceive; rather, it is to produce a compelling arrangement from the data at hand (sayings, stories, traditions, conceptions, beliefs, and so on) that would persuade readers to see the truth of the matter as the author conceived it. This is essentially what Luke describes as his operating procedure in the preface to his Gospel at Luke 1:1–4.

Returning to the account in Luke 7:1–10, it is not only the added Jewish elements that are important with reference to the larger narrative in Luke and Acts, but especially the combination of Jewish and Roman characters. It will emerge that the hope that Luke cultivates in his two works is tied above all to the coexistence of Jews and non-Jews (represented here by a Roman figure) in one community that is the beneficiary of promises made by God to Israel. These concerns are reflected in the construction of the current account in Luke 7:1–10 vis-à-vis its counterpart in Matthew. Thus, in Luke's account, the centurion does not directly approach Jesus, as in Matthew 8:5, but makes his request for the healing of his slave using Jewish elders as his intermediaries. This process may intend to communicate that the centurion was aware of Jewish purity concerns and acted to respect them. Moreover, it is clear that the Jewish intermediaries do not make contact with Jesus through any coercion on the part of the centurion. Rather, the narrative implies that a deep bond exists between these characters, crystallized in the extraordinary disclosure made by the elders that this Roman centurion "loves our nation, and he built us our synagogue" (7:5). As noted above, this whole scenario seems rather incredible, and it possibly provides us with more insight about the group of Christian believers known to Luke during his day (that is, Jewish and Roman believers together in one group) than it does about events during the time of Jesus.

## "JEWISH GENTILES"

Luke 7 is not the only place that Roman soldiers appear in Luke's narrative in a sympathetic portrayal. In his passion account, Luke retains the reference to the centurion at the foot of the cross from Mark 15:39. But the Markan centurion's christological confession of Jesus as "Son of God" gives way at Luke 23:47 to the following declaration: "Certainly this man was innocent!" This alteration signals that from a Roman perspective Jesus has done nothing wrong, and it fits with many other features of Luke and Acts that indicate Luke's eagerness to assert the compatibility of Christian faith with Roman citizenship. He likely does this not for the benefit of any Roman officials who might read his works (an extremely unlikely prospect), but rather to reassure his Christian audience somewhere around the Aegean Sea, who may have been concerned that their religious convictions might be viewed as seditious by the political authorities. A similar impression is fostered by the various centurions and tribunes who appear as Paul's guards in the latter part of Acts. Luke is somehow able to skirt the fact that these military figures restrain Paul's freedom to offer a portrayal that leaves readers with the impression that these Roman soldiers are on Paul's side: saving him from a mob lynching (21:31–32), cooperating to save him from an ambush (23:16–24), writing letters in his defense (23:26–30), treating him kindly while in captivity (27:3), and sparing his life in a situation of crisis (27:42–43). But the most significant centurion of all appears in Acts 10–11 and embodies what for Luke appears to be a perfect combination of Jewish and Roman/Gentile characteristics.

Luke presents the centurion Cornelius in Acts 10–11 as the first Gentile convert to the gospel. What is significant for the current consideration is the profile of Cornelius that Luke sketches for the readers. Cornelius is not just any run-of-the-mill, idol-worshipping Gentile, akin to the people Paul tells us he preached to in Thessalonica (1 Thess 1:9). Like his counterpart in Luke 7, who surely appears there to prepare readers for Acts 10–11, Cornelius is a most unusual centurion. The narrator (that is, Luke) tells us in Acts 10:2 that Cornelius was "a devout man who feared God with all his household, gave alms liberally to the people, and prayed constantly to God." It seems almost unimaginable that there was such a centurion, but by now we are accustomed to the style of Luke's presentation. The description of Cornelius appears as it does because this is the type of Gentile Luke is particularly interested in—a Gentile who practices Jewish piety. That he is a centurion is a bonus, and we see how Luke constructs his narrative to illustrate and suggest how people from the two main groups of humanity from a Jewish perspective, Jews and Gentiles, must join together into one community to realize the hope of salvation that had been promised in the scriptures of Israel.

Luke's interest in Gentiles who display a special interest in Judaism is sustained as the narrative moves on to portray the basic outline of Paul's mission. In Acts, Paul's pattern is to go first to a local synagogue to proclaim his message, and there are indications of a partial Jewish response in these settings (13:43; 17:4, 11–12; 18:8; 19:17–18). But the text also highlights the interest and response of another category of listeners, proselytes and so-called God-fearers, Gentiles who were already attracted to Judaism and, according to Luke, quite receptive to Paul's preaching. It is primarily Gentiles like these whom Luke portrays as the audience responding to Paul's mission (see Acts 13:16, 26, 43; 16:14;

17:4, 17; 18:7). On only two occasions does Acts provide examples of how Paul addresses a strictly Gentile audience without any affiliation to Jews. These accounts occur at Acts 14:8–18 and 17:16–34, the famous Areopagus speech. As the latter narrative indicates, the results are hardly spectacular and we see nothing like the initial conversion of thousands of Jews in Jerusalem portrayed in the early chapters of Acts. These observations should make it clear that Luke operates with a preference for a "Jewish" type of "Christianity."

It is important to remember that during this period neither of these terms, Judaism or Christianity, refers to a clearly defined socio-religious group. The name *Christian* is only just emerging, and although Luke knows it (see Acts 11:26), he does not refer to the movement he is involved in as "Christianity"; rather, he uses the more Jewish-sounding designation, "the Way" (Acts 9:2; 18:25–26; 19:9, 23; 22:4; 24:14, 22). Precisely what *Judaism* signifies during the decades after the destruction of Jerusalem in 70 CE (and likely well into the second century) is not easy to determine. These definitional issues more than complicate the supposition that Judaism and Christianity parted ways relatively soon after the fall of Jerusalem. In fact, a fair amount of ancient data suggests that the long held notion of a relatively quick and clear separation between Judaism and Christianity is a miscalculation by a magnitude of three or four centuries. Thus, there is ample room conceptually, sociologically, temporally, and theologically for Luke's writings to be seen as evidence for a kind of Jewish Christianity (or Christian Judaism) that existed, albeit briefly, around the turn of the first and second centuries in Luke's own group.[2]

In this light, we can make better sense of the fact that the story line of Acts constantly shows Paul initiating his activity in a new place in the local synagogue, while Paul in his own letters highlights his call to work among the Gentiles. Of course, Acts also depicts significant opposition to Paul promoted by "the Jews," who seek to thwart him at every turn by both legal and nonlegal (violent) means. It is a generally accepted principle among scholars that, in terms of historical reliability, preference must be given to the information contained in Paul's own writings and that the data of Acts should be used cautiously. Thus, the emphasis in Acts on Paul's constant appearance in synagogues may have more to do, once again, with Luke's rhetorical presentation directed to the circumstances of his audience vis-à-vis their Jewish affiliations. Consequently, the story Luke puts before his readers is primarily concerned with matters of interest to his and their time and circumstances, as opposed to what may have happened during the days of Paul. In this way, authoritative figures from the past (Paul, Peter, and others) can be depicted in the narrative of Acts in a way that informs, motivates, and prescribes certain behaviors, beliefs, and practices for Luke's contemporaries.

## HOPE IN THE COMMUNITY OF JEWS AND GENTILES

Another area where we may witness Luke's special concern for the relation between Jews and Gentiles coexisting in the same group devoted to Christ and the God of Israel is in the so-called Apostolic Decree of Acts 15. This chapter stands as the ultimate watershed moment in Luke's account, appropriately located at the center of the narrative of Acts, in which the primary authority figures of the early church meet in Jerusalem and agree to the principle of Gentile inclusion in the church without circumcision or strict observance of the Mosaic Law. From a Christian perspective, it is easy to forget that all of these apostles and elders, along with Paul and Barnabas, as well as James the brother of Jesus, were Jews. Of course, they are also believers in Christ, but one should hesitate to suppose that this fact in any way removes them from Judaism in Luke's view. It may separate them from other forms of Judaism that are uninterested in, or perhaps even hostile to, followers of Jesus. But in terms of the full range of Luke's story, these Jews are realizing the hope that was broached at the outset of Luke's Gospel. What is of particular interest is that when these leaders accept that it is God's own action that has brought Gentile believers into the church, they also stipulate, through James, that these same Gentiles should "abstain only from things polluted by idols and from fornication and from whatever has been strangled and from blood" (Acts 15:20). These four prohibitions comprise the Apostolic Decree, and to publicize this decision the Jerusalem authorities are said to have composed a

65

letter to be circulated among Gentile believers in Antioch, Syria, and Cilicia stating things this way:

> For it has seemed good to the Holy Spirit and to us to impose on you no further burden than these essentials: that you abstain from what has been sacrificed to idols and from blood and from what is strangled and from fornication. If you keep yourselves from these, you will do well. (Acts 15:28–29; see 21:25)

Scholarly discussion of the Apostolic Decree is extensive and there are numerous controverted issues with regard to the precise meaning of the various stipulations that cannot be reviewed here. But the association of Paul with this decree according to Acts bears notice. According to Acts 15:30–35, Paul accompanies Barnabas, Judas, and Silas to deliver the letter to Antioch. Next, Acts 16:4 informs us that Paul, now with Timothy, delivers the decree to the various towns he visits at the outset of his so-called second missionary journey. But in Paul's own letters there is no mention or trace of this decree, not even in Galatians 2, which reports on Paul's version of events at the Jerusalem Council that Acts 15 seems to adjust for its own purposes. In fact, Paul is at pains to point out that in Jerusalem "those leaders contributed nothing to me" (Gal 2:6), a statement that stands in great tension with the decree as it is presented in Acts. How can we account for this discrepancy? One possibility is that Luke introduces the notion of the Apostolic Decree as part of his rhetorical strategy to legitimize the current (or prospective) social practices of Christian groups known to him. Scholars have noticed that the four elements found in the decree (Acts 15:20, 29; 21:25) fit well among the laws catalogued in Leviticus 17–18 that apply to Gentiles living in Israel. Among various proposed interpretations, it might be that Luke's objective was to cover situations in which dietary laws were involved. That is, the rationale behind these limitations seems to be that Gentile Christians must commit to the basic standards that will enable a church made up of Jews and Gentiles to share a common table. As the Acts scholar Ernst Haenchen has noted: "These prohibitions must have come into force in a strongly mixed community of the diaspora, where Jewish claims were more moderate and could be satisfied by the four commandments which Moses himself gave to the Gentiles."[3]

## THE HOPE OF GOD'S SALVATION

Now that we have surveyed a collection of significant passages spread over the full narrative of Luke and Acts, it will be helpful to go back to the beginning of the Gospel to see how the opening chapters prepare the reader for the configuration of Jewish and Gentile components that come later. All of the figures who appear in these chapters are Jews who can be described as righteous or devout or finding favor with God. They exemplify a piety that is centered on the Jerusalem Temple and eagerly awaits God's redemptive action on behalf of Israel. Everything about Luke's infancy narrative makes it clear that the story of God's salvation is firmly embedded within the biblical tradition of Israel. In this way, Luke makes it clear that the origins of the Christian movement itself are to be found at the heart of Israel.

Of particular note is the presence of a series of broad statements about God's saving actions on behalf of Israel: three angelic announcements (Luke 1:13–20, 28–37; 2:10–14) and three hymns voiced by Mary (1:46–55), Zechariah (1:68–79), and Simeon (2:29–32), respectively. These declarations provide the context that Luke wants readers to have in mind as they follow the unfolding of Jesus' activity in the rest of the Gospel. One might conclude from these passages that as far as Luke is concerned, the promised salvation of Israel is the only salvation there is. Of course, a major component of the good news is that this salvation will not be limited to Israel but will encompass the whole world. This becomes particularly clear in Simeon's oracle at Luke 2:29–32, where he describes God's salvation in this way: "a light of revelation to the Gentiles and for glory to your people Israel" (2:32). In Luke's view, Jews and Gentiles belong together and share a common hope; the turn to the Gentiles is not a turn away from the glory of Israel. Luke has composed the infancy narrative to underline the continuity between Israel and the church that begins at the very outset and is apparently an essential characteristic of the Christian community.

# REALIZING THE HOPE OF ISRAEL

All of the texts examined here combine to suggest that in Luke's view realizing the hope for the redemption of Israel is connected with the continuing survival of his own mixed group of Gentile and Jewish believers in Christ. Because the boundaries of Judaism during this time were flexible, it is possible that the conflict between believers in Acts and "the Jews" reflects a struggle in Luke's own day between the Christian type of Judaism that Luke knows and espouses, and another form of Jewish Christianity that continued to observe Jewish ceremonial and dietary regulations and viewed Paul's "concessions" to Gentiles as an illegitimate abrogation of God's law.[4] If this supposition has any merit, the plot development of Acts begins to make much more sense as the product of a small Christian Jewish group in the Pauline tradition that was seeking to promote its understanding of how the hope of God's salvation was to be realized in the world.

That Paul was a hero for Luke is clear from the space that Acts devotes to his life and work. It would not be surprising if Luke knew various of Paul's letters, Paul's reflections on hope, detailed by Thomas Stegman elsewhere in this volume, and especially Paul's conviction with regard to Israel, stated in Romans 11:29, that "the gifts and the calling of God are irrevocable." Such a presupposition seems to underlie Luke's arrangement of his Gospel and Acts throughout, and recognizing this brings clarity to the entire presentation. Thus, when one arrives at the final scenes portraying Paul's meeting with the Jews of Rome in Acts 28:17–28, the notice in 28:28 that "this salvation of God has been sent to the Gentiles" may be seen for what it is: yet another in a series of prophetic announcements to particular Jews in a particular place (see 13:46–47; 18:6), and not a final rejection. For in Luke's view, the hope of the redemption of Israel involves a reversal of expectations (that is, the inclusion of Gentiles in the people of Israel), but it would be hope abandoned if it meant the rejection of Israel. One of Luke's tasks over the course of his two books is to make this point in a multitude of ways. Thus, his primary didactic intent was not to communicate a history of the church, but rather to persuade his readers about the configuration of a church that truly embodies the hope of the redemption of Israel.

## Notes

1. For a more thorough discussion of the characteristics of Luke as an author and his historical setting and theological presuppositions, see Christopher R. Matthews, "Acts of the Apostles," in *The Oxford Encyclopedia of the Books of the Bible*, 2 vols., ed. Michael D. Coogan (New York: Oxford University Press, 2011), 1:11–26. See also Christopher R. Matthews, "Luke the Hellenist," in *Early Christian Voices: In Texts, Traditions, and Symbols. Essays in Honor of François Bovon*, eds. David H. Warren, Ann Graham Brock, and David W. Pao, *Biblical Interpretation* 66 (Leiden: Brill, 2003), 99–107.

2. See Marilyn Salmon, "Insider or Outsider? Luke's Relationship with Judaism," in *Luke-Acts and the Jewish People*, ed. Joseph B. Tyson (Minneapolis: Augsburg, 1988), 76–82.

3. Ernst Haenchen, *The Acts of the Apostles: A Commentary* (Philadelphia: Westminster, 1971), 470–71.

4. See the fascinating suggestion of John Gager, although I would not draw the same implications that he does for Luke's narrative and social situation: John G. Gager, "Where Does Luke's Anti-Judaism Come From?" in *Heresy and Identity in Late Antiquity*, eds. Eduard Iricinschi and Holger M. Zellentin (Tübingen: Mohr Siebeck, 2008), 207–11.

6

# Imagining Hope:
# Insights from Pastoral Care and Counseling

## *Philip Browning Helsel*

Persons struggling with long-term difficulties often feel despair about ever being able to change and thus lose hope. This chapter demonstrates how caregivers can foster hope by asking 'miracle' questions in pastoral care and counseling. Using the theological notion of the eschatological self, I show how the exploration of one's future involves more than planning: it is an encounter with the future-self-held-by-God occurring in an atmosphere of imaginative discernment.

According to Mark's Gospel, when a blind man approached Jesus, he promptly asked the man what he could do for him. Rather than assuming that the blind man wanted to have his sight restored, Jesus asked what he wanted. After the man replied that Jesus could restore his sight, Jesus attributed the healing to the man's faith (10:51–52). Therefore, during his earthly ministry the incarnate Son of God asked persons to speak about what they hoped for and honored these hopes as expressions of implicit hope in the One who is the ultimate object of their faith and ours.

It is important to articulate our hopes. Often it can be easier to explain what seems wrong with us than to describe what brings us fulfillment. Part of this is cultural: we have lexicons of pathology that help us describe our ailments. Another aspect of this may be neurological.

Some neurologists have suggested that our minds function like Velcro for negative experiences: negative experience imprints more firmly in memory than positive experience.[1] To balance this tendency, we need a language for hopeful experiences. As we have seen from the Gospel example, articulating what we hope for is essential to transformation.

Nevertheless, at times hope seems far away. Hope needs to be articulated in everyday hopes in order to come to life. As Dominic Doyle has argued elsewhere in this text, our ultimate hope is union with God. With this goal before us, we live the spiritual life by deepening our faith in a series of intermediate steps in which we come closer to union with God in concrete, observable ways.[2] We cultivate hopefulness by progressively becoming more aware of God's presence in our everyday existence. This can be an implicit sign of the grace of God operating in our lives.

This essay takes place in three parts. First, I clarify the nature of hope. Second, I discuss a method for identifying particular hopes and invite the reader to try this method. Finally, I explore how the process of accessing one's hopes reflects the breaking in of a future that we have yet to experience.

In this regard, I connect future-oriented questions in pastoral counseling with eschatology. Traditionally understood as the branch of theology describing *final things*, eschatology has been reoriented in the last fifty years to an examination of how God's kingdom is breaking in even now. This emphasis is in continuity with how early Christians thought about the kingdom of God. As Daniel Harrington illustrates in his chapter in this volume, the Johannine community believed that the promises and presence of God were uniquely available to them in the present through Jesus Christ. Therefore, eschatology is centrally concerned with how the promises of God are being realized in the present.

## THE LIVED EXPERIENCE OF HOPING

In this first section I will describe some qualities of hope and indicate how despair and apathy frequently threaten hope. In his book *Agents of Hope*, pastoral theologian Donald Capps maintains that hope is central to ministry: "Pastors" and, by extension, lay ministers and social service workers inspired by their faith, "view hope as a critical issue in their ministry and...often judge their ministry to be effective to the degree that it supports, instills, or inspires hope."[3]

Hope involves investment in the future in which we envision ourselves in a hoped-for scenario. Thinking that what one longs for will come to pass, a hopeful person's self inhabits both present and future. Likewise, there is a reflexive nature to envisioning hope: by hoping one sees oneself with one's mind's eye in a new situation. Hoping requires imagination and involves discernment.

Even while seeing themselves in the future, persons must name their particular hopes. This naming is a crucial aspect of hopefulness: "Hoping occurs as the identity of that which is desired becomes known to us. In this sense, hope does not exist until desire has been able to 'name' its object, to say, *this* is what I long and yearn for."[4]

People do not have to manufacture hopes. If they find themselves doing this, it is likely that these are not their own hopes. Therefore, "if we find we have to work hard to create [hopes], this is a signal that we either do not desire this outcome as much as we thought, or that we do not have much hope that it will materialize."[5]

Hope is not merely wishful thinking. Hope is a constructive perception that names specific objects and, for this reason, it can transform the future: "Hope is often the decisive element in *changing* the world of facts."[6] Hopeful persons intuit that what they hope for could indeed come to pass, and at times they sense that it is already happening. They often articulate this sense by saying that they can envision something. By contrast, persons whose hope is threatened have difficulty seeing beyond the present.

Many despair when their hopes seem forestalled. Finding themselves incapable of meeting their goals, they end up in a downward spiral of apathy that may threaten hope indefinitely.[7] In such circumstances, difficulty is in the foreground. Apathy may set in for several reasons. Persons may seem unable to reach long-term goals because their goals are poorly defined or too extensive. In such cases, perfectionistic or unrealistic goals block persons from fulfilling their plans. At other times, persons have placed all their hopes in an unreliable other and so they have no ability to bring about on their own initiative that for which they hope. Finally, some grieve because injustice places barriers in the way of their hopes.[8]

Despair threatens persons' hopes because despairing people "believe that [their plans] of action are insufficient for meeting future goals."[9] This belief can become a reinforcing pattern. Persons who despair because of vague or perfectionistic goals need to name small achievable goals and picture themselves achieving them. Meeting smaller goals, rather than focusing on long-term goals, can help persons feel more hopeful. Additionally, the simple process of meeting small goals often leads to long-term change.

## ASKING ABOUT THE FUTURE

In this section, I will propose a way to imagine a positive, hopeful future, but first I need to indicate some obstacles that people experience to such thinking. As we have seen, people despair for a variety of reasons and this despair can lead to apathy. People may seek help from their pastor or counselor when they find themselves caught in seemingly irresolvable dilemmas and exhausted from trying to solve their problems. At times the "solutions" that they have used may have even created new difficulties. It is especially frustrating when a person's plans do not seem to be able to bring about desired long-term change. Additionally, it is difficult for persons to change with vague or generalized goals such as "feeling better" or "not being depressed any longer." When persons try to solve their problems with vague or perfectionistic long-term solutions, these problems often persist. The core of despair is the sense that one's own agency cannot bring about one's goals. Similarly, some expect their religious leader to provide answers, or hope that their counselor— being an expert about problems—will be able to prescribe the right solution to the problem. If problems depend on an outside expert for their resolution and can only be solved one way, this can contribute to a sense of despair because these notions undermine a person's agency.

Just as Jesus asked the blind man what he wanted, persons often need an opportunity to name specific hopes. Because our conscious thinking becomes patterned around problems, people benefit from opportunities to engage their imagination to discover what a solution would look like in their lives. Therefore, people need to witness small and observable changes in their lives. This frequently leads to further small changes that contribute in the end to significant transformation. This approach addresses the frustration that comes from vague or perfectionistic long-term goals.

People often seek help because their typical ways of handling difficulties have been fruitless. In this situation, they need an opportunity to imagine beyond the horizon suggested by their problems and this need invites responses that are unusual, creative, and even extravagant in scope. While typical helping conversations focus on problems, people can be refreshed by encountering a sense of possibility within their lives. To this end, I maintain that people can be asked a *miracle question*. This kind of question can yield small but observable changes and can address the disjunction that occurs when people believe that their plans are insufficient to meet their goals. The use of the religious term *miracle* implies that God is implicitly present when persons are able to enter the possibilities of their lives rather than being trapped in their difficulties. The miracle question is an unusual exercise that helps a person separate a little from a problem's all-encompassing framework.

There is an important formula for asking the question. First, you prepare the person for the odd experience of being asked a somewhat unusual question. Second, you state that a miracle has occurred but you place the miracle beyond the person's reach by suggesting that they will not know when the miracle happened. Finally, you position the person to witness the effects of the miracle in behavioral terms.

Here is a typical formula for asking the miracle question that should be preserved in order to add to the powerful effect of witnessing one's own miracle:

I am going to ask you a rather strange question...[picture yourself going through your typical nightly routine and going to bed]. In the middle of the night, a miracle happens *and the problem that prompted you to talk to me today is solved!*

74

But because this happens while you are sleeping, you have no way of knowing that there was an overnight miracle that solved the problem. [pause] So, when you wake up tomorrow morning, what might be the small change that will make you say to yourself, "Wow, something must have happened—the problem is gone!"[10]

The miracle question creates a paradoxical situation in which the solution is suddenly in the foreground but the client has no idea what the solution looks like. Presented as a gift, the new future slowly unfurls itself in small observable steps, but the final goal of the change remains obscure. The miracle question reverses the typical order of thinking about problems, in which we focus on understanding the problem in order to solve it. Instead, an aura of mystery surrounds the solution as it dawns on a person in an atmosphere separate from a deep consideration of problems.

Suspense is created as the counselor and client together witness the remarkable unfolding of a different future in observable terms. Witnessing their own miracle, the client is cast as an observer on their lives. Asking clients to contrast an imagined video tape in which "the problem was really getting in the way for [them]" and another video tape "sometime in the near future when things are going better" is another way to highlight the observable nature of the miraculous.[11] Watching the miracle unfold in observable terms places the solution in the foreground. Paradoxically, a miracle, which seems like such a tremendous achievement, takes place in small events that could be captured with a video camera.

Another variation on the miracle question highlights the interpersonal nature of the activity of discerning the miracle by placing the report about the miracle in the third person. A counselor might ask, "How would [your significant other] know that a miracle occurred overnight and that your...problem is solved without your telling [them] that?"[12] Watching the miracle through another person's eyes, clients have a chance to conceptualize themselves doing things that could seem miraculous by the standards of previous experience. Furthermore, it is important that the significant other *not* know that the miracle has taken place. The atmosphere of surprise is maintained even in this fantasized witnessing. The miracle question helps persons whose lives seemed to be dominated by problems begin to value how they are seen by others when they are less influenced by these problems. This is effective because people's sense of themselves is influenced by how they perceive others seeing them. By adding this level of distance, placing the witnessing of the miracle in another person's perspective, the counselor contributes to fresh and observable solutions that tend to have positive interpersonal effects.

# ENGAGING THE MIRACLE

Miracle questions are deceptively simple. I will briefly offer some practical direction that may help when answering miracle questions in order to prepare the reader to imagine his or her own miracle. These suggestions will also address some possible objections you may have.

One of the most important aspects of asking the miracle question is waiting for the answer to arrive. In order to keep quiet, counselors can bite their lips for six seconds or more after asking the miracle question. Likewise, it is important that the counselor's body language not indicate that the counselor wants to speak, lest the unique receptive holding space in which the miracle question is answered be broken.

Because the miracle question seeks to build a richly detailed picture of the solution in a person's life, when a person finds herself saying that she will "not" do or feel something, it is important to affirm her response and ask what she will be doing instead. Once she begins to answer the miracle question with small observable signs, the counselor can ask "What else?" until several answers have been given. The counselor can also ask if there is any small way in which the miracle has already started happening now.

Likewise, some may be concerned that the miracle question might provoke mere fantasy or wishful thinking. Instead, people frequently understand all too well the real limitations and conditions of their lives. One man who had lost his arm in a work accident answered the miracle question by stating that:

He'd wake up with his left arm in place. [The counselor] answered "Sure," and since he didn't know how to go on he waited. A long silence ensued and then the man added: "I guess you mean something that could happen," and [the counselor] nodded. The man went on to describe how he would get up and make breakfast with only one arm.[13]

When given the space, people frequently answer the miracle question within the constraints of their lives.

Ideally, responses to the miracle question focus on the client rather than change in another persons' behavior. Nevertheless, if the client answers that someone else will change, the counselor can focus on what will be different *for the client* after the other person changes and thereby focus again on building a rich description of the miracle that would make a difference for the client.

Sometimes the miracle question is asked in groups that are experiencing conflict. In such cases, it is important to allow everyone to answer the miracle question. In addition, when the miracle question is put in the third person it can help persons to envision positive change in one another's lives in ways that lead to the dramatic reduction of conflict and the building of a shared vision for change. Discovering the miracle can be cast as a playful event in which the counselor asks who was first to discover the miracle and how they noticed it had happened, thus dramatizing the telling of the miracle in ways that begin to make it a reality.

In this sense, the miracle question, if asked patiently, playfully, and persistently, can lead to a surprising outcome. It can offer a person a rich and detailed depiction of a solution when all they had before were pictures of problems. Often these images of a solution are small and observable. They may not seem like much to someone else, but they are miniature miracles to the client. Frequently, persons expect to be able to solve their problems by discovering the cause of the problem and seeking to eliminate it. By contrast, the possibility that arises in response to the miracle question may have little to do with solving the problem. This new future often takes seemingly mundane forms: a simple smile or a friendly meal shared with a family member, an unforeseen moment of grace in which a person slows down and communes with nature. The miracle question allows observable glimpses of a new future to take center stage in the counseling. This is rather different from addressing a vague and perfectionistic ideal such as "feeling better."

# A PERSONAL EXERCISE

Perhaps this would be a good time for the reader to put down the text and prepare to be asked a strange question. In answering this question, you may find yourself using a different kind of thinking than you have used thus far in reading the essay:

*Suppose a miracle happened tonight while you were sleeping and you did not know it. What would be the first sign that a pressing problem you have been facing is gone? How would significant other[s] in your life notice without being told?*

Get a pen and paper and list the small observable signs of the miracle, asking yourself, "What else?" after each one. Try to avoid negative responses and bracket answers that assume someone else will have to change. With some patient waiting, in the space of ten minutes or so, you may start to envision small and observable changes that indicate a miniature miracle.

As we saw earlier in this chapter, many of us become discouraged when our problems persist. This is only compounded when we state vague or perfectionistic goals to address this problem. If we do not feel we can change we feel defeated. On the other hand, by practicing the miracle question for yourself, you may have experienced already an element of possibility in relationship to the difficulties that you have had. In order to foster hope, it is crucial to name particular hopes. The miracle question names hope's occurrence in the present and thus brings the future radically to bear in our own situation. As a result, it contributes to a sense of hopefulness among those of us struggling with despair.

# THE COMING OF ONE'S FUTURE SELF

There seems to be something transcendent at work when people are able to place themselves, even for a few minutes, in the realm of a solution instead of the realm of the problem. In order to understand what it feels like to encounter this realm of the solution, I turn to eschatology, a branch of theology that explores how God's promised kingdom is made present to us. A turn to eschatology is justified because our own future is a mystery to us and yet indispensable to our identities.

Through hoping, we envision ourselves in a future scene and thus we invest in the future, coming up with sensory images that indicate what this future is like. In the use of the miracle question, as rich and detailed descriptions of the solution are built, the process of envisioning the future and investing in it becomes clear.

Nevertheless, the miracle question also disrupts temporal categories. Using the miracle question meddles with linear time. Therefore, responding to the miracle question is different from planning: it is an encounter with one's future self as it breaks into the present. While answers given to the miracle question may not initially seem theological, eschatology helps explain the disruption of the progression of past, present, and future that occurs when the miracle question is asked.

Clients who are asked the miracle question often respond in quite dramatic ways. As one therapist noted, they "appear to direct their attention inward as their body relaxes, …the pupils of their eyes become dilated and their eyelids flutter, …some begin to smile as they become absorbed in the experience."[14] Other therapists have described how clients unconsciously rehearse parts of their answer as they give them. One woman, who described drinking tea on her terrace in the sun as part of the miracle, raised her face to the sun; a mother and daughter stretched out their hands to each other as they described the closeness they would experience after the miracle. The future is bodied forth through the miracle question.

In his book *Counseling Troubled Youth*, pastoral theologian Robert Dykstra used Jürgen Moltmann's distinction between *futurum*—the future in linear time that can be the object of planning—and *adventus*—the disruptive future that breaks in on the present—to describe how the future self can transform the present. Arguing that both *futurum* and *adventus* must be held in tension, Dykstra suggested that the transformations occurring in the lives of troubled youth should be understood as having the quality of *adventus*, a rupture or in-breaking from the future.[15]

Therefore, at times we meet our future selves in surprising ways. Being "*in* Christ," we encounter our future eschatological selves that belong in Christ and will culminate only with Christ's return.[16] This interference with the ordinary progression of time defies cause and effect.[17] Transfixed by that which seems to come from beyond, a small glimmer of hope, the wonder of an answer to a suggestive question that disrupts our familiar relationship with our problems, we act as if a miniature miracle had already taken place.

Dykstra wonders, "Is it possible...that a person might be uniquely molded not only by decisive circumstances from prior experience, but also from the formative influences of that person's future, from what has not yet been experienced? Might one's future actually *create* one's present and past experiences?"[18] Therefore, following eschatology, we can say that the self is not simply the product of the past; it also grows from experiences of disruption or reversal that seem to break into linear time from the future. Just as the resurrection "re-created" the disciples of Jesus, persons "come to themselves" in moments of wonder and unanticipated change.[19]

When persons who are asked the miracle question begin to rehearse it within the counseling hour, the future is close at hand. You may have experienced a glimpse of such an encounter when you wrote a response to the miracle question, especially if some of your answers seemed vivid. How much can we compare our eschatological selves— our future selves held in Christ—with our ability to envision the future in response to the miracle question? Can Christ's promise to always be with us "to the end of the age" (Matt 28:20) be equated with the fulfillment that seems to dawn on persons miraculously when they are asked the miracle question?

While it may be troubling to stretch analogies too far, eschatological theology has something to offer psychology. When Dykstra narrated how a youth named "Stan," who had struggled with anxiety attacks, was overcome by a "peace attack," he suggested that an analogy could be made between the eschatological self and this young man's experience of sudden peace: "It may be presumptuous to suggest that, in his experience of *adventus*, Stan was experiencing the Spirit or presence of Jesus Christ, since Stan himself possessed no language for or awareness of any such holy visitation."[20] Nevertheless, Dykstra suggests that eschatology and human development are not necessarily at odds, since both affirm that life is lived most fully when we are open to the complexity of relationships, allowing ourselves to love and be loved. Therefore, "Stan's eschatological self surprises his developing self with a promise of the self Stan may one day cherish—congruent, integrated, peaceful, and capable of suffering rather than defending against the pain of broken relationships."[21] Miracle questions are thus a brief means of discovering some aspect of this future self and some indication of the wholeness that God desires for us.

Dykstra argues that this notion of the eschatological self—the self held by Jesus Christ that may be yet unknown to the person—actually offers a corrective to psychology: "If theology has too long neglected the tremendous impact of early childhood development on personal formation, psychology has not given their due to sudden, unexpected, singular transformations…the advent of God's startling future."[22]

With difficulties in the foreground, people occasionally witness small glimpses of how life may appear when a solution comes into the foreground. In these moments, persons hear from their future self, their as-yet-unknown self that is held by God even as they are in Christ. From this perspective, the future becomes an opportunity to instantiate God's peace and wholeness that one receives in eschatological glimpses.

We are neither the sum of our pathologies nor the prospect of our careful planning. There is something about the human spirit, ungraspable in empirical terms, that surprises us when we encounter the territory of a new wholeness in our lives. For this reason, eschatology is a helpful theological category to approach the mystery of miracle question conversations.

Additionally, the miracle is often a mystery to us. For this reason, it has to be witnessed through the eyes of another. The syllogistic idea that the miracle happened but we are unaware of its occurrence and can only see it through another's eyes also fits closely with the idea that the eschatological self is in some sense unquantifiable. Just as the epistle to the Colossians promises that our lives are "hidden with Christ in God" (3:3), there is something about the *adventus*, the in-breaking of our future selves, that remains ungraspable, firmly hidden in the future even as it comes to us with small, observable signs of a transformed future.

## Notes

1. Kirk A. Bingaman, "The Art of Contemplative and Mindfulness Practice: Incorporating the Findings of Neuroscience into Pastoral Care and Counseling," *Pastoral Psychology*, 60 (2011): 483.

2. Duane Bidwell, "Working Miracles: Goaling for Short-Term Spiritual Care," *Healing Ministry* 12 (2005): 33.

3. Donald Capps, *Agents of Hope: A Pastoral Psychology* (Eugene, OR: Wipf and Stock, 1995), 25.

4. Ibid., 59.

5. Ibid., 69.

6. Ibid., 70.

7. Ibid., 104.

8. Gregory Ellison, "Late-Stylin' in an Ill-Fitting Suit: Donald Capps' Artistic Approach to the Hopeful Self and Its Implications for Unacknowledged African American Young Men," *Pastoral Psychology* 58 (2009): 484.

9. Capps, *Agents of Hope*, 101.

10. Insoo Kim Berg and Yvonne Dolan, *Tales of Solutions: A Collection of Hope-Inspiring Stories* (New York: W. W. Norton, 2001), 7.

11. Frank Thomas and Jack Cockburn, *Competency-Based Counseling: Building on Clients' Strengths* (Minneapolis, MN: Augsburg Fortress, 1998), 67.

12. Berg and Dolan, *Tales of Solutions*, 15.

13. Steve de Shazer and Yvonne Dolan, *More than Miracles: The State of the Art of Solution-Focused-Brief-Therapy* (Binghamton, NY: Haworth Press, 2007), 39–40.

14. Berg and Dolan, *Tales of Solutions*, 7.

15. Robert C. Dykstra, *Counseling Troubled Youth* (Louisville: Westminster/John Knox Press, 1997), 90.

16. Ibid., 16.
17. Ibid., 15.
18. Ibid.
19. Ibid., 16.
20. Ibid., 91.
21. Ibid., 91.
22. Ibid., 18.

7
_____

# Is There Hope for Faith?

## *Thomas H. Groome*

At the end of his public ministry, Luke has Jesus wonder "will there be faith on earth?" upon his return (18:8). Faith, as always, is the foundation of hope, but in our postmodern and secularized era, the more pressing question may be "is there hope for faith?" This essay proposes the rationale why we can have such hope and a pedagogy that, by God's grace, may ensure as much.

There is an obvious logic to Aquinas' sequencing of the three great theological virtues of faith, hope, and love. As Dominic Doyle's essay in this collection lays out so clearly, faith is presumed to come first as what we believe, encourages us to hope for the good we desire, and should result in love for, and in keeping with, our ultimate desire: God. In theory, we move from faith, to hope, to love, or, to quote Thomas' summary: "Faith shows the goal, hope moves towards the goal, charity unites with the goal." Logically at least, faith is the prior foundation, grounding hope and intending charity. By way of the relationship between the first two, Pope Benedict summarizes that "hope is the fruit of faith."

Though all quite logical, their symbiotic relationship prompts me to propose that there are existential times and places in life when faith depends on hope as much as vice versa. This is obviously true when we push beyond the theological *concept* of faith to the *life of faith*, that is, to faith as *lived* by Christians. When it comes to "being" Christian, indeed we need to have *faith for hope*, but oftentimes our greatest need may be to have *hope for faith*. Perhaps Paul had this reversal in mind when he wrote of Abraham, "Hoping against hope, he believed" (Rom 4:18); sounds like the hope came first. The poet Emily Dickinson had a similar sequence in mind when she imagined hope as a bird "That perches in the soul, / And sings the tune—without the words," that is, before explicit faith.[1]

Might we also hear an echo of faith needing hope in the life of Jesus himself? Toward the end of his public ministry, Luke has Jesus wonder, "When the Son of Man comes again, will he find faith on earth?" (18:8). Within the context, Jesus' question reads like rhetorical rumination to himself. But taking it at face value, might it reflect his felt need to have hope for faith? Having traveled throughout Galilee preaching his gospel of God's reign for some three years, and now facing into the culmination in Jerusalem, was Jesus wondering whether his efforts would remain, if his own mission would endure across time? His comment seems to legitimate the question "Is there hope for faith?" in any time.

While hope can sometimes demand priority in our personal lives, and especially as we face our crosses, there is much to suggest that our postmodern era and culture poses a particular challenge to maintain hope for faith. Social scientists generally agree that our cultural conditions do not lend much hope for faith but rather actively work against it, even posing what can look like attractive alternatives. Charles Taylor contends that instead of religious faith being the foundation of life, as it was in former times, postmodern society has embraced an "exclusive humanism,"[2] *exclusive* in that it denies any need for God in order to live humanly. Instead, it emphasizes self-sufficiency without reference to transcendent sources, values, or hopes.

Of course, "faith is the gift of God" (Eph 2:8); it comes by grace. However, rather than emphasizing it as an "infused" virtue, à la Aquinas, the reality is that faith must be nurtured, reflecting the old Catholic conviction that God's grace typically works through human instrumentality. As the pages of history attest—and our daily lives as well—our collaboration with God's grace of faith is far from inevitable. Indeed, history provides many examples that caution us not to be sanguine in our hope for faith. There was a large Christian community in North Africa at the time of Augustine of Hippo (354–430); it has disappeared. Much of Europe, which once had a deep Christian faith, now seems to be thoroughly sec-ularized. Note, too, the rapid decline of church participation in what had been, until recently, deeply Catholic contexts like Quebec and Ireland. A recent report from the Pew Forum (April 2009) indicates that there are as many as 30 million "former" Catholics in the United States.[3]

So, how might we proactively encourage *hope for faith* in our sec-ular age? From my perspective as a religious educator, I respond that much depends on *what faith* we teach and *how we teach it*—a fairly obvi-ous proposal. To both of these questions, I will offer an equally obvious response. Using Paul's summary, I propose that "Christ Jesus [is] our hope" (1 Tim 1:1). However, this Christ-centered emphasis represents something of a new departure in the practice of Catholic catechesis.[4]

Though our practice may lag, the centrality of Jesus Christ as our best hope for faith is now well reflected in the church's official cate-chetical documents. For example, the *General Directory for Catechesis* (GDC, 1997) summarizes well what is now the "mind of the church" on how to keep hope alive for faith in our time: it champions the cen-trality of Jesus Christ for both *what* and *how* to teach.

## WHAT FAITH? JESUS CHRIST AS THE HEART

So, *what faith* holds the best hope of being taught effectively by contemporary Christian religious educators? The comprehensive answer, of course, must be the full, rich legacy of spiritual wisdom that is Christian faith, its whole Story and Vision. I use *Story* as a metaphor for all the scriptures and traditions that make up Christian faith over time. By *Vision* I intend the hopes and demands, the promises and responsibilities that Christian Story means for people's lives. To have hope for faith, we must present the whole Christian Story and Vision with a persuasive apologetic as an extraordinarily life-giving spiritual wisdom, as the best possible "way, truth, and life" (see John 14:6) by which to live.[5]

This being said, the question remains, what will be the defining core of the Christian faith we teach? What will be "the canon within the canon" of this great faith tradition, which will constitute the heart of its hope in our postmodern world? To this, I believe, we can give only one resounding answer: Jesus Christ.

Though patently obvious, this is worth stating and particularly, perhaps, for Catholic Christians (see note 6): *the most hopeful heart of Christian faith is Jesus Christ.* For the heart—and thus the hope—of Christian faith is not the church, nor the scriptures, nor the dogmas and doctrines, nor the commandments, nor the sacraments, nor any other one "thing"—important and vital as all these are to our faith. Rather, as the *Catechism of the Catholic Church* (CCC) so well summarizes, "At the heart…we find a Person, the Person of Jesus of Nazareth, the only Son from the Father" (CCC #426).[6]

Note well that the Catechism names the core "Person" as both *the Jesus of history*, the one "of Nazareth," and *the Christ of faith*, "the only Son from the Father." So, Christians are called to be disciples of that carpenter from Nazareth who walked the roads of Galilee, who preached the reign of God with its rule of radical love, even of enemies, who fed the hungry, cured the sick, consoled the sorrowing, and welcomed the marginalized, who claimed to be the kind of Messiah that brings liberty to captives, sight to the blind, good news to the poor, and sets free the oppressed (see Isa 61:1 and Luke 4:21), who presented himself as "the way, the truth and the life" (John 14:6), and invited all and sundry to "come follow me" (for example, Matt 19:21, Mark 1:17). Such is *the way* that the historical Jesus modeled for us. Presenting his gospel in its fullness, its joys and challenges, is our best hope for attracting people to Christian faith, and more than ever in our time.

To have hope, however, of following *the way* of Jesus we need him also to be *the Christ of faith* for us, the Son of God, the second person of the Blessed Trinity, who by his life, death, and resurrection makes it possible for disciples to so live. The paschal mystery forever mediates to us that abundant grace that grounds our hope of living as Christians. Because of his dying and rising, we *can* live as disciples of Jesus. In sum, to educate with hope for Christian faith, Jesus the Christ must be the defining center of *what* we teach.

I have a friend who likes to play association of ideas at social gatherings. He claims that when played around Christian denominations, if he says, "Baptist" people typically associate "Bible"; when he says "Evangelical," people tend to say "Jesus"; and when he says "Catholic," people most often say "church." Our best hope is to educate in faith so that the first association that Catholics will have with being *Catholic* is Jesus Christ.

This is certainly the clear intent of the church's contemporary catechetical documents, epitomized in the summary statement from the Catechism just cited. The GDC describes the primary purpose of catechesis as to "put people in communion and intimacy with Jesus Christ" (#80), presenting "Christian faith as the following of his person" (#41). Note well that such conversion demands "full and sincere adherence to his person and the decision to walk in his footsteps" (#53), albeit entailing an apprenticeship (a favorite GDC term) that takes a lifetime. "Adhering to Jesus Christ sets in motion a process of continuing conversion, which lasts for the whole of life" (#56).

The GDC makes clear that this renewed emphasis in Catholic catechesis should not fall into a christomonism, as if Jesus were the beginning and end of Christian faith. Instead, he is the key to how we understand and come to share in the triune life of God; Jesus represents the fullness of divine revelation and embodies God's overflowing trinitarian love toward us. As always, "the Word of God, incarnate in Jesus of Nazareth, is the Word of the Father who speaks to the world through his Spirit" (#99). This means that "every mode of presentation [of faith] must always be christocentric-trinitarian: 'Through Christ to the Father in the Holy Spirit'" (#100). Thus, the GDC repeatedly makes clear that Jesus reveals God's unconditional love for all people, and that God's work of salvation in Jesus continues in the world through the Holy Spirit. All catechesis, then, must reflect "the trinitarian christocentricity of the Gospel message" (#99–100).

In catechetical practice, too, the centrality of Jesus and discipleship to him has prompted a more holistic sense of the faith for which we are to catechize. As the Doyle essay summarizes, for Aquinas "faith encounters God in the primal terms of *truth*," and thus the primary function of faith is belief. Although Aquinas never intended as much, this encouraged a catechesis that presented Catholic faith simply as a list of teachings that people are called to believe. Indeed, the *Catechism of the Council of Trent* defined faith as "that by which we yield our unhesitating assent to whatever the authority of our Holy Mother the Church teaches us to have been revealed by God."[7] Thereafter, formal catechesis was crafted primarily around question-and-answer catechisms that summarized "the beliefs" and taught them to be simply memorized.

In keeping with the sentiments of the Second Vatican Council, the GDC returns to a holistic sense of Christian faith as if it should shape people's whole way of *being* in the world. So, Christian faith has "cognitive, experiential, [and] behavioral" aspects (#35); it engages people's minds, emotions, and wills; it is to permeate how we make meaning out of life, the quality of our relationships, and the ethic by which we live (#16). Summarizing, the GDC echoes the traditional tripod of Christian faith as *lex credendi, lex orandi,* and *lex vivendi,* that is, shaping our norms for believing, praying, and living. For this reason, though knowledge of the faith is vitally important (#85), "formation for the Christian life comprises but surpasses mere instruction" (#68). As I elaborate in the section to follow, this suggests a catechesis that re-integrates "faith" with "life" toward a "life of faith."

## HOW TO TEACH? PERHAPS AS JESUS DID

Now the pressing practical question is what kind of pedagogy might offer the best hope for effective education in holistic Christian faith for our postmodern context. In struggling with this question, I have learned much from the great Brazilian educator, Paulo Freire (1921–97).[8] A central theme in Freire is that education that shapes people's lives must engage their everyday praxis by crafting curriculum around "generative themes," in other words, around the issues of life that matter to them. I am convinced that we can detect this kind of pedagogy long before Freire in the teaching ministry of Jesus of Nazareth. He constantly engaged the everyday of people's lives in order to teach his gospel of God's reign, inviting the integration and integrity of a lived faith. So, might the hope engendered by placing Jesus at the center of *what* we teach be enhanced all the more if we also aspire *to teach as Jesus did*?[9]

For *how* he taught, we have only hints from the Gospels, which are the memories of the first Christian communities. Yet we can detect a pattern of pedagogy that is so consistently described that we can take it as reliable. Indeed, the Gospels refer to his public ministry as "teaching" some 150 times. Nicodemus had it right: "we know you are a *teacher* who has come from God" (John 3:2). By way of Jesus' overall approach, we can readily recognize: a) his *inclusive outreach and welcome toward all*— men, women, and children—including ordinary people, farmers, shepherds, merchants, homemakers, fishermen, with special outreach to the marginalized; b) his *respect for the learners*—empowering people to be agents of their own faith (for example, "you are the light of the world" [Matt 5:14]); and c) his whole life was a parable of *compassion for all*. How hopeful our catechesis will be if we can imitate Jesus' inclusion, empowerment, and compassion.

## Jesus' Pedagogy

Focusing on Jesus' pedagogy, I propose that his dynamic was to lead people *from life to faith to life-in-faith*. He did so by:

* Beginning with people's lives
* Encouraging their own reflections
* Teaching his gospel with authority and for lived faith
* Inviting people to see for themselves, to take his teaching to heart
* Encouraging their decisions for faith as disciples

*Beginning with People's Lives*: First, Jesus most often began a teaching event by inviting people to look at their present lives, at their reality in the world. He turned his listeners to their own experiences, to their feelings, thoughts, and values, to creation around them, to the beliefs, practices, attitudes, and mores of their religious tradition and culture, to their work and social arrangements, to their joys and sorrows, fears and hopes, sins and goodness—to life. His favorite teaching method in this regard was through use of parables in Matthew, Mark, and Luke, and through allegories (for example, the Good Shepherd [John 10:11]) or "signs" (for example, the wedding at Cana [John

2:1–11]) in John's Gospel. All of these begin with symbols of everyday life through which people could recognize their own lives and stories. His pedagogy was to reach into the very souls of his listeners in order to actively engage them.

For example, Jesus' parables were engaging stories—as good stories always are—through which people could recognize some aspect of their own experience and later see for themselves how to appropriate his teaching back to their everyday lives. When he taught the parable of the sower, I imagine he was talking to farmers; the parable of fine pearls was likely to pearl merchants; the lost coin to a group of women, perhaps gathered at the village well; and so on. Jesus engaged people's interests and made them active participants in the teaching/learning dynamic by raising up real life themes and issues of concern.

*Encouraging People's Own Reflections*: Second, Jesus invited people to think about their lives in a whole new way. He wanted his listeners to recognize that great things like the reign of God and their own eternal destiny were being negotiated in the ordinary and everyday of life, even while sorting fish. He wanted them to reflect on the falsehood of hypocrisy, the emptiness of ritual detached from doing God's will, the faith contradiction in hating any group or class, the unconditional love of God regardless of one's worthiness.

Again, Jesus' commitment to encourage people's own reflection was epitomized in his use of parables. Indeed, his parables often turned people's perspectives upside down. None of Jesus' first hearers would have expected the Samaritan to be neighbor, nor the father to welcome home the prodigal, nor the prostitutes and tax collectors to enter the reign of God before the religious leaders. Such *reversals* were Jesus' way of getting people to reflect critically, perhaps to change their minds and hearts, to see their lives and possibilities with fresh hope and in a whole new way. Freire would say that his teaching style invited people to a *critical* consciousness, to reflect on and question their own reality and to imagine how to live more faithfully as people of God.

*Teaching His Gospel with Authority and for Lived Faith*: Third, from the very beginning of Jesus' public ministry, people recognized that he "taught them as one with authority" (Mark 1:22). Clearly, Jesus took strong positions in teaching his gospel. Jesus deeply appreciated his Jewish tradition, never intending to abolish the Law and the Prophets but "to make their teaching come true" (Matt 5:17). Yet he also claimed the authority to propose a new vision for living as a people of God: "You have heard it said...but I say..." (Matt 5:21–22).

Likewise, Jesus taught for faith in ways that were meaningful to people's lives. Notice that so many of his statements inviting faith in himself have a follow-up that lends hope. So, "I am the light of the world" is immediately followed by "Whoever follows me will have the light of life" (John 8:12). He presented himself as the good shepherd and this means that we can "have life, and have it abundantly" (John 10:10–11). Even as he says, "I am the living bread that came down from heaven," he adds that this is all given "for the life of the world" (John 6:51). Faith in Jesus calls disciples to a lived and living faith that is wonderfully hopeful for ourselves and for society.

*Inviting People to See for Themselves*: Fourth, Jesus taught in a way that invited people to recognize for themselves his spiritual wisdom for life, to take to heart and personally embrace the truth he was teaching. Jesus often blest those "with the eyes to see and the ears to hear" (Matt 13:16). Referring surely to more than physical seeing and hearing, he wanted people to open their hearts and make their own what he was teaching. He enabled the Samaritan woman to come to see for herself: "Could this be the Messiah?" (John 4:29). The same was true for her friends; they, too, came to recognize him for themselves: "It is no longer because of what you said that we believe, for we have heard for ourselves and we know that this is truly the Savior of the world" (John 4:42). Of course, the greatest example of Jesus' pedagogy for people to "see for themselves" is the story of the risen Christ and the two disciples on the road to Emmaus (check Luke 24:13–35), which Chris Matthews explores in his essay elsewhere in this volume. Indeed, that story perfectly reflects Jesus' whole *life to faith to life* approach.

*Encouraging Their Decisions for Lived Faith*: Fifth, Jesus' invitation to discipleship—to lived faith—was ever on offer. The intended outcome of his entire public ministry was that people might decide to live for the reign of God—the ultimate symbol of hope—to follow his way as disciples. Jesus was adamant that to belong to God's reign, people cannot simply confess faith with their lips, saying "Lord, Lord," but must "do the will of my Father in heaven" (Matt 7:21). That surely requires decision. Jesus even went so far as to say, "Whoever does the will of God is my brother and sister and mother" (Mark 3:35). From his opening statement inviting people to "repent and believe in the Gospel" (Mark 1:15) to his farewell discourse, "live on in my love…keep my commandments" (John 15:9–10), Jesus invited people to decision for lived faith.

In summary, Jesus engaged people's own lives and encouraged their reflections on them. He preached with authority the old-and-new faith that was his gospel. He invited would-be disciples to see for themselves how to integrate "life" and "faith" and to make decisions for lived, living, and life-giving faith. Jesus' pedagogy was one of bringing *life to faith to life*. Our best hope for faith in our time is to do likewise.

## This Life to Faith to Life Approach

The Second Vatican Council declared that the "split" that Christians maintain "between the faith which many profess and the practice of their daily lives" ranks as "one of the gravest errors of our time."[10] This is a rather amazing statement, given all the candidates there are for "error." Clearly, to have hope for Christian faith in our time, we need a way to teach it that consistently integrates *life* and *faith* into a lived faith. Here again, we find a contemporary source of hope in the GDC. Throughout the latter part of the twentieth century, a debate raged as to whether catechesis should be "kerygmatic" or "experiential," often pitting these approaches as opposites. The GDC states repeatedly that catechesis must be both, that is, it must teach faithfully the faith handed down *and* engage people's lives—toward integrating the two.

So, in the pedagogy of catechesis, "every dimension of the faith, like the faith itself as a whole, must be rooted in human experience" (GDC #87). For the fact is that "experience promotes the intelligibility of the Christian message"; thus, "experience is a necessary medium for exploring and assimilating the truths which constitute the objective content of Revelation" (#152). Catechetical education is most effective when it presents every aspect of the faith tradition "to refer clearly to the fundamental experiences of people's lives" (#133). Such statements are surely consistent with the pedagogy of Jesus.

For almost forty years now, I have been attempting to develop, articulate, and practice a *life to faith to life* approach to Christian religious education and catechesis. I have written about it more formally as a "shared Christian praxis approach."[11] I now refer to it with the more user-friendly *bringing life to faith and faith to life.*[12]

In sum:

1. *A life to faith to life approach encourages a teaching-learning community of active participation, conversation, and presentation;* in other words, the primary paradigm is of community and conversation before classroom and "didaction";
2. *...in which people share their reflections on their own lives in the world around a generative theme of life or of life-in-faith;* the theme for reflection and conversation must be of real consequence to participants' lives;
3. *...are given persuasive and hope-filled access to the truths and spiritual wisdom of Christian Story and Vision regarding the theme;* this is the prime moment of accessing the formal content of Christian faith;
4. *...are encouraged to personally integrate their lives and their faith, and to make decisions accordingly;* such integration of life and faith is the intended "learning outcome" throughout but is fostered explicitly here.

I have organized this approach more deliberately around a focusing activity and five pedagogical movements:

*Focusing Activity—Establishing the Curriculum around a Life/Faith Theme*: Here, the educator's intent is twofold: a) to engage people as active participants in the teaching-learning event, and b) to focus them on a generative theme of life, of faith, or of life-in-faith, that is of real interest to them. For example, a unit on Jesus with adolescents might have them imagine themselves on the road to Caesarea Philippi (Matt 13:13–20 and Mark 8:27–30) and invite them to begin to wonder who *their* Jesus is.

*Movement One (M1)—Expressing the Theme as in Present Praxis*: The educator encourages participants to express themselves around the generative theme as reflected in their present lives and situations. They can express what they do or see others doing, their own feelings or thoughts or interpretations, and/or their perception of what is going on around them in their socio-cultural context. Their expressions here can be mediated through any means of communication—spoken words, art, writing, movement, construction, and so on. One might invite the teenagers, "Imagine Jesus put the question to you, 'who do *you* say that I am'" and then, "how would you respond?" (their own praxis of Jesus).

*Movement Two (M2)—Reflecting Critically on the Theme of Life/Faith*: The intent here is to encourage participants to reflect critically—discerningly—on the praxis they expressed in M1. Critical reflection can engage reason, memory, imagination, or a combination of them; such reflection can be both personal and socio-cultural. Here, the teenagers might reflect on "who or what has shaped my image of Jesus?" and "What difference does Jesus make to my life?"

*Movement Three (M3)—Accessing Christian Story and Vision*: Here, the pedagogical task is to teach persuasively the Christian Story and Vision around the particular theme, and to do so with hope. The key is that participants have ready access to the truth and spiritual wisdom of Christian faith around the theme and what it might mean for their lives and world. For our example, M3 is the most overtly catechetical moment; now is the time to lay out an understanding of Jesus, appropriate to age level, highlighting both who Jesus is from the perspective of Christian faith and what it means to live as a disciple of Jesus (that is, both Story and Vision).

*Movement Four (M4)—Appropriating the Truths and Wisdom of Christian Faith to Life*: M4 begins the dynamic of moving back to life again with renewed Christian commitment (M5). Here, the pedagogy encourages people to see for themselves what the truths and wisdom of Christian faith might mean for their everyday lives, to personally appropriate the faith with hope for who they are and how to live. For our example, the reflective activities here could invite participants to express their emerging/developing image of

Jesus as they take the instruction to heart, what discipleship to him might ask of their lives, and so on.

*Movement Five (M5)—Making Decisions in Light of Christian Faith*: Here, participants are invited to choose how to respond to the truths and spiritual wisdom of Christian faith, and to do so with hope for their lives. Decisions can be cognitive, affective, or behavioral—what people believe, how they might relate with God or others, or the ethics by which to live. The questions and reflective activities for the adolescents in our example would invite explicit decision at some level, for example, "if a person professes faith in Jesus, what would this mean for their lives?" or, depending on the context, "do you want to live as a disciple of Jesus?" and if so, then "so what?"

After many years of working with it and with other religious educators who use it consistently, I am convinced that a pedagogy that enables people to bring their lives to their faith and their faith to their lives can lend hope for faith in our time. Of course, there is no one sure-fire way of insuring that Christians integrate their lives and faith into lived faith. But a *life to Faith to life* approach seems to be a fitting instrument for the workings of God's grace in our time. It puts Christ Jesus at the center and reflects his own pedagogy. Therein lies our hope for faith.

## Notes

1. Emily Dickinson, "Hope," in *Selected Poems* (New York: Dover Publications, 1990), 5.

2. Charles Taylor, *A Secular Age* (Cambridge, MA: Harvard University Press), 2007. See pages 25–28 for Taylor's summary of why "exclusive humanism" has emerged in postmodern cultures.

3. See the Pew Report, *US Religious Landscape Survey*, April 2009; available online at http://religions.pewforum.org.

4. One reason why Catholics don't immediately associate Jesus as "the heart" of their faith is the enduring legacy of the old catechisms. With the doctrinal section built around the Apostles' Creed, there was almost no attention to the Jesus of history. Recall that the Creed jumps from "born of the Virgin Mary" to "suffered under Pontius Pilate." In consequence, the catechisms literally skipped over Jesus' public life and

preaching. Even regarding the Christ of faith, the intent was much more to state technical dogmas than what Christ means for our lives. For example, the *Baltimore Catechism* had no explicit Q&A on the meaning of Easter for Christian faith. By way of pedagogy, it is patently obvious that the question-and-answer doctrinal summaries of the catechism were a long way from the approach of the storytelling Jesus.

5. For further reflection on "a persuasive apologetic," see Thomas H. Groome, *Will There Be Faith: A New Vision of Educating and Growing Christians* (San Francisco: Harper One, 2011), 145–53.

6. The Latin text of the *Catechism of the Catholic Church* was promulgated in 1997. I cite from the second edition, English translation (Washington, DC: USCCB, 2000).

7. *Catechism of the Council of Trent*, John McHugh, ed. (New York: Wagner, 1923), 11.

8. Building a praxis-based pedagogy around the "generative themes" of people's lives is a central aspect of Freire's approach. See Paulo Freire, *Pedagogy of the Oppressed* (New York: Seabury Press, 1970).

9. This phrase reflects the fine pastoral letter issued by the US Catholic Bishops; see *To Teach as Jesus Did* (Washington, DC: USCCB, 1973).

10. Vatican II, *Gaudium et Spes*, "Pastoral Constitution on the Church in the Modern World," art. 43.

11. The most complete account of a *shared Christian praxis approach* can be found in Thomas H. Groome, *Sharing Faith: A Comprehensive Approach to Religious Education & Pastoral Ministry* (San Francisco: HarperSanFrancisco, 1991).

12. For the best and less technical explanation of the *life to faith to life* approach, see Groome, *Will There Be Faith*, especially chapters 8 and 9.

# 8

# Glimpses of Christian Hope along the Migrant Journey

## Hosffman Ospino

This chapter is a practical theological reflection on Christian hope in light of the experience of Latin American migrants on their journey to the United States. The essay explores the various moments of the migrant journey, namely, preparation, the journey itself, and arrival; it identifies theological themes emerging in each of these moments. Migration is treated here as a theological category that has the potential of revealing something new about hope and the overall Christian experience.

Millions of people every year make the difficult decision to leave their homeland to go somewhere else. Only a small number do so to study, undertake well-paying jobs, conduct business, or enjoy their wealth. The vast majority must leave to survive; most are poor. Countless people have to leave family, friends, and cultural roots behind, understanding that they may never reconnect with them. They cross borders, legally and illegally, into other countries, with the dream of finding better opportunities to fulfill their most basic needs and intimate hopes. There is no assurance that they will succeed in their quest. Many do; many do not. Despite this uncertainty, countless people embark on the journey and take their chances anyway. Lives are at stake, their own and those of the people they love. For many, there is no other option.

This practical theological reflection takes the experience of migration as its starting point.[1] The term *migrant* is used here to name people who journey from one nation to another searching for better living conditions (for example, food, job, medicine, shelter). I focus primarily on recent research and analyses about the experience of Latin American migrants on their way to North America. This essay is an exploration of how the migrant experience, as well as the presence of immigrants in our midst, can compel Christians to examine with new and critical eyes how we live our faith here and now. I argue that the migrant experience challenges the believing community to interpret Christian hope from a unique perspective. It challenges unexamined assumptions about what it means to be a community of faith and opens perhaps unfamiliar windows into the mystery of the divine revealed in history.

## THE REALISTIC AND METAPHORIC POWER OF THE MIGRANT EXPERIENCE

To state the obvious: migrants are real people, flesh-and-blood women and men of all ages whose hopes and desire for fulfillment point to the drive of the human spirit not to succumb to that which makes us less. Migrants have names and identities shaped by the cultures in which they were born and raised. They have families who often depend on them for survival, as well as spouses, children, parents, relatives, and friends who miss them and hope that one day they may be together again. The suffering of migrants, along with the perils of journeying across frontiers, is exacerbated when they realize that those whom they most love are left behind, that distance can erase important memories, that they are traveling into the unknown. Yet the joys of a migrant seem to offset some of that suffering in a rather inscrutable way. The smallest achievement along the journey raises hope, despite the wounds that cause pain and scars, which serve as constant reminders of the cost of migrating. The fact that others have "made it" often justifies the risks. Migrants are very likely to reconnect with their religious roots more intentionally, renewing their relationship with God. God emerges on the migrant journey as companion, protector, guide, and even consoler. The unique relationship of the migrant with God and all those involved in the migration experience offers the theologian and the believing community a great resource to learn more about God's presence in history.

99

# Nurturing Hope

No theological reflection about hope in light of the migrant experience can dispense with the "faces" and "voices" of migrants.[2] Neither can it ignore the experience, questions, and concerns of the communities that are directly confronted by the presence and the demands of the migrant *other*. The realistic character of these experiences, in fact, turns the tables on all attempts to advance conversations—theological, ministerial, and even political—under the guise of (naïve) neutrality or the presumption of disengaged objectivity. The presence of the migrant constantly invites the Christian community to revisit how the gift of hope, in its human and religious dimensions, is interpreted, lived, and appropriated here and now—of course, without losing sight of its transcendent dimension.

Hope is "the desire for a future, difficult, yet possible good," writes Dominic Doyle in this collection. Furthermore, "For believers, hope is the desire for unending union with God....The goal of religious hope is thus called *eternal happiness*." Gabriela, a Catholic immigrant mother of two, would have no quarrel with this classical definition of hope. As a woman of faith she trusts in the promise of eternal happiness and would agree with Doyle when he notes that Christian hope "envelops all ordinary hopes within a transcendent horizon of meaning and dignity." But it is possible that human hopes, even when fragile and historically limited, may lead to fresher understandings of Christian hope. In an interview about her migrant experience, Gabriela stated: "there was no hope that things would improve in Guatemala. We either had to leave or we would starve."[3] What makes Gabriela's words uniquely compelling is that hope for her is mediated through deeply existential concerns: her children, the need to survive (to beat hunger), and the realization that human hope may be no more where she lived. It is not a question of hopelessness—much less of theological despair—but a realistic awareness of reality as she experienced it and the emergence of a renewed sense of hope in God, who can lead her somewhere else to enjoy what was denied to her and her children.

It is this kind of realism that has the potential to lead theologians and pastoral ministers to draw important insights to read the larger Christian tradition in creative ways. In this case, the migration experience lends itself as a metaphor to examine our understanding of Christian hope in the here and now of our historical experience. It can help Christians to revisit the question of what it means to be a prophetic community through the practice of hospitality and advocacy, or it can challenge a particular group of believers to get out of their comfort zone and act as instruments of hope for the migrant other.

Biblical and more classical definitions of hope inform the praxis of the Christian community by presenting not only a vision, but also distinct appropriations of what God wants humanity to know about this theological virtue through revelation. Nevertheless, the presence of migrants in any community introduces particular questions, raises new concerns, and makes distinctive demands. The migrant experience, then, as a metaphor challenges us to read biblical and classical definitions of hope from the perspective of "the particular." Such reading—along with the questions, concerns, and demands born out of the migrant experience—invites us to assess the convictions and practices that we claim embody Christian hope. At the same time, such reading summons us to learn from how others—in this case migrants—live and interpret hope, humanly and religiously, in the complexity of their everyday experience.

Is there, then, a major distinction between the human hope that drives the Christian migrant onto a journey in search for a better life and Christian hope as a theological virtue? These hopes are distinct insofar as the degree of fulfillment to which each points—within and beyond history. It is our conviction as Christians, however, that hope in eternal life through Jesus Christ is first experienced in the present of our immediate historical existence. For this we must allow God's reign to become a reality in our midst. Christian hope, the fruit of faith, informs our human hopes.

## THREE MOMENTS FOR HOPE

It is possible to identify three key moments as part of the migrant journey: preparation, transit, and arrival. The decision to leave one's land, family, and social networks to live in a different nation—crossing not only geographical, but also cultural boundaries—implies a complex process of *up*-rooting and *re*-rooting oneself. Such process is usually accompanied by faith that sustains and hope that moves hundreds of thousands of Christians from Latin America to search for a better life. Many of these believers refuse to accept that they and their families cannot enjoy God's plan of fulfillment for humanity *in history* because of conditions that often are contrary to such plan. If searching for better life conditions implies making major sacrifices, they are willing to do so and trust that the God of their faith will not abandon them in the process. Isn't this similar to what drove the people of Israel at various moments in the scriptures?[4]

Sociologist and migration scholar Jacqueline Maria Hagan rightly observes that most efforts to understand the migration dynamics of Latin Americans traveling to the United States have failed to recognize the central role that religion plays.[5] Religion, and more particularly Catholic Christianity, has much to say to interpret the experience of this particular body of migrants. As a sociologist, Hagan documents religious practices and convictions among Latin American immigrants from the time they prepare for the journey to the time they cross borders. Building on her research, I propose that we focus on the three moments of the migrant journey—preparation, transit, and arrival—and see how each moment provides glimpses of human and religious hope. These glimpses allow us to embrace the migrant experience as a metaphor to enter more deeply into the beauty of the mystery of the Christian faith here and now.

## Hope Preparing the Journey

Religion comes into play when millions of Latin Americans realize that their own societies, supposedly influenced by Christian values over the centuries, have failed to provide opportunities for all to live with dignity. They often hear about this dignity in church. They have been told for generations that every person enjoys a unique dignity because every human person has been created in God's image and likeness. They trust that God's promises for humanity are true, that God's reign has already begun in history, a reign of "righteousness and peace and joy in the Holy Spirit" (Rom 14:17). But the sinfulness of abject poverty, injustice, oppression, and prejudice contradict their God-given dignity and the presence of God's reign. Gabriela's words quoted earlier seem to hint that these circumstances can lead many to think that hope, humanly speaking, is not possible in certain circumstances. Departing to another land is actually an indictment of sin in society. From a theological perspective then, we see the Holy Spirit raising prophetic awareness among God's people in these societies.[6]

The process of discernment leading to the decision to leave behind their roots is for many migrants a profoundly religious experience.[7] Some look for signs "from God" that indicate the most appropriate time to leave. It could be a scripture passage, the granting of a visa, sometimes a dream, a phone call, or the promise of a job. Soon-to-be migrants usually look for priests and other ministers to confirm such signs or simply to get their blessing. They will carry those blessings with them as protection and with a sense of certainty that God walks with them. Clergy face a constant dilemma since they know about the dangers that migrants can encounter, the families they leave behind, and how difficult it is to "make it" across the border. But they also know that for many in their flocks this is the best option. Hagan cites Fr. Rigoberto España, who ministers in Guatemala:

> It is not the Catholic way to tell them not to go. We support migration as a human right…in a better world, they would never leave their communities. So, when they say "Father, please advise me, please let me go," what can I say? I must let them go. I must bless their decision.[8]

Seeking the blessing of a priest is quite common. However, there are other rituals that also accompany the process of decision-making among soon-to-be migrants. Masses are regularly offered for a successful journey. Women and men from all ages in Mexico visit the Basilica of Our Lady of Guadalupe, where they place themselves under the protection of the Virgin before the journey. The sanctuary of El Señor de Esquipulas in Guatemala and the Basilica of Nuestra Señora de Suyapa in Honduras serve a similar purpose. A number of shrines have emerged in various parts of Mexico and Central America in recent decades where those who are ready to migrate go to pray. Worth mentioning among many others are the chapel of Juan Soldado[9] in Tijuana, the Shrine of St. Toribio Romo[10] in Jalisco, and the Church of St. Francisco in Antigua, Guatemala, where *el Santo Hermano Pedro*[11] is venerated.

The ritualizing of the discernment process does not happen in isolation. Although the person who will migrate may be readying herself for a rather lonely journey, she is not alone in her preparation. Families and communities come together in a unique process of reflection, prayer, and support. Community prayer services, family rituals around home altars, and candles lit by relatives and friends to symbolize a spiritual communion are a few examples of "being with" the migrant as people of faith. Sometimes the family and the community gather to raise funds, give something that would remind the migrant that he is not alone, and provide advice to stay safe. All these moments are reminders that the particular exigencies of the everyday constantly call the church to be an authentic community of hope.

Hagan's research highlights the importance of migrants' *promesas* (promises), covenantal pledges between the person and the divine mediation of choice based on personal devotion (for example, Jesus, the Virgin, a saint, and so on). She observes: "In exchange for divine intervention on an issue of concern or granting of a request, the believer promises to perform certain acts, usually devotional, in gratitude."[12] She identifies four kinds of *promesas* to be fulfilled after a successful journey: to be better Christians; to engage in religious practices intentionally as a sign of gratefulness; to return home to a familiar shrine or church, perhaps where a beloved saint is venerated; and to send money to buy something to honor the object of their devotion when a prompt return is not in sight.[13]

In preparing for their journey, many Christian migrants reconnect with the depths of their faith not only as a source of hope, but as a practice of hope. Christian hope is experienced in at least four different ways at this stage. Hope that prophetically reminds society that sin does not have the ultimate word; hope that God listens to the plea of those who call on divine providence; hope that sustains families and communities in solidarity; and hope that invites to a covenantal relationship in always-new ways.

## Hope during the Journey

The greatest hope that someone has while journeying as a migrant in the midst of difficult situations is to arrive at their desired destination…safely. This hope turns into a quest for survival when the circumstances defining the journey threaten not only the possibility of getting to the ultimate destination, but also one's physical integrity. This is what millions of migrants from Latin America have experienced in the last decades on their way to the United States in hope for a better life. It is certainly more difficult for undocumented immigrants who often risk their lives crossing unfriendly deserts, rivers, and roads. Yet it is not less difficult for those migrants who journey with legal documents knowing that they will be taking low-paying jobs that will keep them living in poverty or those who will be forced to engaging in degrading activities (for example, victims of human trafficking). Neither is it less difficult for those who know that poverty and low educational levels—not to mention skin color and poor knowledge of the language of the new land—will put them in a position of tremendous social disadvantage. For them the migratory journey has almost no end, the sense of arrival is constantly fleeting.

Journalists, scholars, and activists have done a remarkable job documenting the dangers and risks that migrants from Latin America face on their journey to the U.S.-Mexico border.[14] Stories of migrants being robbed, exploited, and assaulted are well known. Some get very sick on the journey and cannot continue; others suffer permanent injuries that prevent them from reaching their goal; some die or disappear leaving no trace. But the hope for a better chance in life for them and their families still drives millions to face these challenges with religious resolve.

Not every migrant turns to faith during the journey; yet most do. Before the threat of nonexistence or harm that may change the migrant's life forever, it is not uncommon to search for signs that point to God's presence. For many, there is already the conviction that God walks with them because they received a special blessing back home, their relatives and friends are praying for them to arrive safely, and they know that the saints to whom they entrusted their journey are doing their part. This unique instantiation of the communion of saints in the historical present turns the journey into a sort of religious pilgrimage. The sacred images and mementos that many carry, the prayers they constantly say, are vivid reminders of such communion.

But the solace of communion is often tested by the solitariness of being in unfamiliar geographies, away from home and the people one loves. As they move along on their journey, it does not take long for most of these migrants to realize that they are on their own. It is a personal, lonely quest. In the midst of this quest, God is perhaps the closest companion. Migrants do not hesitate to avail themselves of every devotional resource at hand. When formal spiritual guidance and official places for worship are not available, popular religiosity fills the gap. Along the migrant trail, particularly in more deserted areas, it is not unusual to find traces of makeshift altars and improvised shrines built by migrants who long for a place of encounter with a comforting God.[15] Some of these are memorial shrines built to honor migrants who have died on the way. Prayers, devotions, and the scriptures constantly sustain the spiritual life of Christian migrants. *El devocionario del migrante* (the Migrant's Prayer Book) is a well-known resource that facilitates a life of prayer during this stage of the journey. Traditional or spontaneous rituals give migrants the assurance that, even in the loneliest of moments, God is with them.

The large number of migrants traveling through Central America and Mexico on their way to the United States has inspired NGOs and many other organizations to provide humanitarian services to these women and men. Churches clearly stand out in this regard. Dozens of Catholic parishes along the migrant corridor not only have adapted to serve the spiritual needs of these itinerant women and men, but many have actually become centers of social outreach. Sometimes associated with parishes, sometimes not, the public dining rooms, shelters, clinics, migrant homes (*casas del migrante*), and legal centers run by Catholics— laity, vowed religious, clergy, and missionaries—are oases of hope for the journeyers. Worth mentioning is the work of the Scalabrinian congregation, whose large network of migrant houses and various partnerships with local dioceses constitute the most robust Catholic effort to accompany transit migrants in this part of the world.[16] Shared solidarity toward migrants has also engendered ecumenical and interreligious initiatives such as *Humane Borders*, founded in 2000 to prevent migrant deaths by deploying emergency water stations on routes known to be used by migrants coming to the United States through the desert.[17] Other major interfaith initiatives like *Samaritan* and *No More Deaths*[18] also offer food and assistance to distressed immigrants along the U.S.–Mexico border. Hagan rightly observes: "the religious actors that work the migrant trail foster spirituality and play an important role in sustaining the migration process."[19] For Catholics, all efforts to assist migrants, support their right to migrate, and advocate for their just treatment are rooted in the best principles of Catholic social teaching,[20] as Thomas Massaro's essay in this collection makes clear. At the same time, the fact that most Latin American migrants on the way to the United States are Christian invites some serious reflection about the ecclesial implications of how we treat them during their journey and how we welcome them while they settle in our communities. More specifically, Catholics are faced with the decision of welcoming—or rejecting—other Catholics.[21]

During the migrant journey, Christian hope emerges as a quest for life as well as a renewed desire to be in intimate relationship with others and with God. It is hope to be safe, to stay alive as one traverses dangerous paths; hope to change the circumstances that prevent many from living life to the fullest. It is hope that reminds us that prayer binds Christians together in unique ways, that communion is something that we already enjoy but still need to pursue, and that God is the companion par excellence of those on the move.

## Hope after the Journey

Most migrants would agree that the journey is far from over upon arrival. Now they are *im*-migrants, they are in. Once in a foreign land, the journey takes on new dimensions: finding a place, being accepted, securing some stability, and often dreaming about a potential return to the loved ones left behind. One fulfilled hope makes way for many other hopes. That is the human experience. And faith continues to play a significant role in the life of the now immigrant.

For the many Gabrielas who once left their homelands because "there was no hope" and now live in our midst, new challenges await.

Whether some of their human hopes find fulfillment and their lives enjoy glimpses of Christian hope will largely depend on the experience of authentic hospitality that our communities of faith can provide. Upon arrival, immigrants proceed to search for familiar settings and communities where they can find support as they begin a new stage in their lives. After checking in with relatives and friends, and perhaps an employer, churches are among the first places that immigrants seek. The rituals, language, images, sacred texts, and even the leaders have a lot in common with what they left behind. Churches and shrines are also the first places that many visit to fulfill the *promesas* made before their journey.[22] They know that churches are, in principle, welcoming communities, places where they should be welcomed. This fundamental hope for life in community on the part of the immigrant believer is at the same time a calling for the church to live up to its own principles.

The Catholic Church in the United States has always been an immigrant church. Although awareness of this immigrant identity has not always been at the forefront of our shared historical consciousness, today it is. Catholicism in the United States is being renewed and profoundly transformed by immigrants from all over the world, particularly from Latin America. As immigrants settle in society and in the church, a new set of hopes arises. My sense is that the ultimate hope for community, an authentic Christian community, becomes actualized in a twofold hopeful desire that has much to do with how we understand ourselves in relationship with God. On the one hand, the immigrant desires to be part of the community not as a stranger or a visitor but as a member, someone whose presence is sincerely appreciated and embraced, someone without whom the community would feel incomplete. On the other hand, because the community desires to grow as a body of witnesses of God's love in Jesus Christ here and now, immigrants not only are welcome into this vision, but also are responsible for making such a vision real. The ultimate hope of the immigrant *for* community and the ultimate hope *of* the community to become what it is called to be are one and the same in a spirit of faithful mutuality guided by God's Holy Spirit. Both hopes are, in the end, expressions of the desire to allow God's reign to become truly present here and now.

When some believers lose sight of the hope that engenders mutuality in the community of faith, or when certain forces in society threaten the sacredness of the immigrant's dignity, Christians are compelled to speak up with prophetic voice. We do so led by that same Spirit who continues to inspire the denunciation of structures of sin in Latin America and other parts of the world as well as their roots, structures that rob many of the opportunity to find fulfillment for themselves and their families in their homelands. The many voices of Christian leaders and organizations throughout the United States who advocate for the rights of immigrants to be treated with respect, love, and justice, welcoming them as welcoming Christ (see Matt 25:35), are truly signs of Christian hope in our midst.[23]

After the journey, Christian hope becomes actualized in the life of the community. It is hope that strengthens relationships and creates new ones as the migrants are welcomed into a new home; hope that has a prophetic dimension and continues to denounce sin; hope that longs for healing after a long journey; and hope that anticipates a better, perhaps somewhat difficult, future than the past left behind.

## Notes

1. This essay builds on a year of conversations with Rev. Alejandro Olayo, SJ, and Rev. Manuel Clavijo as I led them through an experience of directed study on the theology of migration. Their commitment to working with immigrant communities is truly inspiring.

2. Catholic theologians Dan Groody and Gioacchino Campese make a similar argument. See Daniel Groody, *Border of Death, Valley of Life: An Immigrant Journey of Heart and Spirit* (Lanham, MD: Rowman & Littlefield, 2002), 6; Gioacchino Campese, "Beyond Ethnic and National Imagination: Toward a Catholic Theology of U.S. Immigration," in *Religion and Social Justice for Immigrants*, ed. Pierrette Hondagneu-Sotelo (New Brunswick, NJ: Rutgers University Press, 2007), 180.

3. Quoted in Jacqueline Maria Hagan, *Migration Miracle: Faith, Hope, and Meaning on the Undocumented Journey* (Cambridge, MA: Harvard University Press, 2008), 25.

4. See Walter Brueggemann, *The Land: Place as Gift, Promise, and Challenge in Biblical Faith* (Minneapolis: Fortress Press, 2002).

5. See Hagan, *Migration Miracle*, 3.

6. See Hosffman Ospino, "Entre fronteras, límites y umbrales: aproximaciones teológico-prácticas a la experiencia religiosa a partir del fenómeno migratorio," *Revista de Ciencias Religiosas, Universidad Católica Cardenal Raúl Silva Henríquez, Chile*, 16 (2009): 37–58.

7. See Hagan, *Migration Miracle*, 20–58.

8. Quoted in Hagan, *Migration Miracle*, 30.

9. A soldier executed in Tijuana, Mexico, in 1938 for a serious crime, yet the people believed that he was wrongly accused and was innocent until the last moment. Immigrants and others who have difficulties bring their prayers to the shrines where he is venerated.

10. Venerated as the patron saint of immigrants, Fr. Toribio Romo was known for his devotional life and dedication to catechesis. He was killed in 1928 during the time of the Cristero War in Mexico and canonized in 2000. Some immigrants crossing the U.S.-Mexico border claim to have seen his presence. His devotion among immigrants has grown rapidly in the last few decades.

11. Hermano Pedro de San José Betancurt was a Spanish Franciscan brother who lived in Guatemala during the seventeenth century. Brother Pedro dedicated his life to charitable works and was known for performing miracles. He was canonized in 2002. Devotion to him is very popular in Central America.

12. Hagan, *Migration Miracle*, 53.

13. See Hagan, *Migration Miracle*, 53–56.

14. See for instance John Annerino, *Dead in Their Tracks: Crossing America's Desert Borderlands* (New York: Four Walls Eight Windows, 1999); Margaret Regan, *The Death of Josseline: Immigration Stories from the Arizona-Mexico Borderlands* (Boston: Beacon Press, 2010); Hagan, *Migration Miracle*, 59–81.

15. See Hagan, *Migration Miracle*, 114–32.

16. See Hagan, *Migration Miracle*, 95–103.

17. See http://www.humaneborders.net/.

18. See http://nomoredeaths.org/.

19. Hagan, *Migration Miracle*, 84.

20. See Pontifical Council for the Pastoral Care of Migrants and Itinerant People, *Erga Migrantes Caritas Christi* (Vatican City, 2004). Accessed on September 5, 2012, at http://www.vatican.va/roman_

curia/pontifical_councils/migrants/documents/rc_pc_migrants_doc_
20040514_erga-migrantes-caritas-christi_en.html.

21. This is in many ways part of the message that the Catholic bishops of the United States and Mexico shared in 2003 with their communities in both countries. See United States Conference of Catholic Bishops and Conferencia del Episcopado Mexicano, *Strangers No Longer: Together on the Journey of Hope. A Pastoral Letter Concerning Migration from the Catholic Bishops of Mexico and the United States* (Washington, DC: USCCB, 2003).

22. On the fulfillment of *promesas*, see Hagan, *Migration Miracle*, 133–54.

23. See for instance the essays in Hondagneu-Sotelo, *Religion and Social Justice for Immigrants*; also, Donald Kerwin and Jill Marie Gerschutz, eds., *And You Welcomed Me: Migration and Catholic Social Teaching* (Lanham, MD: Lexington Books, 2009); Miguel A. De La Torre, *Trails of Hope and Terror: Testimonies on Immigration* (Maryknoll, NY: Orbis Books, 2009).

III

———

# SUSTAINING
# HOPE

# 9

# Hope and Salvation in the Shadow of Tragedy

## Nancy Pineda-Madrid

How we engage tragedy matters; if we do not come to terms with it, we will severely limit our capacity to be people of hope. When our account of hope looms larger than our temptation to despair, only then can God's gift of salvation break anew into our world. This essay examines the meaning of tragedy, and how our response to it offers an account of our hope that may reveal God's saving presence active in our world.

The evils and barbarities of the twentieth and early twenty-first centuries are overwhelmingly numerous and widely documented. The Holocaust, the ongoing wars on every continent, the Armenian and Darfur genocides, the ecological destruction of the planet, are only some of the many. We, U.S. citizens and other westerners, nonetheless remain out of tune with our times and resist any serious consideration of tragedy and evil. In the words of theologian Wendy Farley:

> The sweetness of insanity is our truest consolation. Surely it is insanity that in the face of massive evil and imminent destruction, many Americans' primary preoccupation is to be entertained—and not really entertained, merely distracted. The passionate need to escape—through drugs, alcohol, relentless work, or the banalities of the media—has become a national pathology.[1]

Why, we may wonder, do we so easily overlook massive evil? For centuries now we have imbibed the sensibilities of the Enlightenment project with its overly confident belief in the inevitability of human progress, often unaware of how profoundly and blindly this shapes our thinking, acting, and being. We take for granted American exceptionalism, the supposed infinitude of human progress, our seemingly limitless horizons. Resting quietly in an occluded light is the shadow side of our history—that is, the enslavement of African Americans, the savagery we unleashed on Native Americans, the Ciudad Juárez feminicide (the systematic killing of women) that our drug habit has had a hand in creating, and many other atrocities.[2] We have a hard time allowing such tragedies to penetrate our consciousness fully.[3]

How we engage tragedy matters; if we do not come to terms with it, we will severely limit our capacity to be people of hope. Indeed, our response to tragedy carries the possibility of breaking open hope in history. If we endeavor to recognize and address what is tragic in our world, and if we, in response to the tragic, labor on behalf of the victims of history in our own time, then we give an account of our hope (see 1 Pet 3:15). When our account of hope looms larger than our temptation to despair, only then can God's gift of salvation break anew into our world. Hope enables us to catch a glimpse of the salvation that we will know in full at the end of time.

This essay begins with a discussion of what tragedy is and how tragedy provokes a response from us. Our response to tragedy reveals our capacity for hope. When our response is one of resisting the evil that is the source of tragedy, then our response offers a tangible and robust account of our hope. This is the focus of my second section. The third and final section shows that with an account of our hope we may catch a glimpse of God's gift of salvation, even become part of this gift as it breaks into our present.

## ON TRAGEDY AND OUR RESPONSE

Tragedy may be distinguished by necessity, intense suffering, and an active response to intense suffering. These three elements orient my approach to tragedy, which builds on the work of David Tracy and others.[4]

The first element, *necessity*, calls our attention to the way we are thrown into life and confronted with the need and opportunity to respond.[5] Life as it comes to us is identified by various names: fate, chance, force, luck, fortune, and providence, among others. We are born into many circumstances not of our choosing: a given family; at a given historical moment; in a particular city and country; with a given race, class, gender, sexual orientation, and so forth. What we need to recognize is that the contingencies of life are often beyond our control. Some contingencies are benign, some not. Nevertheless, we must deal with them one way or another. For example, a twenty-one-year-old woman may one day discover that she has cancer and will not be able to bear children, a circumstance not of her choosing but one to which she must respond.

Necessity refers not only to our personal experience, but also to the way in which our world is ordered. Indeed, some tragedies are the product of human choices that damage the order of the universe. For example, prior to the 1930s, many poor European American settlers moved west into the panhandle of Oklahoma to farm and provide a living for their families, but their method of farming damaged the ecology of the Great Plains. When drought and severe dust storms came in the 1930s, the settlers' farms and crops were left in utter ruin. Their endeavor to provide for their families, and in many cases their lives as well, were destroyed.

In our attempts to do what is good and just we can find ourselves faced with having to choose between two essentially irreconcilable obligations or goods. While in pursuit of a fundamental good in one realm, we betray another fundamental good that we hold equally dear. For example, during World War I, World War II, and even the Vietnam War, pacifists were often forced to choose between a desire to serve their country and their commitment to pacifism. Many were isolated from their communities, ostracized for their choice, and/or incarcerated. A conflict among values can mean that we will suffer regardless of our choice. These examples challenge "ethical descriptions of the world order in which the righteous person prospers and the wicked perish. Tragedy not only introduces the anomaly of unjust suffering into the moral order of the cosmos, it questions whether such a moral order exists."[6]

Second, *intense suffering* further distinguishes tragedy. Intense suffering "is distinguished by its destructive power and its irreducibility to fault."[7] Intense suffering is such that a good person can be destroyed by an evil that is beyond their control, and accordingly, this suffering cannot in any sense be viewed as a punishment for their failing. No biblical figure captures this experience more profoundly than Job, who in his suffering turns to God and asks, "Why?" A righteous man, Job offers God an account of his life and of the injustices he has been made to suffer through no fault of his own (Job 29–31). Job reminds us that the intense suffering of the innocent serves no purpose and does not reflect a larger moral order; it can, and often does, call into question the belief that the universe is ultimately good. In coming to grips with tragedy, we find ourselves facing the question: is there a basis for our believing in a morally ordered universe?

Intense suffering has the ability to seize one's soul. While Tracy calls this kind of suffering "intense suffering," Farley names it "radical suffering" and Simone Weil identifies it in its most acute form as "affliction."[8] This kind of suffering can destroy the human spirit to such an extent that the sufferer may no longer be capable of defying evil. It can launch such an assault on its victim that they may no longer be able "to exercise freedom, to feel affection, to hope, to love God."[9] What is distinctive about intense suffering is its power to take possession of the sufferer's spirit and soul. Weil underscores the significance of this extreme experience of suffering:

> The great enigma of human life is not suffering but affliction. It is not surprising that the innocent are killed, tortured, driven from their country, made destitute, or reduced to slavery, imprisoned in camps or cells, since there are criminals to perform such actions. It is not surprising either that disease is the cause of long sufferings, which paralyze life and make it into an image of death, since nature is at the mercy of the blind play of mechanical necessities. But it *is* surprising that God should have given affliction the power to seize the very souls of the innocent and to take possession of them as their

sovereign lord. At the very best, he who is branded by affliction will keep only half his soul.[10]

Intense suffering invariably runs the risk of devolving into affliction,
even though it does not always do so. Affliction is akin to a prolonged,
severe depression, but Weil uses this term to focus our attention on its
spiritual dimensions. When sufferers find a way to defy the evil that haunts
them and when they refuse to give in to despair, then they meet intense
suffering with grace-filled hope, denying affliction its prize.

An *active human response to intense suffering* constitutes the third element of our guiding definition of *tragedy*. The Greek tragedies, and indeed
the writers of tragedy throughout history, attempt to shift our attention
away from the question "Why do we suffer?" which has no satisfactory
final answer, to the questions "How can I respond to suffering?" and
"How can I come to terms with the suffering I know in my life?" Writers
of tragedy recognize that we need to grow in our capacity to embrace the
whole of life: the pain we know in suffering (an experience that eventually comes to us all) as well as the joy that we know through our experience of beauty. In a real sense this is an invitation to cling less tightly to
the question "Why suffering?" and, in turn, to learn to let go of our need
to control. This does not mean passivity in the face of evil, for we must
strive to blunt the effects of evil to the best of our ability. However, we
also need to recognize that evil and sin are part of life, a part we must face
squarely. How can we become clearer and more starkly honest about the
suffering and the joy present in our lives?[11]

An active response includes coming to grips with our suffering,
and in spite of that suffering still choosing to struggle for a more just
and compassionate world. Choosing to fight evil and injustice is not a
denial of evil, but a refusal to grant finality to evil. The struggle for justice gives witness to our conviction that there is an ethical order beyond
the most heinous and systematic evils known in our world. Even if "suffering and destruction cannot be overcome, they can be resisted. It is in
the resistance itself, in this refusal to give up the passion for justice, that
tragedy is transcended."[12] When tragedy is transcended, we see grace at
work, not to remove tragedy but certainly to offer a "yes" to life in spite
of tragedy. Surrendering to suffering says "no" to life. It abandons any

struggle for what is just and true. An active response is one that confronts the evil in life and offers a "yes" to life and to God in the midst of sorrow as well as joy.[13] Even so, this "yes" to life, this hope, is fragile as Christopher Matthews' chapter in this volume amply demonstrates.

Having developed a description of tragedy, we now turn our attention to our response to tragedy. Evil presents us with more than the problem of how to eliminate or destroy the cause that furthers intense suffering.[14] This "more" demands attention. It takes us to the heart of tragedy.

Two responses to intense suffering, despair and egocentrism, fail to integrate our experience of tragedy and thus undermine the possibility of giving an account of our hope, of acting in accord with God's will. These two responses represent a "no" to life. To give in to either of these responses is to deny that there is reason for hope and that hope matters. Both of these responses take one down a path that ultimately destroys the self and community, and grants victory to a malignant power. In the process, hope appears to ring hollow.

Despair grows when those who experience intense suffering become defeatist in the face of evil. This response means withdrawing from the world and resigning oneself to the world as it is. It is a form of self-denial in that it idealizes passivity not only in relation to the world, but also in relation to the self. Accordingly, it means the absence of a purpose in life, which is in effect the denial of the self. This attitude stifles hope. Despair also distorts the historical process of salvation by denying the possibility of our efforts to cooperate with God so that the world becomes more in line with God's will.[15]

Egocentrism emerges when those who experience intense suffering choose to make themselves the center of the world, viewing everyone and everything else in the world as extensions of themselves. Here, their purpose in life so determines everything in the world that other people are merely a means to an end. In this case, those who suffer move through the world with the expectation that their own personal loss and pain orient the world of everyone with whom they come into contact. Egocentrism destroys the communal dimension of hope, which seeks to envision a more just world for all of us.[16] In contrast with the "no" to life of despair and egocentrism, a third kind of response to intense suffering enables us to give a tangible account of our hope.

## GIVING A TANGIBLE ACCOUNT OF OUR HOPE

To claim that in the face of tragedy we can offer an account of our hope necessitates first that we clarify the meaning of hope, as Dominic Doyle does in this volume when he develops Thomas Aquinas' definition of hope: "the desire for a future, difficult, yet possible good." Our longing for and working toward a difficult good suggests that hope has both a contemplative and an active dimension. It remains ever attentive and responsive to God. "[Hope] is less eloquent than either optimism or despair (both of which, knowing the outcome, confidently complete the story). Sometimes in silence, sometimes in more articulate agony or Job-like anger, the mood of the discourse of Christian hope is less that of assertion than request: its form is prayer."[17] But as Richard Lennan also points out, a comprehensive understanding of hope requires not only the contemplative, but also the active dimension of hope as well. Theological hope requires that we work with God as co-workers, as disciples of Christ ever vigilant to the "in-breaking of God's reign."[18] It is the victims of the world's injustices, Jon Sobrino argues, who are invariably the primary subjects of the hope that is God's protest against suffering. In his words, "the hope that has to be rebuilt now is not just any hope but *hope in the power of God over the injustice that produces victims.*"[19]

In light of our reticence to engage tragedy, any credible conception of Christian hope needs to include attention to the tragic. Accordingly, hope must be distinguished from optimism. As Lennan argues:

> the characteristics of theological hope not only transcend confidence in our ability to construct a satisfying environment; they are even free of the requirement that the world and its history be benign. Indeed, hope, far from being synonymous with positive thinking about one's present circumstances, 'stirs when the secure system shows signs of breaking

down,' when we are no longer able to maintain even the pretense of being able to regulate life comprehensively.[20]

Always, but particularly in the ebb of life, God continuously invites us into a deeper relationship. Thus, our inclination to hope is fundamentally our response to God and God's initiative rather than an independent act of our will. Conversion is central to hope. We become increasingly freer to engage a world beyond our control precisely because of God's presence to and unconditional love for us, which we know in the life, death, and resurrection of Jesus Christ. Moreover, as already noted, hope invariably bears a communal dimension. Not only do we come to hope as our response to an offer from God, but also as our recognition of our interdependence with each other and our call to act in solidarity with one another,[21] a point that Richard Lennan develops in his chapter in this collection.

With this understanding of hope in mind, what does it mean to give a tangible account of our hope in response to intense suffering? This kind of response is described variously. Tracy identifies it as an "active human response," Farley refers to it as "resistance," and Josiah Royce names it "the subversion of evil."[22] I will call it *resistance to evil*. This response does not seek to destroy the person judged to be the source of evil, but rather is a response that attempts to thwart evil so as to realize the greater good. When faced with senseless tragedy, if we respond by attempting to subvert evil, then we contribute to the ongoing transformation of this world so that it becomes more just and more humane. Thus, this response furthers God's saving action because it contributes to the fulfillment of the self, of humanity, and of history. Conversion is at the heart of this third response because it requires that we see the world in a manner ever more faithful to the reign of God. Within the reign of God, the poor themselves are the favored locus of God's love and thus the locus by which we come to see hope made real in history. It

> ...is not those innocent of evil who are fullest of the life of
> God, but those who in their own case have experienced the
> triumph over evil....The knowing of the good, in the higher

122

sense, depends upon contemplating the overcoming and sub-ordination of a less significant impulse, which survives even in order that it should be subordinated.[23]

Hope takes on flesh when we directly face real situations of ongoing crucifixions and then act on behalf of those who are being crucified today, demanding an end to their crucifixion. We experience a tangible account of hope when those who suffer nonetheless actively work to bring about a realization of the reign of God that is fuller than what they have known. This work, when born out of prayer, directs our attention toward God's final destiny for human beings. When we work to bring the crucified down from the cross, we give hope expression and support the resurrection of the many, as Jon Sobrino has so eloquently observed.

> *Materially*, the mission that expresses the content of hope is that justice be done to the victims of this world, as justice was done to the crucified Jesus, and so the course of action called for is to take the crucified people down from the cross. This is action on behalf of the victims, of those crucified in history, that tries in a small way—with of course no hubris—to do what God himself [sic] does: to take the victim Jesus down from the cross. As this course of action is on behalf of the crucified it is also automatically against the executioners and so a conflictive course, being conscious of the risks and accepting of them, on the side of the victims and open to becoming a victim oneself. Finally, being a course of action at the service of the resurrection of the dead, so of the resurrection of *many*, it should also be social, political, seeking to transform structures, *to raise them up*.[24]

Without doubt, taking the crucified down from the cross exacts a high cost from anyone—the crucified themselves or any others—who dare to challenge the ongoing crucifixions. For as long as those who suffer do so in silence, they are praised for their "goodness" and their "pious ways." But the moment they begin to speak out and demand that they be set free, they are branded as subversives, criminals, unbelievers, and worse.[25] Much is at stake when we choose to give a tangible account of our hope, which is why doing so provokes such a forceful and swift reaction from those who enthusiastically encourage piety, but do all in their power to crush transformation. Giving such an account carries power because through it we expand our capacity to dream a transformed world—one more in keeping with the reign of God. The dream of a transformed world spurs us to act with courage to nudge our world a little closer to that dream—Ernesto Valiente's chapter in this book explores the import of utopic dreams in the greater realization of God's reign.

To give an account of our hope, to subvert the evil that confronts us, to bring the crucified down from the cross necessarily means seeking out the precarious occasions when hope and history come together. Far too often, we are much more inclined to keep hope detached from history. We may be tempted to see hope as God's plan hidden from our view, as a future experience that overrides the reality of our human experience and thus remains untainted by historical realities: this is not theological hope. Similarly, driven by a vision of what might be, we may decide to confront and transform the historical injustices of our time, but then fall into disillusionment when what we realize falls short of what we hoped for. This too is not theological hope.[26] Theological hope must be grounded in the ongoing journey of conversion, at both the personal and social levels.

## HOPE AND GOD'S GIFT OF SALVATION

Theological hope, grounded in personal and social conversion, grounded in prayer and prophetic action, opens out like a doorway to the possibility of salvation breaking in on our present. Salvation can only be understood through our communion with one another, with God, and with creation. Without a love for community, without an active drive to make more visible and vital the many ways we are interrelated, the partial realization of salvation in this world becomes impossible. While we need to interpret salvation through a personal and individual lens, Christian salvation is always more than an individualist matter.

Salvation is always also social. When we strive to bring the crucified peoples of our time down from the cross, we not only give an account of our hope, but we may also catch glimpses of God's saving presence revealed in human acts of resisting injustice and evil. Through these acts our interrelated nature becomes more visible. We see how we are bound to one another.

The historical destiny of humanity rests not in an overly confident understanding of human progress. Rather, it rests in the belief that we, through prayer and action inspired by God, strive to build up love and justice in this world, despite history's irrational, contingent nature and the enduring presence of evil. In doing so, we walk in the footsteps of Jesus, who through his earthly ministry enabled "fragments of salvation to gain a foothold in history."[27] At Pentecost, we received the gift of Jesus' Spirit, which incessantly moves freely in history urging every generation to walk faithfully in the footsteps of Jesus. When we open ourselves as fully as possible to God's self-gift, a fragment of salvation may break into our present.

Even when our actions incarnate our hope, this account of hope is nevertheless fragile. Our attempts to subvert evil and to bring the crucified down from the cross remain, at best, fragmentary and subject to defeat. God is a God who comes to us, prodding us to resist evil, inviting us into a more intimate relationship. Yet our ongoing struggle against injustice and evil does not defeat evil. Nevertheless, it is the resistance to evil that reveals the presence of God in history. That resistance suggests to us that evil is not final.

When in the face of tragedy we choose to act on behalf of the victims of history, we affirm hope, forging a world more receptive to God's ever-saving presence.

## Notes

1. Wendy Farley, *Tragic Vision and Divine Compassion: A Contemporary Theodicy* (Louisville: Westminster John Knox, 1990), 11.

2. For a study of the feminicide on the U.S.-Mexican border see, Nancy Pineda-Madrid, *Suffering and Salvation in Ciudad Juárez* (Minneapolis, MN: Fortress Press, 2011).

3. For a discussion of the underpinnings of our contemporary aversion toward tragedy and evil, see John Gray, *Enlightenment's Wake: Politics and Culture at the Close of the Modern Age* (London & New York: Routledge, 1995).

4. David Tracy, Lecturer, *Tragic Vision: The Abandoned Vision of the West*, lecture available at http://frontrow.bc.edu/program/tracy1/ (March 30, 2005), Boston College.

5. Here, David Tracy's notion of our being "thrown into life" builds on the work of Martin Heidegger. See Martin Heidegger, *Being and Time*, 1927, trans. John Macquarrie and Edward Robinson (New York: Harper & Row, 1962), section 31.

6. Farley, *Tragic Vision and Divine Compassion*, 27.

7. Ibid., 24.

8. Tracy, *Tragic Vision*; Farley, *Tragic Vision and Divine Compassion*; Simone Weil, "The Love of God and Affliction," trans. Emma Craufurd, in *Waiting for God* (New York: G. P. Putnam's Sons, 1951).

9. Farley, *Tragic Vision and Divine Compassion*, 53.

10. Weil, "The Love of God and Affliction," 119–20.

11. Tracy, *Tragic Vision*.

12. Farley, *Tragic Vision and Divine Compassion*, 27.

13. Tracy, *Tragic Vision*.

14. Josiah Royce, *The Sources of Religious Insight*, 1912 (Washington, DC: Catholic University of America Press, 2001), 226.

15. Josiah Royce, *The Problem of Christianity*, 1913 (Washington, DC: Catholic University of America Press, 2001), 354–55.

16. Royce, *The Problem of Christianity*, 351–54.

17. Nicholas Lash, *The Beginning and End of "Religion"* (New York: Cambridge University Press, 1996), 229. Quoted in Richard Lennan, "The Church as a Sacrament of Hope," *Theological Studies* 72 (2011), 254.

18. Richard Lennan, "The Church as a Sacrament of Hope," *Theological Studies* 72 (2011), 254.

19. Quoted in Lennan, "The Church as a Sacrament of Hope," 256–57, emphasis original.

20. Lennan, "The Church as a Sacrament of Hope," 251–52.

21. Ibid., 252–53, 258.

22. Tracy, *Tragic Vision*; Farley, *Tragic Vision and Divine Compassion*, 27; Royce, *The Sources of Religious Insight*, 215–54; Royce, *The Problem of Christianity*, 355–58.

23. Josiah Royce, "The Problem of Job," in *Studies of Good and Evil: A Series of Essays upon Problems of Philosophy and of Life* (New York: D. Appleton and Company, 1898), 23, 24.

24. Jon Sobrino, *Christ the Liberator: A View from the Victims*, 1999, trans. Paul Burns (Maryknoll, NY: Orbis Books, 2001), 48, emphasis original.

25. Jon Sobrino, *The Principle of Mercy: Taking the Crucified People from the Cross*, 1992, trans. Dinah Livingstone (Maryknoll, NY: Orbis Books, 1994), 52.

26. Walter Brueggemann, *Hope within History* (Atlanta: John Knox Press, 1987), 1–26.

27. Elizabeth A. Johnson, "Jesus and Salvation," in *CTSA Proceedings*, ed. Paul Crowley, vol. 49 (Santa Clara, CA: CTSA, 1994), 11.

# 10

# "Happy Are Those Who Fear the LORD": Hope, Desire, and Transformative Worship

## *Christopher Frechette, SJ*

The biblical concept of fearing God promotes worship that fosters right relationship with God. Such worship cultivates emotional investment in our relationship with God, which is important as God is the source of our hope and freedom. This freedom contrasts with the compulsions that accompany attachment to other objects of desire. This chapter portrays the hope that helps us to navigate the difficult feelings that accompany letting go of compulsive desires.

"Praise the LORD! Happy are those who fear the LORD."[1] Thus begins Psalm 112. Yet how can fear lead to happiness? What does fearing God have to do with hope? To address both questions requires an inquiry beyond the ordinary meanings of the three key words: *fear, happiness*, and *hope*. Taking up the religious meanings of these words within the biblical world, this essay will explore how emotionally engaged worship can cultivate Christian hope.

As odd as it may sound to modern ears, in the biblical context *fearing God* refers to worshipping in a way that cultivates living in right relationship with God. *Happiness* here refers to two types of satisfaction: that which *may* occur as a result of attaining one's desires regarding physical welfare and human relationships, and that which *will* result from being in right relationship with God. The latter brings its own deep satisfaction, and the Bible depicts God as desiring that people also experience the former. For instance, God shares the delight that humans receive from ordinary joys; as we shall see, such joys can even count as praising God! Moreover, God instructs us to attend to one another's ordinary desires, as in the command to love one's neighbor (Lev 19:18; Matt 22:39; Mark 12:31), and God insists on the establishment of a social order in which no one is oppressed, and the poor are cared for. However, while ordinary human flourishing can be taken as a sign of God's care, the absence of that flourishing cannot be taken as indicating an absence of right relationship with God.

In ordinary usage, *hope* denotes the sense that the good things one desires for a satisfying life are possible to attain, even though doing so may be uncertain or difficult: one hopes for good health, rewarding work, a suitable spouse, a faithful friend. Because Christian hope prioritizes the desire for a healthy relationship with God, it echoes the sort of happiness that is envisioned for those who fear God. Distinguishing between ordinary desires and desire for relationship with God is crucial for understanding what fearing God has to do with hope.

As we all know, life entails suffering that results from all manner of unmet ordinary desires. The lack of ordinary hope that results when ordinary desires do not seem attainable may prompt a diminishing of desire for any relationship with God. Nancy Pineda-Madrid's essay in this volume discusses how tragedy can have this effect. For instance, when a terminally ill woman recognizes that her desire to recover is unattainable, she may withdraw from God. Some may conclude that their desires are not attainable because they believe that they have done wrong (guilt) or that they lack human value (shame). Such people may find it difficult to maintain a sense that desire for a healthy relationship with God is possible. The cultivation of Christian hope, then, involves negotiating the sometimes-turbulent waters in which one's unmet ordinary desires churn alongside one's desire for relationship with God.

Unconventional as it may seem, *fearing God* refers to a kind of worship that offers a way to negotiate those waters. How this is so becomes clear if we understand the central role that the investment of emotional energy plays both in the way in which desires come into existence and in the manner in which people worshipped in the biblical world. Humans negotiate their desires by choosing how to invest emotional energy in the objects of those desires. Worship in the biblical world enabled people to invest emotional energy in a way that helped them to cultivate a desire for relationship with God over all other desires. Ritual activities and prayers paradoxically expressed the goodness of ordinary desires as well as the anger, pain, and isolation those desires can prompt, if they are not met. These kinds of rituals and prayers evocatively affirmed the desirability and accessibility of communion with God.

The first part of this essay uses insight from contemporary psychology to explain how the investment of emotional energy shapes desires; it also shows how people tend to become compulsively attached to ordinary desires because they expect them to satisfy their desire for relationship with God. The second part of the essay examines the cultural context of God-fearing worship in the Bible, identifying its fundamentally embodied, emotional, and communal dimensions. This sort of worship includes drawing emotional satisfaction from being in relationship with God. Such satisfaction facilitates hope, because even during situations of difficulty resulting from unmet desires, it shapes and strengthens both a desire for right relationship with God and a sense that this is attainable.

## THE PROBLEM: COMPULSIVE ATTACHMENT TO ORDINARY DESIRES ERODES HOPE

Christian hope is a gift of the Holy Spirit, as Colleen Griffith elucidates in her essay in this volume. Insight from contemporary psychology into the dynamics of human desire can help us to grasp how our behaviors may enhance or hinder our reception and expression of that gift.

The central problem posed here concerns maintaining both a desire for right relationship with God and a sense that it is attainable, even while experiencing the aftermath of one's unmet ordinary desires. The root of this problem involves confusion between these two types of desire, an issue addressed by the late Christian psychiatrist Gerald May.[2]

Integrating insights from psychology, neurology, and spirituality, May constructed a model of the dynamics of desire in embodied terms.[3]

This model distinguishes between two fundamental kinds of desire: one's deepest desires and ordinary desires to which one can become compulsively attached. At the deepest level, humans desire to love, to be loved, and to move closer to the divine source of love. These desires all involve ways of being in relationship to other people and to God that resist one's control. At the same time, human beings desire objects that they can control in some way, even if only in their minds. Here, *objects* include anything that one can desire in any aspect of experience, including beliefs, activities, relationships, and self-image. Aside from whether such objects in themselves are healthy or harmful, the fundamental problem is that people tend to cling compulsively to the use of any number of objects that give them a sense of control. For example, being in a marriage can satisfy both deep desires and ordinary desires; when one's spouse dies, experiencing intense pain and difficulty in letting go can indicate both deep love and compulsive attachment to particular experiences that are no longer available. To be human and alive is to be compulsively attached in various ways. May's discussion of *compulsive attachment* as *addiction* provides a compelling metaphor for the human condition.

Compulsive attachment creates idols, which are counterfeit religious presences. In other words, we create idols when we confuse ordinary desires with desire for relationship with God by imbuing ordinary objects of desire with an aura of *ultimate* necessity. Compulsive attachments breed hopelessness because through them we turn to controllable objects for what they cannot provide: the fulfillment of our deepest desires to love and be loved, including a desire for relationship with God. People rarely recognize that this confusion of desires is occurring, since the intensity of compulsive attachment clouds their perception. Such blindness is often perpetuated by various rationalizations or denials, under which lie mistaken notions about both desire and freedom.

Insight into how desires are formed illuminates a way of reducing compulsive attachments and disposing one to hope. According to an understanding cultivated particularly in consumerist cultures, objects of desire simply have power over people. Like Gollum in J.R.R. Tolkien's *The Lord of the Rings*, once we experience desire for an object, fulfilling that desire becomes equated with our fulfillment as people. Freedom, then, is equated with the ability to act in ways that fulfill our desires. By contrast, an insight from classic psychoanalytic theory affirms that our attachment to an object results not from any power inherent in the object, but from our investment of emotional energy in it, a process called cathexis.[4] The more we invest emotionally in an object, the more we desire it, increasing our attachment. Conversely, as we withdraw such investment, our attachment diminishes.

Freedom derives from our ability to choose whether to invest emotionally in a particular object of ordinary desire. May refers to this ability as freedom *of* desire. Broadly speaking, freedom is becoming what we were created to be by giving priority to pursuing our deepest desires, while allowing our ordinary desires to be transformed by shifting our investment of energy from certain desires to others as necessary. Such freedom includes passionate investment in ordinary desires, but only those that support loving relationships with God and with others. It also includes reliance on grace to bear the consequent pain, when those good desires are not—or perhaps are no longer—satisfied.

To the degree that we are compulsively attached to our ordinary desires, our capacity for freedom and hope is diminished. Yet those desires remain malleable, increasing or decreasing in proportion to our emotional investment in them. Moreover, even while remaining compulsively attached in many ways, we may at the same time cultivate investment in our deepest desires, including relationship with God. As we do so, the capacity of ordinary objects of desire to enslave us decreases.

However, the intensity of our attachments can pose a formidable obstacle to our growth in freedom. Often we are able to relinquish compulsive attachments only after experiences of loss or failure force us to do so. In addition, if we conclude that the necessity to relinquish compulsive attachments results from God's initiative, we are likely to feel fear, anxiety, and perhaps anger toward God. This is because we tend to see our compulsive attachments as necessary and justified and so are likely to perceive any prod to abandon them, even if it comes from God, as an affront. Such feelings and perceptions result from our fear of freedom.

Cultivating hope in this situation demands a process that helps us let go of certain ordinary desires when necessary while allowing us to acknowledge honestly our feelings and perceptions, as harsh as these may be. Because people who must let go of compulsive attachments are often inclined to withdraw at some level from God and from their faith community, they need a process that can nurture a desire for relationship to both. The kind of worship to which fearing God refers entails such a process.

## A PATH TOWARD HOPE: EMOTIONALLY ENGAGED WORSHIP

Thus far, we have seen that desires are malleable, waxing or waning over time, and that how we cultivate both our deepest desires and our ordinary desires affects our disposition to receive and to express the gift of hope. That disposition is strengthened by: (1) cultivating desire for relationship with God as ultimate; (2) cultivating desires for ordinary objects that are in harmony with God's design; (3) lessening compulsive attachments, which easily become obstacles to our relationship to God; and (4) allowing for honest acknowledgement of the fear, sadness, or anger that the necessary relinquishment of desires can elicit. The biblical concept of fearing God refers to emotionally engaged communal worship that supports these four processes.

The cultural gap separating our contemporary world from the world out of which the biblical texts emerged is always a challenge for any reader of the Bible. Even the best translations of certain words cannot communicate the nuances of meaning necessary to prevent misunderstanding. Given the ordinary sense of *fear* as a feeling of anxiety prompted by imminent danger, the *fear of God* might easily evoke a sense of anxiety prompted by an angry, misanthropic deity who is eager to punish. Although the Hebrew verb (*yr'*) employed in *to fear God* can express such ordinary fear, when it takes God as its object, the context significantly alters its meaning. Although the biblical concept of the fear of God is commonly understood to refer to an attitude of utmost awe and respect, it, in fact, refers fundamentally to emotionally engaged worship that fosters the four processes just described.

To fear God is a central biblical concept for how people are to relate to God.[5] The Israelite understanding of this concept shares much in common with that of its neighboring ancient Near Eastern cultures. These cultures presumed that all aspects of creation shared an all-pervasive, divinely determined orderliness. To prosper in life, one would have to accept this fact and learn to live according to that order. Failure to do so would have dire consequences. According to one common rationale —but not the only one—events that cause suffering were thought to result from such failure. In order to gain the knowledge and ability necessary to prosper, people must maintain a proper relationship with the divine. The concept of fear served as the starting point for maintaining a proper relationship with the Lord in Israel and with the gods in the polytheistic religions of the ancient Near East.

In many Old Testament texts that have parallels from Mesopotamia and Egypt, *to fear God* means to worship God.[6] This is so in Deuteronomy, in the historical books that share its theological outlook (Joshua, Judges, 1 and 2 Samuel, 1 and 2 Kings), and in the Psalter. Even in biblical contexts such as wisdom teaching, in which the fear of the Lord may refer more immediately to an attitude or way of behaving, the necessity of worship to cultivate such attitudes and behaviors would nevertheless have been presumed.[7]

But what is the tone of Israel's relationship with God? As among its neighbors, in Israel the failure to be in right relationship with God was considered likely to bring punishment, and some biblical texts describe such punishment in harsh detail.

On the one hand, we ought to see such texts not as literal descriptions of what God actually does, but as interpretations of events according to cultural assumptions that we are not obligated to share. When biblical texts describe God or God's deeds as *awesome* (in Hebrew, *nôrā'* from the verb *yr'*), such deeds often involve the destruction of Israel's enemies or those who act unjustly and so inherently convey an element of warning. Nevertheless, the dominant force of such accounts is to evoke admiration for God's capacity to restore a harmonious order.

On the other hand, ancient Israelite worship cultivated desire for relationship with God not primarily out of fear of punishment for disobedience. The Bible's portrayal of God's power to punish is vastly outweighed by its emphasis on God's love manifest throughout Israelite history. The passionate love of God for Israel is compared to that of an ideal parent for a child as well as that of a compassionate husband for his wife. The people could turn to this loving God in worship to sustain their dignity when they were violated by others or assailed by illness. When they persisted in their compulsive attachments, God would call them to the dignity of freedom, sometimes harshly and sometimes gently, but always motivated by love. Nevertheless, the people's compulsive attachments could cause them to resist the Lord's invitations to freedom, a tendency captured in the story of their desire to return to slavery in Egypt when facing uncertain deliverance from Pharaoh's army (Exod 14:10–14). Still, Israelite worship aimed not to deny or suppress difficult feelings, but to help people to navigate them.

## Israelite Worship and the Transformation of Desire

Worship in ancient Israel could take many particular forms. Yet a fundamental capacity to foster the four processes described above is supported by practices described in the Pentateuch and the Psalter.

The ancient Israelites believed that the Jerusalem Temple housed the Lord's presence in a way unparalleled by any other geographic location. Despite the Israelite prohibition against making images to be worshipped (Exod 20:4; Deut 5:9), the Temple and its immediate environs, Mount Zion, were understood to offer worshippers a visual experience of the Lord.[8] The Temple, its precursor the portable sanctuary, and their associated ritual objects would have evoked intense emotion in worshippers and cultivated in them a desire for relationship with God. Evidence from ancient Israel and related cultures indicates that the ancients perceived such evocative capacity to result in part from the expert craftsmanship and the abundance of gold, silver, and bronze that went into the Temple's architecture and objects.

135

Ancient Mesopotamian descriptions of how they perceived their ritual objects and architecture show that they understood them to evoke an almost overwhelming emotional response.[9] Such objects, often described as finely crafted with precious metals, are said to evoke in worshippers awe and admiration, which art historian Irene Winter translates as "ad+miration" in order to convey the intensified visual response indicated by the ancient Sumerian terms.[10] According to one Sumerian expression, one response that such objects evoked was a sudden intake of breath.[11] Winter has demonstrated that the strikingly large, staring eyes in certain Mesopotamian statues of worshippers reflect the intense affect understood to be aroused by visual contact with representations of the divine.[12] Entire temples could also evoke such a response.[13]

The Jerusalem Temple manifested in a preeminent way God's presence and care for the Israelites, as well as an ability to elicit intense positive emotion from worshippers. For instance, Psalm 48 recounts how enemy kings are terrified, thrown into panic at the sight of the Temple (verses 5–8), but the faithful rejoice as they meditate on the Lord's care for them and take in visually the features of Mt. Zion (verses 10–15). Jon Levenson observes, "Zion, the Temple Mount, is the visible form, the 'incarnation,' so to speak, of the sacred story of YHWH's commitment to rescue those loyal to Him" (verse 9).[14] This sacred story includes multiple traditions of the Lord's powerful acts of creating both the world and Israel. The Temple and its ritual objects manifested these traditions in various ways, contributing to their capacity to inspire worshippers.[15]

Whether enacted within the sacred precincts of the Temple or not, the manner of Israelite worship strengthened the people's disposition to hope by integrating their emotional investment both in relationship with God and in ordinary desires. Two biblical sources provide a view of Israelite worship that reveals key factors in its ability to accomplish this integration: the instructions in the Pentateuch concerning worship, and prayers in the Psalter that reflect practices, attitudes, and language of worship. These sources point to a polarity between joyful activities celebrating relationship with God and sorrowful activities that acknowledge the difficulty of unmet desires while affirming desire for relationship with God. Not limited simply to speech, these expressions of sorrow and joy intensified emotions both by the nature of the activities themselves, and by being enacted publicly and communally.[16] Many psalms suggest that a fundamental inclination of Israelite worship was to hold the poles of sorrow and joy in relationship to each other: prayers of distress often anticipate an end to distress and full communion with God, to be celebrated with praise. In addition, prayers reflecting such praise typically recall the former distress that has been alleviated.

The common instruction to *rejoice* before the Lord was not a directive simply to summon feelings. Fundamentally, such rejoicing would entail either sacrifice or praise, or both together, and both were understood in terms of pleasurable public activities. Such sacrifices entailed offering only a small portion of the animal to God by burning, while the remainder was eaten in celebratory feasting by the people. (Think of a communal barbecue.) Praise was understood as a public proclamation of the deeds of God in conjunction with enjoyable activities such as singing, dancing, feasting, wearing fine garments, and being anointed with fragrant oil.

Ideally, rejoicing by means of sacrifice and praise was to be enacted at the Jerusalem Temple. Thus, these concrete expressions of joy would have been augmented by that emotionally evocative environment. By contrast, times of suffering and penitence are characterized as participation in death and as isolation from God and from the community. The inverse of practices expressing joy, those associated with periods of suffering or penitence, include crying out in lamentation, fasting, wearing sackcloth or torn clothes, covering one's head with ashes or dust, and sexual continence.

Such expressions gave voice to the common human perception that suffering feels isolating, yet paradoxically they also cultivated solidarity. Biblical prayers of lament may articulate alienation from people and from God, sometimes expressing a sense of God's absence or unresponsiveness and even angry protest at God as a result. The fact that the community provided people with authoritative prayers for addressing God in such situations, however, would have mitigated people's sense of isolation. Although prayers and practices of sorrow express isolation, they cultivate solidarity because of their shared observance by friends and family during personal suffering, and by the entire community during communal catastrophe. Moreover, in many prayers of lament, even while expressing present suffering, the speaker recounts a basis for trust in God and affirms a desire to again find full communion with God. In effect, such worship accomplished what Colleen Griffith considers necessary practices for choosing hope: stretching ourselves beyond our feelings of isolation and our problems, and cultivating our capacity to celebrate our relationship with God.

Israelite worship provided an effective means of cultivating desire for relationship with God as a priority over ordinary desires, without discounting their goodness. This was accomplished, in part, by associating ordinary pleasurable experiences such as feasting and singing with the joy of relationship with God and by using these experiences to celebrate the fulfillment of ordinary desires as evidence of God's care. At the same time, many prayers embrace the loss of compulsive attachments as opportunities to deepen a desire for relationship with God, emphasizing the superior value of that relationship over even the finest ordinary pleasures. Sorrowful behaviors such as fasting and lamenting associated unmet ordinary desires with a felt absence of God, even while prayers associated with those sorrowful practices affirmed both ability and desire to relate to God.

In this way, the ordinary desires of the people for welfare and their emotional responses to the lack of fulfillment of those desires were continuously voiced in communal solidarity, while at the same time being placed in the larger context of desire for relationship with God. Such continual fostering of emotional investment in relationship with God as the only ultimate desire cultivated in the people an ability to transform ordinary desires, to shift investment of energy from former desires to new ones. The simultaneous recognition of present suffering and anticipation of future union with God resonates with the eschatological dimension of hope reflected in Christian worship, as discussed by John Baldovin elsewhere in this volume.

If we understand the biblical concept of fearing God only in terms of maintaining the proper attitude of respect toward God, we can be left wondering how to sort through feelings that may seem incompatible with that attitude. This concept points not merely to awe and respect for God, but to ongoing, emotionally engaged worship capable both of shaping desires and of making room for the expression of feelings that result from having to let go of compulsive attachments. To consider such worship the "beginning of wisdom" (Ps 111:10) and the path to "happiness" (Ps 112:1) makes sense because it actually helps people to desire relationship with God above all else and to live in relationship with others according to God's vision for the world. By allowing for recognition and integration of the difficult feelings that letting go of desires can prompt, such worship manifests a tone of nurture and healing.

## The Fear of God and Christian Hope

We human beings feel hope when we sense that our difficult or uncertain desires are attainable, and we maintain those desires by investing emotional energy in them. Unfortunately, we tend to invest compulsively in our ordinary desires with the mistaken expectation that they can meet our deepest desires. Such fixation of desire erodes a disposition to receive the gift of hope. However, we have seen how the biblical concept of fearing God offers a model for integrating emotions into worship that can help us navigate between our desire for relationship with God and our ordinary desires.

As John Baldovin emphasizes, the manner in which the liturgy is celebrated strongly affects the experience of liturgy as the embodiment of hope. Christians worship in many different styles and cultural settings, and the manner in which they integrate emotions into their worship will vary accordingly. Nevertheless, the biblical concept of fearing God discussed here has implications for contemporary worship: (1) Emotional engagement in worship and attention to the aesthetics that facilitate it are not peripheral, but central to helping people navigate experiences that otherwise might erode their desire to relate to God or their ability to maintain central Christian beliefs. (2) In worship, we need to attend to the sadness, anger, or fear that may result from unmet ordinary desires and to do so in a way that simultaneously directs our energy toward a relationship with God in Christ. (3) As intensely as people may invest energy in clutching their disappointment or frustration over unmet desires concerning the church, the world, or their personal lives, emotionally engaged worship can help them to loosen that grasp and to redirect their energy.

Efforts to allow Christian worship of whatever style to engage the emotions can foster hope in several ways: by cultivating desires for relationship with God in Christ and for the ordinary goods that embody the justice and mercy of God; by cultivating these desires as a community of members in solidarity with one another even while struggling with unmet desires; and by allowing people to acknowledge whatever sadness, fear, or anger they may feel at having to let go of various desires, while remaining in the faith community and in Christ.

We rely on liturgists and other ecclesial ministers to enhance our experience of liturgy and to help us reflect and pray in ways that integrate that experience into our lives. For instance, careful preparation of music that captures both the pain of grief and the comfort of God's care can enhance the quality of a funeral Mass. Some parishes even organize choirs especially for funerals. Through preaching, counseling, religious education, or spiritual direction, ecclesial ministers can offer us safe ways to imagine allowing even difficult feelings to surface during liturgy and subsequently to pray or talk with others about them.

We may conclude: *hopeful* are those who fear the Lord, for through their worship they will find solidarity in cultivating their desires for relationship with God and for constructing a world that embodies God's justice and compassion. When those desires go unmet, their communal witness will help them to remain with Christ, whose strength will support them along the way.

## Notes

1. "LORD" is a standard translation for the proper name of God when quoting the Old Testament directly, "YHWH" in Hebrew.

2. Gerald G. May, Addiction and Grace: *Love and Spirituality in the Healing of Addictions* (San Francisco: Harper & Row, 1988).

3. The present summary of May's model and the subsequent discussion of compulsive attachment and freedom of desire draws from May, *Addiction and Grace*, 1–20.

4. For a definition and discussion of cathexis, see May, *Addiction and Grace*, 52–54.

5. The following paragraph draws from Michael Barré, "'Fear of God' and the World View of Wisdom," *Biblical Theology Bulletin* 11 (1981): 41–43.

6. H. F. Fuhs, "*yārē'*," in G. Botterweck and H. Ringgren, eds., *Theological Dictionary of the Old Testament* (Grand Rapids: Eerdmans, 1974), 290–315, at 306–9.

7. See Barré, "Fear of God," 42.

8. Jon D. Levenson, "The Jerusalem Temple in Devotional and Visionary Experience," in A. Green, ed., *Jewish Spirituality from the Bible through the Middle Ages* (New York: Crossroad, 1986), 32–61; Jon D. Levenson, *The Death and Resurrection of the Beloved Son: The Transformation of Child Sacrifice in Judaism and Christianity* (New Haven: Yale University Press, 1993), 111–24.

9. Irene J. Winter, "The Eyes Have It: Votive Statuary, Gilgamesh's Axe, and Cathected Viewing in the Ancient Near East," in R. Nelson, ed., *Visuality Before and Beyond the Renaissance: Seeing as Others Saw* (New York: Cambridge University Press, 2000), 22–44.

10. Winter, "Eyes," 30–31.

11. Ibid., 35.

12. Ibid., 22–24, figs. 2–4, 36.

13. Ibid., 31–32.

14. Levenson, "Jerusalem Temple," 47.

15. See Levenson, "Jerusalem Temple," 51–53; Jon D. Levenson, *Creation and the Persistence of Evil: The Jewish Drama of Divine Omnipotence* (Princeton, NJ: Princeton University Press, 1994), 78–99.

16. The present discussion of expressions of joy and sorrow draws on the work of Gary Anderson, "The Praise of God as a Cultic Event," in G. Anderson and S. Olyan, eds., *Priesthood and Cult in Ancient Israel* (Sheffield, England: JSOT Press, 1991), 15–33, and Gary Anderson, *A Time to Mourn, a Time to Dance: The Expression of Grief and Joy in Israelite Religion* (University Park, PA: Pennsylvania State University Press, 1991).

11

# *Pignus Futurae Gloriae*: Liturgy, Eschatology, and Hope

## *John F. Baldovin, SJ*

Christian hope for God's ultimate victory over evil, sin, and death has been a constant feature in worship; it has inspired both consolation in the here-and-now and commitment to a vision of a world filled with divine justice. This essay deals with the contours of that hope in the history of the liturgy, the Eucharist, the rite of the anointing of the sick, and the rite of Christian funerals.

> *O sacrum convivium: in quo Christus sumitur:*
> *recolitur memoria passionis eius: mens impletur gratia:*
> *et futurae gloriae nobis pignus datur.*
>
> O sacred banquet!
> in which Christ is received,
> the memory of his Passion is renewed,
> the mind is filled with grace,
> and a pledge of future glory to us is given.
>
> —Antiphon for Magnificat, Vespers of Corpus Christi

What are people looking for when they participate in the church's liturgical worship? No doubt there are dozens of good answers to this question: wisdom to get through a difficult time, an opportunity to pray for their loved ones living and dead, an oppor-

tunity to share their faith with others, a chance to express their gratitude for gifts and graces received or to repent for their sins and negli-
gence, help in knowing how to live their lives as Christians. These are
but a few of the fine motivations that inspire people to participate in the
liturgy. But I wonder if by digging deeper we would discover that
people come to church because of their conviction that God is God,
and that God will ultimately reign over the earth. In other words, they
come not only because of their immediate hopes for themselves and
those they care about, but because of the ultimate hope that grounds
these hopes: what we would more formally call eschatological hope, the
kind of hope that Pope Benedict XVI emphasizes in his encyclical,
*Saved by Hope* (2007).[1]

This essay will discuss how prominently that eschatological hope
is expressed in Roman Catholic worship today. I will begin with the
eschatological dimension of Christian liturgy in general and then turn
to three particular liturgies: the Eucharist; the anointing of the sick; and
the rite of Christian funerals.

## HOPE AND THE LITURGY IN GENERAL

As the British Methodist theologian Geoffrey Wainwright demonstrated in his important work, *Eucharist and Eschatology*, the dimension of
hope has long been neglected in liturgical and sacramental theology in
favor of questions that deal with the past (especially the Eucharist as sacrifice) and the present (real presence and holy communion).[2] And yet,
as St. Thomas Aquinas' lovely antiphon that heads this essay expresses so
well, the liturgy is memorial, present grace, *and* a pledge of future glory.[3]

Twentieth-century scholars struggled over the issue of whether
the liturgy lost its eschatological focus in the course of history, especially
after acceptance of Christian faith throughout the Roman Empire in
the fourth century. In 1945, Gregory Dix, an Anglican Benedictine,
published a book, *The Shape of the Liturgy*,[4] which had a very significant
impact on mid-twentieth-century liturgical reform in the Anglican
Communion and well beyond. Dix influenced, among other important
issues, the way that scholars thought about the relation between liturgy

and time. He argued that the early liturgy was profoundly and thoroughly eschatological, but that this emphasis was transformed in the course of the fourth century with the end of the era of persecutions into a historical interest in the events of Christ's life.[5]

This view was challenged by Thomas Talley, who showed that history and eschatology are by no means mutually exclusive. In the second century, a debate, known as the Quartodeciman Controversy, arose with regard to the date of the celebration of the Christian *Pascha* (Easter). This is a period well known for its vibrant sense of eschatological expectation, but in fact, there was a good deal of interest in historical remembrance among the Quartodecimans: a debate arose among the churches of Asia Minor and the West with regard to the desire of some to celebrate the death and resurrection of Christ annually on the actual date of his crucifixion, the fourteenth of Nisan on the Jewish calendar. The West insisted that the Lord's resurrection be celebrated exclusively on Sunday, which many referred to as the Eighth Day, the eschatological day beyond ordinary earthly time.[6] Talley argued that like the Jewish Passover, the Christian Easter Vigil (and other more common Sunday vigils as well) was a moment of expectation for the bridegroom who would come in the middle of the night (Matt 25:10). The issue was resolved by the common acceptance of an annual celebration of the *Pascha* on the first Sunday after the first full moon of spring.

Another scholar, Robert Taft, picked up this theme and argued that historical and eschatological themes have coexisted in the liturgy from the very beginning, and that liturgical tradition has always manifested a tension between future and realized eschatology.[7] A good example of this tension can be found in the traditional liturgy of Advent, which has a twofold focus: the fulfillment of the kingdom at the end of time and the coming of Christ in the incarnation. In addition, we can point to the fact that one of the earliest Christian liturgical acclamations (for example, in the late first-century *Didache*) was *Maranatha—Come, Lord (Jesus)*, usually understood as a plea for the second coming.

In other words, eschatological hope has always been present in the liturgical traditions of East and West, however muted it may have been by a post-twelfth-century obsession with eucharistic presence and eucharistic sacrifice in the West.

Although eschatology has often been associated, strictly speaking, with the four last things (death, judgment, heaven, and hell), it is useful to adopt a broader perspective, especially when dealing with the liturgy which, as Aidan Kavanagh has argued, is thoroughly eschatological in the sense that it presents us here and now with our hoped for future.[8] This future is realized in a ritual way. Along with Kavanagh, I would argue that the very structure and content of the liturgy are meant to be a manifestation, an epiphany of God's reign. Of course, greater attention to that epiphany would make our liturgies more hope-filled in practice.

The Christian East has retained this eschatological experience of the liturgy far better than the West. A good example is be found in the story about Prince Vladimir of Kiev sending envoys to Latin Christians, Muslims, and Greek Christians in the tenth century to discover which was the "best religion." They visited the Latin Christians and the Muslims first, but after their visit to Constantinople they returned with a glowing description of the liturgy of Hagia Sophia, Constantinople's Great Church, saying, "we knew not whether we were in heaven or on earth."[9] Clearly, the ambassadors appreciated the celebration of the liturgy as the embodiment of Christian hope.

In the late twentieth century, renewed interest in eschatology bore fruit in a landmark ecumenical convergence document, *Baptism, Eucharist and Ministry*.[10] The Eucharist section of the document refers specifically to the eschatological significance of the Eucharist:

> Christ himself with all that he has accomplished for us and for all creation (in his incarnation, servant-hood, ministry, teaching, suffering, sacrifice, resurrection, ascension and sending of the Spirit) is present in this *anamnesis* [that is, remembering], granting us communion with himself. The eucharist is also the foretaste of his *parousia* [second coming] and of the final kingdom.... The eucharist opens up the vision of the divine rule which has been promised as the final renewal of creation, and is a foretaste of it. Signs of this renewal are present in the world wherever the grace of God

145

is manifest and human beings work for justice, love and peace. The eucharist is the feast at which the Church gives thanks to God for these signs and joyfully celebrates and anticipates the coming of the Kingdom in Christ. (1 Cor 11:26; Matt 26:29)[11]

It is a major contention of this essay that the Eucharist as anticipation of the kingdom is one of the most important ways that the liturgy expresses Christian hope. Moreover, as the document just quoted makes clear, that hope is inextricably bound up with a vision of social justice and well-being at the heart of the kingdom—how God wants the world to look. In this vein, the late pastoral theologian Robert Hovda called the liturgy "kingdom play."[12]

Pope John Paul II made the same connection between liturgy, hope, and justice clear in his last encyclical, *Ecclesia de Eucharistia* ("On the Eucharist," 2003). The Pope associated the eschatological dimension of the Eucharist with the social justice obligations that the Eucharist implies:

> A significant consequence of the eschatological tension inherent in the Eucharist is also the fact that it spurs us on our journey through history and plants a seed of living hope in our daily commitment to the work before us. Certainly the Christian vision leads to the expectation of 'new heavens' and a 'new earth' (Rev 21:1), but this increases, rather than lessens, our sense of responsibility for the world today. And what should we say of the thousand inconsistencies of a "globalized" world where the weakest, the most powerless and the poorest appear to have so little hope! It is in this world that Christian hope must shine forth! For this reason too, the Lord wished to remain with us in the Eucharist, making his presence in meal and sacrifice the promise of a humanity renewed by his love.[13]

I will turn to three specific examples of how this hope for the divine vision of the future manifests itself in Catholic liturgy.

# THE EUCHARIST AS A CELEBRATION OF HOPE

That the Eucharist is itself intended to be an experience of Christian hope is quite evident in a number of liturgical texts. Some important examples can be found in the Ordinary of the Mass, which is, of course, repeated every time the Eucharist is celebrated. Both creeds used on Sundays and solemnities proclaim Christian belief in the "resurrection of the dead" (Nicene) and the "resurrection of the body" (Apostles'). The priest's addition to the conclusion of the Lord's Prayer prays for deliverance from distress "as we await the blessed hope and the coming of our Savior, Jesus Christ." The Lord's Prayer is itself a constant reminder of the eschatological plea "Thy kingdom come," and two of the three options for the memorial acclamation following the institution narrative in the Eucharistic Prayer—"We proclaim your death, O Lord and profess your resurrection" and "When we eat this bread and drink this cup we proclaim your death, O Lord"—conclude with "until you come again."[14]

The current Roman Catholic liturgy contains a number of Eucharistic Prayers in which profound eschatological hope is expressed. For example, "Even now you set before your people a time of grace and reconciliation, and, as they turn back to you in spirit, you grant them hope in Christ Jesus and a desire to be of service to all, while they entrust themselves more fully to the Holy Spirit" (Eucharistic Prayer for Reconciliation I) and "Bring us to share with them the unending banquet of unity in a new heaven and a new earth where the fullness of your peace will shine forth in Christ Jesus our Lord" (Eucharistic Prayer for Reconciliation II). In our "desire to be of service to all," our ultimate (future) hope is clearly joined to our hope for a truly just world.

The numerous prefaces for the Eucharistic Prayer specify the motive for giving thanks on a particular feast or in a particular liturgical season. Here are a number of phrases in these prefaces that point to Christian hope: "that we who watch for that day may inherit the great promise in which we now dare to hope" (Advent 1); "the pledge of life eternal" (Sundays in Ordinary Time 6); "bathed in the sweetness of your grace, we may pass over to the heavenly realms here foreshadowed"

(Holy Eucharist 2); "In him the hope of blessed resurrection has dawned, that those saddened by the certainty of dying might be consoled by the promise of immortality to come" (For the Dead 1); "For today the Virgin Mother of God was assumed into heaven as the beginning and image of your Church's coming to perfection and a sign of sure hope and comfort to your pilgrim people" (Assumption of the Virgin Mary); "For today by your gift we celebrate the festival of your city, the heavenly Jerusalem, our mother, where the great array of our brothers and sisters already gives you eternal praise" (All Saints); that "he might present to the immensity of your majesty an eternal and universal kingdom, a kingdom of truth and life, a kingdom of holiness and grace, a kingdom of justice, love and peace" (Christ the King).

These are but a few examples of how the language of the liturgy reflects Christian hope, but I also need to note that the *manner* in which the liturgy is celebrated will strongly affect the experience of the liturgy as the embodiment of eschatological hope. Few commentators have expressed this as well as Robert Hovda:

> To celebrate a sacrament is not merely to say the words associated with the rite, but it is rather to act out the rite, to perform a choreography. The power of sacramental action is the whole experience....Our placing ourselves and our imaginations at the Lord's Table, in the holy city, the new creation of God's reign, is altogether for the sake of transforming us and our world. God reveals in symbolic word and deed what the liberated and reconciled community of humanity must become, asks us to act it out in rite.[15]

What Hovda describes is "kingdom play" in action. Therefore, even beyond the ordinary and occasional eucharistic texts that have been cited, the very *experience* of contemporary Roman Catholic worship celebrates the hope to which we are called. In addition to the choreography to which Hovda refers, a fuller investigation of this subject would have to consider ways in which the changing styles of liturgical music, liturgical architecture, even vesture, have reflected a more positive sense of Christian hope in Catholic Church assemblies. I suspect that, as with so much in ritual, these nonverbal aspects have an even greater impact on developing people's Christian hope. In fact in a number of faith communities this hope is palpable in a way that would be hard to articulate on the basis of the texts alone. In my experience this has been true in communities like St. Paschal Baylon Parish in East Oakland, California, where serious concern for liturgical celebration is joined to passionate commitment for social justice.

Up to this point, we have been considering how people experience Christian hope in what we might call the ordinary liturgical life of the Catholic. But perhaps an even more striking example of hope (and the challenge to Christian hope) can be found in life's crisis moments: sickness and death.

# HOPE AND THE RITE OF THE ANOINTING OF THE SICK

As is well known, the Second Vatican Council's Constitution on the Sacred Liturgy (*Sacrosanctum Concilium*) called for a renewed understanding and celebration of the anointing of the sick. For centuries, the sacrament had been called *extreme unction* and was the last element in a series of rituals (penance, viaticum) that prepared a Christian for a good death.[16] The current rite has significantly shifted the emphasis of the sacrament to the strengthening and healing of the sick person as well as to the sick person's witness to our eschatological hope.[17] The introduction to the rite does not neglect caregivers: "This message of hope and comfort is also needed by those who care for the sick, especially those who are closely bound in love to them."[18] This sacramental rite is intended to encourage hope in several senses of the word, that is, not only eschatological hope, but also a more immediate hope for recovery and well-being. This is clear in the first of the options provided as a prayer after the anointing:

> Father in heaven, through this holy anointing grant N. comfort in his/her suffering. When he/she is afraid, give him/her courage, when afflicted, give him/her patience, when

dejected, afford him/her hope, and when alone, assure him/her of the support of your holy people.[19]

Although penance is still provided for in the liturgical celebration and is certainly not completely missing from the prayer texts for this sacrament, the tenor of the anointing of the sick is oriented more clearly toward healing and hope.[20]

# HOPE IN THE ORDER OF CHRISTIAN FUNERALS

"In sure and certain hope of the resurrection to eternal life through our Lord Jesus Christ...." One of the optional prayers for the committal of the body of the deceased begins with these words that affirm the Christian's ultimate hope for eternal life.[21] It has been argued, with good reason, that there has been a significant shift in Catholic funeral liturgy from a preoccupation with the dire fate of the deceased, penance, and the forgiveness of sin to confidence in eternal life and the consolation of the grieving mourners.[22] Part of this transformation may well reflect the shift in the eschatological imagination from the four last things to the more comprehensive vision of the kingdom of God discussed above.

Of course, there is ample concern in the funeral ritual that the deceased may be freed from sin, but the funeral Mass connotes a much more positive and hope-filled approach as in the following collects:

> O God, almighty Father, our faith professes that your Son died and rose again; mercifully grant, that through this mystery your servant N. who has fallen asleep in Christ, may rejoice to rise again through him....Listen kindly to our prayers, O Lord: as our faith in your Son, raised from the dead, is deepened, may our hope of resurrection for your departed servant N., also find new strength.[23]

We find a significant contrast with the collect in the pre–Vatican II Roman Missal:

O God, your nature is ever merciful and forgiving, and we beseech you on behalf of your servant N, whom you have just called out of this world. Do not give him over to the enemy nor forget him forever, but bid your holy angels take him and lead him home to Paradise. He put his hope and trust in you: do not then let him undergo the pains of Hell, but bring him to happiness without end.[24]

The pre–Vatican II Missal contained a number of poetic *sequences* that were eliminated from the Missal of Paul VI, among them the forbidding *Dies Irae* (Day of Wrath), which has served as inspiration for so many composers. The preoccupation of the pre–Vatican II liturgy with the dire fate of the deceased was underlined by the *absolution* that introduced the rite of final commendation and pleaded for forgiveness for him or her. This somber note is completely lacking in the post–Vatican II introductions to the final commendation, which speak of strengthening the hope of the mourners and comforting the mourners in their hope. If the grave is to be blessed, the prayer addresses Christ who "made the grave a sign of hope."

One of the particularly tragic and challenging situations we sometimes face is the death of an infant. The pre–Vatican II liturgy dealt with this situation with great sensitivity by providing Mass prayers from the Votive Mass of the Angels. In the new Roman Missal, a particularly lovely and hope-filled prayer is provided for a child who has died before baptism: "Receive the prayers of your faithful, Lord, and grant that those you allow to be weighed down by their longing for the child taken from them may be raised up by faith to hope in your compassion."

As I pointed out at the end of the first section of this essay, not only do the texts of the liturgy reflect and encourage the eschatological Christian hope of believers, but also—and perhaps even especially—the nonverbal dimension of the liturgy. Certainly what we sing, which combines words with musical expression, is one of the more important aspects of liturgy. In the past fifty years or so, metrical hymns and other songs have become a staple of Roman Catholic liturgical celebration. I began this essay with a beautiful text from a thirteenth-century author. I will end with the words of another piece, "All My Hope on God Is Founded," written in the seventeenth century by Joachim Neander, translated in 1899 by Robert Bridges, and set to music by Herbert Howells:

All my hope on God is founded;
He doth still my trust renew,
Me through change and chance He guideth,
Only good and only true.
God unknown, He alone
Calls my heart to be His own.

## Notes

1. Pope Benedict XVI, Encyclical Letter, *Spe Salvi* #31–32. Accessed August 16, 2012, at http://www.vatican.va/holy_father/bene dict_xvi/encyclicals/documents/hf_ben-xvi_enc_20071130_spe-salvi _en.html.

2. Geoffrey Wainwright, *Eucharist and Eschatology* (New York: Oxford University Press, 1981).

3. See also Thomas Aquinas, *Summa Theologiae*, IIIa, Q. 60, a.3 resp.; Q.74, a. 4 resp. The latter reads with regard to the Eucharist: "It has a third significance with regard to the future. It prefigures that enjoyment of God which will be ours in heaven. That is why it is called 'viaticum', because it keeps us on the way to heaven. For the same reason it is called 'eucharist', that is 'desirable gift or grace', because the free gift of God is eternal life, as we read in Romans, or because it contains Christ, who is full of grace." St. Thomas Aquinas, *Summa Theologiae, vol. 58: The Eucharistic Presence*, trans. William Barden, OP (Cambridge: Cambridge University Press, 1965), 15–17.

4. Gregory Dix, *The Shape of the Liturgy* (London: Dacre Press, 1945). A new edition was published with revised footnotes in 2005 by Continuum Press (London).

5. Ibid., 303–19, 347–60.

6. Thomas Talley, "History and Eschatology in the Primitive Pascha," *Worship* 47 (1973): 212–21; see also Thomas Talley, *The Origins of the Liturgical Year*, 2nd ed. (Collegeville, MN: Liturgical Press, 1991), 18–40.

7. Robert Taft, "Historicism Revisited," in *Beyond East and West: Problems in the Liturgical Understanding*, 2nd ed. (Rome: Pontifical

Oriental Institute, 1997), 31–49. On "The Eighth Day," see Paul Bradshaw and Maxwell Johnson, *The Origins of Feasts, Fasts and Seasons in Early Christianity* (Collegeville, MN: Liturgical Press, 2011), 7, 13.

    8. Aidan Kavanagh, *On Liturgical Theology* (New York: Pueblo Publishing Co., 1984), 142–44. On the past, present, and future dimensions of the liturgy, see also Louis-Marie Chauvet, *Symbol and Sacrament*, trans. P. Madigan and M. Beaumont (Collegeville, MN: Liturgical Press, 1995), 239–61.

    9. S. H. Cross and O. P. Sherbowitz-Weltzor, *The Russian Primary Chronicle. Laurentian Text* (Cambridge, MA: The Medieval Academy of America, 1953), 111. See Robert Taft, "The Spirit of Eastern Christian Worship," in Robert Taft, *Beyond East and West*, 143–44.

    10. World Council of Churches, Faith and Order Commission, *Baptism, Eucharist and Ministry* [*Faith and Order Paper No. 111*] (Geneva: World Council of Churches, 1982). This document is often referred to as "The Lima Document."

    11. Ibid., no. 6 and no. 22.

    12. Robert Hovda, "Celebrating Sacraments: For the Life of the World," in John Baldovin, ed., *Robert Hovda: The Amen Corner* (Collegeville, MN: Liturgical Press, 1994), 19–20.

    13. Pope John Paul II, Encyclical Letter, *Ecclesia de Eucharistia* #20. Accessed August 16, 2012, at http://www.vatican.va/holy_father/john_paul_ii/encyclicals/documents/hf_jp-ii_enc_20030417_eccl-de-euch_en.html. Emphasis in original. See Thomas Rausch, *Eschatology, Liturgy and Christology: Toward Recovering an Eschatological Imagination* (Collegeville, MN: Liturgical Press, 2012), 130–40. For a similar argument, see Pope Benedict's 2007 exhortation on the Eucharist, *Sacramentum Caritatis*, #30, accessed August 14, 2012, at http://www.vatican.va/holy_father/benedict_xvi/apost_exhortations/documents/hf_ben-xvi_exh_20070222_sacramentum-caritatis_en.html#The_Eucharist_and_Eschatology.

    14. All quotations from the Roman Catholic eucharistic liturgy are taken from the 2011 International Commission for English in the Liturgy (ICEL) translation of the third edition of the Roman Missal, 2002.

    15. Hovda, *The Amen Corner*, 22–23.

    16. Constitution on the Sacred Liturgy, 73: "Extreme unction," which may also and more fittingly be called "anointing of the sick," is

not a sacrament for those only who are at the point of death. Hence, as soon as any one of the faithful begins to be in danger of death from sickness or old age, the fitting time for him to receive this sacrament has certainly already arrived. For the former rite, which centered on death, see "The Sacrament of Last Anointing," in *The Roman Ritual: Vol. I, The Sacraments and Processions*, trans. P. Weller (Milwaukee: Bruce Publ. Co., 1950), 330–43. For a brief historical overview, see Philippe Rouillard, "The Anointing of the Sick in the West," in Anscar Chupungco, ed., *Handbook for Liturgical Studies: Volume IV, Sacraments and Sacramentals* (Collegeville, MN: Liturgical Press, 2000), 171–92.

17. See "Pastoral Care of the Sick: Rites of Anointing and Viaticum" (1972/1982), General Introduction, #3, in A. Bouley, ed., *Catholic Rites Today* (Collegeville, MN: Liturgical Press, 1992), 493.

18. Ibid., 511 (*Anointing of the Sick*, #98).

19. Ibid., 518 (*Anointing of the Sick*, #125).

20. Important issues like the recipients of the sacrament and the minister of the sacrament are outside the scope of this essay. See Lizette Larson-Miller, *The Sacrament of Anointing of the Sick* (Lex Orandi series) (Collegeville, MN: Liturgical Press, 2005).

21. The prayer is actually taken from the American Episcopal 1979 Book of Common Prayer.

22. See Ansgar Franz, "'Everything Is Worthwhile at the End'? Christian Funeral Liturgy amidst Ecclesial Tradition and Secular Ritual," *Studia Liturgica* 32 (2002): 48–68.

23. The first collect is taken from prayers for the dead outside of Eastertide, the second during the season of Easter.

24. The translation is from the *Layman's Missal and Prayer Book*, a bilingual version of the pre–Vatican II Roman Missal (London: Burns and Oates, 2008).

# 12

# Hope for a More Just Future: Wisdom from Catholic Social Teaching

## *Thomas Massaro, SJ*

Hope is central to Catholic social teaching. This teaching encourages the hope that looks toward a more equitable distribution of resources and opportunities. At the heart of such hope is the divine call for solidarity, charity, and justice. Catholic social teaching also challenges us not to succumb to discouragement in the face of the continued failure of human society to achieve the justice for which we long.

For well over a century, the Roman Catholic Church has produced, published, and implemented a body of teaching documents regarding social ethics. These documents include papal encyclicals on social justice and numerous statements on peace and justice from national bishops' conferences and other church councils. Among the themes covered in this large, and still growing, body of literature are human rights, worker justice, the reduction of poverty, and care for the environment.

It is not hard at all to locate the theme of hope in these often stirring writings. They embody hope by exhorting readers to take up works of justice and charity and by appealing for social transformation in the troubled economic and political systems of our world today. Readers will find in these documents a complex mix of idealism and realism—features that make them authentic carriers of theological hope, as we shall explore below.

# DEFINING SOCIAL ETHICS

Like all the essays in this volume, this chapter relates the theme of hope to one specific branch of theology; in this case, Christian social ethics. The term *social ethics* refers to any tradition of reflection on the meaning of proper social order, as well as the conditions for its attainment. The modifier *social* signals that this topic involves how people relate with one another. More specifically, social ethics deal with the public and private institutions of the wider circles of human society, rather than the intimate level of face-to-face interaction, such as in family relationships. How one treats a spouse or sibling is certainly a matter of ethics, but social ethics normally concerns our judgments about the policies of larger groupings, such as governments, business corporations, or voluntary organizations.

The commanding concept governing social ethics in Western thought is the notion of *social justice*, that is, the proper distribution of social goods such as material success, security, political influence, good reputation, and social recognition. It is notoriously difficult to assess achievements regarding social justice. It is never as simple as measuring the current allocation of money and power, although those items are common shorthand terms for describing what members of society distribute to one another in various direct and indirect ways. Justice in social contexts is a highly dynamic and relational reality, not a static thing easily captured by quantifiable measures. Whether we are considering religious or strictly secular versions of social ethics, the search for social justice in both procedures and outcomes dominates most conversations about ethics in human society.

Christian social teaching documents consistently emphasize that true social progress is inevitably a divine work, not merely a human work. Left to ourselves, we all stumble on the path of justice. For the Christian, any authentic hope for social justice is ultimately grounded in God's loving purposes for the world, with which we are invited to cooperate. Official Catholic social teaching recognizes the rich interplay of divine initiative and human response, of grace working through nature.

The key to this chapter, then, is the search to maintain a balanced position that avoids utter despair, on one hand, and naïve optimism, on the other. Neither extreme captures the authentic Christian stance on social ethics and the struggle for social justice. We join observers throughout Christian history who have been discouraged by cruelty and injustice, but who have resisted the temptation to abandon their hope for a world of greater fairness and equity. It is also wise to avoid the illusion that just a bit more technical tinkering with social arrangements will quickly, easily, and thoroughly heal all the wounds and repair all the injustices of our contemporary economic and political systems. Those who aspire to be people of hope work to maintain a balanced set of expectations regarding the promise and limits of social progress— what is possible in this life, and how it relates to the reign of God that is yet to come, but in some ways is already present, as both Daniel Harrington and Ernesto Valiente discuss in their chapters in this book.

## THE NATURE OF HOPE IN THE CONTEXT OF SOCIAL RELATIONS

In his recent appraisal of the constructive role that faith can play in the public life of contemporary society, theologian Miroslav Volf describes hope as "the expectation of good things that don't come to us as a matter of course."[1] Rather, Volf writes, "the expectation of good things that come as a gift from God—that is hope....At the heart of the hoped-for future, which comes from the God of love, is the flourishing of individuals, communities, and our whole globe."[2] Volf's insights do us the great service of distinguishing hope from mere optimism. Contrary to ordinary linguistic convention, hope for the Christian is not an expectation that everything will turn out just fine in the end. Rather, this Christian virtue acknowledges that the results we might desire (typically, for a life of happiness for oneself, but also for social virtues such as true justice) are very much in doubt, at least during our time on earth. This doubt is all the more reason for us to embrace our identity as people of hope, people who dare to look beyond a very imperfect present order in a world that so easily falls prey to the temptations of fatalism, apathy, or indifference—the powerful enemies of social activism and change.

Nearly two thousand years ago, St. Paul made a related point, one that remains crucial to the consideration of the project of Catholic social teaching. In his Letter to the Romans he reminds us: "Now hope that is seen is not hope. For who hopes for what is seen? But if we hope for what we do not see, we wait for it with patience" (Rom 8:24–25). In the context of religious social ethics, this passage, which Thomas Stegman's chapter in this text also discusses, sheds particularly helpful light. St. Paul here highlights the tensions that inevitably exist between our legitimate desires for social reform (however sincere or even ardent they might be) and the difficulty of projecting constructive change as a likely outcome from what we know of human history thus far.

If there is one field where hope seems especially elusive, social ethics is probably the one. To begin with, the track record of humankind regarding questions of basic justice in society is highly discouraging. History is full of failed experiments to establish utopian societies, providing ample evidence against the prospect of human perfectibility and unlimited progress by means of our own efforts—conceits that crop up in a recurring way throughout history. Greed, favoritism, and corruption creep into human affairs with distressing predictability. No society has ever achieved a full and complete measure of justice. The gap between what should be and what actually is seems only to grow wider.

In the contemporary United States, to cite just one example, the richest ten percent of the population holds approximately seventy percent of the wealth of the nation, while the poorest thirty percent possesses merely two percent of national wealth. In fact, "the 400 richest Americans have more wealth than the bottom 150 million of us put together."[3] The richest society in human history allows millions of its members to go without health insurance, adequate nutrition, and even permanent housing, while unprecedented wealth is concentrated in a few hands. It is hard to gainsay the cliché, "the rich get richer and the poor get poorer." But the problem transcends the shortcomings of any one place and time; indeed, it appears to be a lamentable part of the human condition itself. Particularly pernicious is the interaction of wealth and power, as power so often begets money and money begets power. Whether we think of corruption in ancient Rome, influence pedaling at the court of the Chinese emperor during any of the great dynasties, or the abuses of the lobbying industry that prompt calls for comprehensive campaign finance reform in the United States today, the message is the same. Sharp and discouraging social hierarchies— pyramids of power and money that reinforce great disparities that involve race, class, and gender identities—work to the disadvantage of the majority of the disenfranchised and benefit the privileged few.

One need not be a leveler, a radical egalitarian who favors absolute equality of outcomes regardless of one's effort or social contribution, to acknowledge the sting of these observations. All too frequently it is the poorest who work hardest, often laboring in difficult circumstances for long hours for inadequate wages. Profound questions about the system of economic competition rightly hang in the air: Why are some types of human efforts largely unrewarded, or at least seriously under-rewarded, compared with others? Why do unjustifiable social privileges so seldom undergo serious or successful challenge? Why do so few voices champion the exploited laborers throughout our world? We all have dreams of the good life, yet some people seem to cruise down a super-highway on the way to their dreams while others struggle to hack a path with heavy machetes through thick brush to make only minimal progress toward realizing their dreams.

# THE AUGUSTINIAN INHERITANCE:
# A BALANCED VIEW OF HOPE IN HISTORY

At the heart of questions about hope and social justice is the notion of human agency—the possibilities and limits of what people can expect to accomplish given their free will and determination. Of course, nobody possesses adequate power to control all the factors that shape his or her life, such as health, natural disasters, and the sheer luck of our genetic endowments. Nevertheless, even in the face of these con-straints, each of us has the power to make meaningful moral choices, and to put our own personal stamp on our lives and our world.

Catholic social thought has consistently maintained a carefully bal-anced view of human agency, one that accounts for many factors related to hope and how it plays out in the lives of individuals and groups. The documents of popes and bishops, as well as the reflections of influential theologians working on social issues, recognize the limits of what we can realistically expect to accomplish through moral appeals and educa-tion for justice. We cannot stop floodwaters or epidemics by means of our moral teachings and preaching, but we can work for a conversion of hearts that will mitigate the exploitation of workers and the needless resort to force in situations of conflict, to cite a few examples of what may and may not be possible in church advocacy for peace and justice.

A particular strength of Catholic social teaching is the fact that it builds on a two-thousand-year tradition of reflection on the ways that hope and history interact. A dazzling early milestone in the theological tradition is *City of God*, a treatise written by St. Augustine of Hippo (354–430) as the Roman Empire was crumbling around him early in the fifth century, as my colleague Francine Cardman discusses in her chapter in this volume.[4] Among Augustine's many accomplishments in this lengthy work was a careful delineation between what can rightly be expected from temporal affairs (the mundane world of economy and politics, governed by fallible and sinful people) and from spiritual affairs (governed by the all-powerful God, whose presence remains hidden or mediated in the present order of history). We must not confuse the Earthly City with the Heavenly City, Augustine warns, nor conflate the hopes we might have for an imperfect order such as the Roman Empire (or any modern state) with the more profound and truly lasting hopes we rightly place in God alone.

Furthermore, we look to both God and Caesar for appropriate benefits, but we are ever aware that the semblance of peace and pros-perity achieved by even the best political leaders and systems in the course of human history is infinitely surpassed by the promise of divine redemption. To cite one of St. Augustine's favorite images, the appropri-ate ethical response for a person of faith is to exercise the patience of a pilgrim—someone who keeps one eye fixed on the holy destination, in eager anticipation, and the other eye directed toward the road being trod, with care for the practicalities of the present moment. A good pilgrim is attentive to the current conditions of life, ever eager to make improvements in the present order for the benefit of self and others, but is also aware that the ultimate hope we maintain transcends any current realities. In our temporary home in this world, there is surely more going on than meets the eye. But we must not focus so much on salvation history that we neglect human history, or become so other worldly in focus that we pass up opportunities to meet the material needs of our neighbors in this world. The pilgrim lives with one foot in each of two worlds, the *already* and the *not yet*. Hope and history are not identical, but on a good day, they might manage to rhyme, as the Irish poet Seamus Heaney cleverly phrased this insight.[5]

The division of labor regarding temporal and ultimate hope that emerges from St. Augustine sounds simple enough, but of course sixteen centuries of subsequent Christian history have demonstrated how elusive these insights can be. How easy it is to expect too much or too little hope in history! What happens when we place too much hope in human history? Periodically, political and social movements have arisen featuring an exaggerated sense of their own possibilities, attributing inflated hopes and claims for social improvement or even human perfection to favored programs of action. Some of these messianic movements became death-dealing ideologies; after all, if you persuade enough people that the stakes associated with your success are high enough, then any means to that end, even extremely violent means like brutal revolutions and genocides, might seem justified. The cost of straying too far from the middle path laid out by Augustine is often measured in blood, and the root of this error lies in human hubris that seeks to rush history by distorting the true basis for lasting hope.

The corresponding error of the other extreme, of placing too little hope in history, is an odd brand of quietism or passivity that aims too low, or fails to strive at all for human progress or social justice. To do nothing to improve the conditions of human life and the attainment of justice is clearly to wander off the path defined by Augustine, who in his own life as bishop of Hippo took great pains to advance peace and prosperity and to protect the people of his region from a range of physical as well as spiritual harms. He cared deeply about the water supply, security forces, and public works, for example, not just about combating heresies like Pelagianism, Manichaeism, and Donatism. Nevertheless, the history of Christianity includes many sectarian groups who are so focused on maintaining the holiness of their own members that they disavow most or all involvements with public affairs, often for fear of being corrupted by the mechanisms of power. While the desire for personal holiness of such sects may be commendable, their disavowal of social responsibility places them outside the mainstream of Christian positions on the nature of the virtue of hope. Thanks to Augustine and his later interpreters, most Christian communities have maintained a thoughtful balance on these matters, one that continues to seek some of the bases of their hope within historical events and some beyond history, in God alone.

## MAKING HOPE EFFECTIVE

Our inquiry into the theme of hope in the field of Christian social ethics would not be complete without some exploration of how our collective hopes for the attainment of greater social justice might become effective in our world today, and particularly in the economic and political systems we inhabit. Of all the branches of theology, social ethics is known as an eminently practical field, one where church and world intersect in ways that demand effective action and attention to the details and structures that can improve or destroy the lives of people.

Two key social institutions that help determine just or unjust outcomes for all people are government and private corporations. While any complete treatment of society must also consider a range of organizations that go beyond these two (including the so-called "third sector" of voluntary and nonprofit groups), the institutions that project the greatest political and economic power set the tone for all social relations. One key observation in this regard is the precarious balance of governmental and corporate power. We live in what is aptly termed a market society, and the power of government to check and regulate the operations of the economy and its major actors, the largest business firms, is a crucial dynamic for any of our hopes for social justice. For this reason, the documents of Catholic social teaching have consistently addressed ethical aspects of the operations of both governments and corporations, and especially the proper interaction of the private and public sectors. In short, if we can place the workings of government and business on the right track, this can encourage our hopes for the attainment of a solid measure of social justice.

Perhaps the most creative new concept to emerge from the documents of official Catholic social teaching in recent decades is the notion of *social sin,* also referred to as structures of sin or structural evil. The concept first appeared in 1971 in *Justice in the World,* a document from the worldwide Synod of Bishops.[6] Pope John Paul II utilized the notion extensively in his 1987 social encyclical *Sollicitudo Rei Socialis* ("On Social Concern"), mentioning the term over a dozen times in the latter half of that document. Much of the document consists of a survey of disturbing world events and trends; it highlights the proxy wars of the late Cold War, the exploitation of developing economies by affluent nations, as well as the distortions of consumerism, militarism, and imperialism. When John Paul II steps back from the description and seeks to offer a diagnosis, in a section of the letter called "A Theological Reading of Modern Problems," he presents a theory of how the world came to be so distorted. Personal sins on a small scale have a way of accumulating, as they build on themselves and come to be embedded in economic and political structures that perpetuate themselves, and in turn influence the perceptions and choices of other people down the line. As the late pontiff phrased it:

> If the present situation can be attributed to difficulties of various kinds, it is not out of place to speak of "structures of sin" which...are rooted in personal sin and thus always linked to the concrete acts of individuals who introduce these structures, consolidate them and make them difficult to remove. And thus they grow stronger, spread and become the source of other sins and so influence people's behavior. (paragraph 36)

For John Paul II, the virtue of solidarity emerges as the perfect antidote to the wreckage left by social sin. When we begin to recognize our obligation to others, and especially to the poor and marginalized, we are motivated to pursue what is best for their well-being, not just our own selfish interests. What is most significant for present purposes is how a consideration of social sin directs our gaze beyond the micro-level of person-to-person relations to the larger context of massive social institutions and the various systems of thought and behavior (sexism, racism, among many others) that demand to be addressed and corrected in the pursuit of social justice. If we are to maintain hope in social betterment and progress toward a more socially just world, then structures of sin must be identified, confronted, and defeated.

The key instrument of these hopes addressed by John Paul II, namely, solidarity, may be joined by an array of other cultural forces that raise our collective awareness of injustice and motivate us to organize for constructive social change. In the presence of powerful structures of sin, those practicing socially responsible strategies for justice must take a long view and exhibit great patience. Turning back the accumulation of evil choices over the course of history is not something that happens overnight. But the great patience required to forge a more ethical world in the future, one worthy of our hopes, will repay the costs many times over.

Catholic theology can learn much in this regard from, among other sources, one of the premier Protestant theologians of the twentieth century, Reinhold Niebuhr (1892–1971). Known as the father of the school of thought called Christian Realism, Niebuhr's voluminous writings commented on the human condition and world affairs with a distinctly pessimistic mood. Niebuhr was a keen observer of the human tendency to act in defensive, even tribalistic ways to protect the interests of one's own group or nation, despite the possibility of acting altruistically in face-to-face relations. Operating within an Augustinian framework that issues a firm reminder not to fall into naïve fantasies that exaggerate human goodness, Niebuhr explores at great length the implications of human finitude and sinfulness. Among other works, his 1932 book *Moral Man and Immoral Society* constitutes a clarion call for realism within a Christian anthropological framework.[7] Catholics in recent decades have gained from his work a sober appreciation of the complexities of the workings of structures of power in contemporary society. Catholic social theory had previously been accused of lacking an adequate structural analysis of power relations, and in fact may still need to consider further the many ways in which political and economic power is so often abused and our initial hopes so often frustrated. In any case, we emerge from Niebuhr's work still possessing abiding hope in a world that may someday be transformed, but also with a hope chastened and tested by a deeper knowledge of what is not likely to change as long as human nature remains as it is.

If Catholic social thought has benefitted through its contact with Niebuhr and other voices within Protestant theology, it can also rightly take pride in what it brings to the table of reflection on social issues. Without a doubt, the master concept of Catholic social thought is the common good. The Second Vatican Council's *Gaudium et Spes* (GS) defines the common good as "the sum of those conditions of social life which allow social groups and their individual social members relatively thorough and ready access to their own fulfillment" (GS, 26). We all have an obligation to consider the needs of others, and especially to prioritize the poorest. We are called to pursue the legitimate needs of others through private actions of a voluntary nature, such as volunteering at soup kitchens or donating to clothing drives, but also through public and collective action, such as in paying taxes to support state, county, and national social services.

In Catholic social theory, government emerges as the key agent whose purpose is to serve the common good, and specifically to undertake necessary functions that no other agent in society is likely to perform. While we are all called to do more than the minimum required of us by public authorities, and while our obligations to our neighbors are not exhausted by our participation in the political system, there is no substitute for supporting public actions in service to the common good. By pooling our efforts through the instruments of government and public life, we participate in the sharing of burdens and benefits that makes society possible. In the very willingness of members of society to sacrifice substantially for the good of others in a spirit of solidarity lies our hope for a society that is fair and just. As musician Bruce Springsteen frequently reminds his concert audiences, "Nobody wins unless everybody wins."

## Sustaining Hope

Catholic social teaching is a living tradition, a body of teachings and social analysis that is constantly being revised and updated. The last major document in this tradition is *Caritas in Veritate*, a 2009 social encyclical of Pope Benedict XVI. As long and complex as this document is, its agenda is exactly what any person of hope might expect: it identifies and responds to the most important issues regarding social justice and the common good in the opening years of this third millennium. Pope Benedict devoted much space to an appeal for a renewal of business ethics, a direct response to the deep-seated causes of the financial crisis that shook the global economy in 2008. In doing so, he demonstrated that the Catholic Church still dares to hope that the economy, as complex and distorted as it has become in this age of globalization, can indeed be reformed in such a way that it will truly serve the human needs of all, not just the exaggerated wants of those in luxury. Benedict also included the longest treatment of the ecological crisis that any pope had ever lodged within the pages of an encyclical, indicating that he retains hope in a reversal of the environmental degradation that threatens life on our planet. Perhaps the best summary of the entire 30,000-word document is a section that mentions hope explicitly:

> The complexity and gravity of the present situation rightly cause us concern, but we must adopt a realistic attitude as we take up with confidence and hope the new responsibilities to which we are called by the prospect of a world in need of profound cultural renewal, a world that needs to rediscover fundamental values on which to build a better future. (paragraph 21)

It is not hard to imagine Christians around the world responding to this call for moral renewal by taking up important projects of social activism, always in the spirit of hope. Whether these involve the promotion of human rights on the global level, advocacy for the poor on a national level, or antipollution efforts on a local level, such efforts for social justice at once reflect the tradition of Christian hope we have inherited and contribute to the enactment of hope, which Christians perceive as a privileged way that God dwells in the world.

The likelihood of experiencing frustration in our hopes for social justice does not prevent us from aspiring even now for some measure of participation in God's ultimate plan for our redemption, an initiative that fully invites our cooperation. Even the most sobering consideration of the hurdles that threaten to continue blocking our progress toward a more just society is no excuse for passivity or inaction. Rather, we find here a challenge to take up the struggle for social justice that has eluded humankind throughout its history. Even in the face of our past failures, Christians discover the energy to pursue a more just world. If our hope is to be effective, it must be incarnated in concrete actions of justice that witness to our Christian faith. Within the church today, in official social teachings and through the ardent social activism of millions of sincere Christians, the seeds for this desired social change are already sprouting.

## Notes

1. Miroslav Volf, *A Public Faith: How Followers of Christ Should Serve the Common Good* (Grand Rapids, MI: Brazos Press, 2011), 55.

2. Ibid., 56.

3. Robert B. Reich, "Ryan Exhumes a Dark Age," *San Francisco Chronicle*, August 19, 2012, F8.

4. Augustine, *City of God*, ed. David Knowles (New York: Penguin Books, 1972).

5. Seamus Heaney's poem "The Cure at Troy" includes the lines: "History says, Don't hope on this side of the grave. But then, once in a lifetime the longed for tidal wave of justice can rise up, and hope and history rhyme."

6. The official English-language versions of the documents of Catholic social teaching mentioned here can be found in Thomas A. Shannon and David J. O'Brien, eds., *Catholic Social Thought: The Documentary Heritage: Expanded Edition* (Maryknoll, NY: Orbis Books, 2010). The website of the Holy See (www.vatican.va) also provides all these texts.

7. Reinhold Niebuhr, *Moral Man and Immoral Society* (New York: Charles Scribner's Sons, 1932).

# 13

# Hope Springs:
# Shaping the Moral Life

## Andrea Vicini, SJ

Hope shapes our moral life and manifests itself as a gift and a choice. Moreover, we experience that "hope springs." The essay discusses these dimensions of hope and verifies them by reflecting on an ethical issue in which hopelessness seems to prevail: environmental sustainability. By attention to the Kenyan activist Wangari Maathai and to various Catholic voices, the essay illustrates how "hope springs" in exemplary commitments and fosters the well-being of humankind and of the earth.

Hope springs. This opening statement on the relationship of hope to the moral life might sound puzzling. It is more likely to evoke the bucolic image of refreshing spring water in the middle of a beautiful landscape, than the rigor of moral reasoning and the challenges of living ethically. To affirm that "hope springs," however, confirms that in the moral life, just as in the spiritual life, hope is a gift and a choice, as my colleague Colleen Griffith suggests in her essay in this collection. "Hope springs" integrates gift and choice, but also provides further insight into how hope helps us to live morally and to address today's ethical challenges.

We need to consider concretely, however, how hope shapes the moral life by being a gift and a choice, and by springing within us. One way to do so is to consider hope in relation to *sustainability*. In recent decades, many researchers, individual citizens, and organizations have stressed that the protection of sustainable conditions for life on the planet is the most pressing ethical task facing humankind. Hence, sustainability is a vital issue that tests our hope.

In his encyclical letter *Caritas in Veritate*, Pope Benedict XVI reflects on sustainability by confirming that both gift and choice are essential: "The environment is God's gift to everyone, and in our use of it we have a responsibility towards the poor, towards future generations and towards humanity as a whole."[1] We receive our world as a gift given to us, and we make personal and social choices that have an impact on the whole earth. Still, gift and choice do not seem sufficient to ensure that we will act morally or be people of hope. This inadequacy is evident when we consider our reluctance to engage in efforts to preserve our environment. We hide behind the various analyses, the contrasting hypotheses on what might happen, and the proposed solutions that scientists are articulating and debating. We are disappointed by the political inability, both nationally and internationally, to come up with appropriate regulations that could successfully foster sustainable living conditions on the planet. If there is to be an alternative to discouragement in the face of such disappointment, we need to experience how hope can spring within us and the current global context.

"Hope springs" stands as a modest ethical proposal. It assumes hope as a gift and a choice. At the same time, it points to another way in which hope shapes our moral life by promoting concrete actions. To articulate my approach, I rely, first, on the moral tradition and on its ability to reflect both on our being and doing: ethically, what do we know about ourselves and our way of acting that will help us to understand how hope works? Second, I consider sustainability to test the practical implications of hope.

# HOPE AND THEOLOGICAL ETHICS

## The Dimensions of Hope

In reflecting on hope in the moral life, I begin by considering the virtue of hope itself. As in the case of every virtue, we notice that it is a gift in our lives. It is given to us. Both the spiritual and moral traditions

169

forcefully affirm it. Hope does not solely depend on what we do. It requires our desires, struggles, and efforts and it grows out of them, but it is more than the fruit of our good will and engagement. We receive hope through others, through experiences, and through our longing for hope. What comes to us as a gift helps to make us who we are and influences what we do. The gift of hope makes us hopeful.

To stop here, however, by highlighting exclusively the dynamic of receiving, would greatly impoverish our self-understanding and appreciation of what constitutes the moral life. We make choices. Using our conscience and freedom, we respond to any ethical question and situation by examining personal and social norms, principles, virtues, and experiences (including the contributions of the sciences). All these moral elements help us in our reasoning, discerning, and deciding. Believers also rely on their religious sources and authorities. For Christians, the Bible—God's word in history—stands as an essential moral resource that calls for enlightened interpretation. For Catholics, the whole Christian tradition and the church's teaching authority also serve as moral guides.

Within the context of moral life, hope is a choice in two ways. First, we choose hope by preferring it to its opposites—despair, presumption, and lethargy of the heart.[2] Second, hope guides our choosing and thus becomes a constitutive element of our choices. In both cases, hope enhances our ability to act.

To sum up, hope involves receiving and acting. We should not be surprised by the existence of these two dimensions and the tension that can exist between them. Hope is not alone in being illumined by various elements and in incorporating them. A simple look at ourselves as moral beings, and at our own actions, would confirm that multiple aspects characterize who we are and what we do—sometimes even in conflicting ways. In other words, the multifaceted character of the virtue of hope matches our own personal complexity, whether we consider our moral identities, our actions, or both.

## Our Moral Identity

Our reflection on hope leads us to consider who we are, what we ought to do, and how we make it happen.[3] Let us begin by reflecting on our moral identity. Our moral lives are rich and complex, but consideration of one representative trait can offer us insight into our moral being: we long for what is good and just. This longing is part of who we are and it also depends on what we have experienced, both in receiving and in doing. It is also rooted in our commitment to the good throughout our whole life story, with its joys, struggles, and sufferings.[4] Finally, such a longing leads us to action and, particularly, to act justly. In Christian discourse, good and justice characterize God's kingdom here on earth and in eternity.

What is good and what is just: this is what we ought to do. In the last century, Catholic moral teaching and theological reflection have repeatedly and increasingly affirmed the urgency of promoting social justice and the common good—as Thomas Massaro indicates in this volume.

We are well aware, however, that the journey to implement this teaching, by making our world a better place, is still unfinished. We might know what is good and just, but we struggle to embody it concretely because of personal resistance or sinfulness and, within civil society, because social dynamics depend on other values and logics—mostly power and money.

In this context, how do we hope? Can hope help us to promote the good and the justice that we want for the whole world and ourselves? To understand hope as a gift and a choice does not seem to be sufficient—at least if we consider them separately. I suggest that, in moral life, these two dimensions of hope are dynamically integrated in a synthetic moment during which hope springs. Let me explain.

## The Dynamic of Hope: Hope Springs

The moral tradition tells us that, within the continuum of moral life, there are events with a specific importance and relevance. They are instances in which we make a synthesis from among multiple dimensions, gain new insight into ourselves and the situation at hand, experience a renewed moral freedom, resolutely pursue the good, and promote justice. These occurrences have been identified with occasions of conversion, because of the transformations that they can bring about in one's life.[5] We could also call them a sort of moral *eureka* moment, in which we grow in awareness, clarity, ability to act, goodness, and succeed in living what was previously out of our moral reach.

Two images allow me to express such an experience of synthesis, insight, freedom, pursuit of the good, and achievement of justice. The first image concerns education. In teaching and advising students, we recognize some of those moments. In many cases, all the needed elements are there, present in their lives, and for all students equally. But something happens and one student begins to flourish, to think creatively, speak her own voice, and articulate her original contribution. The image of a spring comes to mind. The change is noticeable. One wonders what made it possible. The student had received and assimilated information by making it her own. What was given to her as a gift (for example, through teaching and advising), still exterior, was integrated in her life through personal choice, engagement, and hard work. But the creative moment is not a given. It just springs. Sometimes, it is an isolated instance—once in a lifetime—and, after that, the spring seems to stop or at least is reduced. For other students, however, the spring continues to flow. They grow out of being students and gradually become scholars or creative moral agents in other social settings. In his essay in this volume, Thomas Groome shares how our pedagogical choices can support this.

The second example concerns these pages. I experienced the opportunity of this writing as a gift. It prompted my desire to reflect on hope and share something about its importance in shaping our moral life. I have chosen to do it. More was needed, however, for the creative process to occur. I found helpful the insights of other authors and colleagues, as well as personal experiences, together with the sources of moral reasoning. To describe the final result, however, the image of a spring is most fitting.

These two images suggest that in the moral life we experience something specific and unique. We recognize this distinctive element both in others and in ourselves. It is more than the sum of the single constituents that make us who we are and what we do. It goes beyond all our gifts and choices. It is a dynamic and open-ended process. Images can help us to describe it.

What might prepare the transformative instances and moments that mark our moral lives? What makes hope spring? Should we also pay attention to something else besides gifts and choices? My first thought goes to what we usually consider morally irrelevant and worthy of being discarded. Our life stories are filled with what we did not desire, we missed, and we lack.

Theological ethics tells us that we should incorporate these dimensions within our moral character and agency. In emotionally vivid ways, persons with disabilities help us to realize that even our own vulnerabilities and inabilities should be integrated in a more holistic understanding of our being and acting. Moreover, this unifying process could include our personal and social sinfulness.

To sum up, moral theology reminds us that the ethical ground that will make hope spring includes our whole being and doing, as well as our inability to be who we would like to be and to do what we would like to do. In such a way, to become aware of our failed commitments will not necessarily lead us to despair or lethargy. In the next section, this inclusive disposition will appear relevant and valuable, particularly when we acknowledge our major gaps in promoting sustainable conditions of living on our planet.

Hope can also spring in practices that address injustice. Within the Roman Catholic Church, Bryan Massingale, writing on racism, repeatedly called us to lament as an essential and initial moral response to injustice, as one step in our long journey toward justice.[6] Lament sounds ethically appropriate even when we reflect on sustainability. Addressing his religious community, the United Methodist Church, Richard Randolph writes that "Christian prophetic leadership must begin with the Church confessing, lamenting, and repenting from its own failures to be good stewards of God's creation, both in the past and in the present."[7] In a very biblical manner, lamenting our racial discrimination and our lack of care for creation can lead us to commit ourselves to a greater justice, both in our relationships and systemically, as well as to protect the environment.

Hope springs in a person at a certain point of one's life journey. This focus on one's story and context does not betray an individualistic bias or an understanding of the self that is disconnected from specific relational, historical, and geographical locations. On the contrary, each personal narrative reveals how we are all profoundly relational and embedded in social contexts. Relationships make us who we are and help us to become who we want to be. The moral tradition is well aware of the presence and importance of others, from our neighbors, to communities, to future generations.

The communal dimension of moral life is striking. We can name persons who are gifts in our lives. They are powerful and inspiring exemplary figures—from Mahatma Gandhi to Martin Luther King, Jr., from Archbishop Oscar Romero to many more persons less known to the world but dear to us. They embody hope in the concrete actions that marked their lives and in the good that they promoted within society. All of them become our beacons of hope. They are witnesses. With their lives, they confirm that positive radical transformations do occur in individual lives and in history. We see how hope springs in them and, through them, within our world. They inspire us and make us hopeful. They become as intimate to us as dear friends. They make us trust that hope can spring in us too. Somehow we can follow in their steps with creativity and imagination in our own historical, cultural, and religious contexts.

Finally, what happens when hope springs? What are the fruits of hope for the person and society? The witnesses of hope, those in whom we recognize hope springing, allow us to answer. They embody moral leadership that is characterized, as James Keenan indicates, by moral praxes of reconciliation, just relationships, humility, modesty, solidarity with those in need, and the ability to ask for forgiveness.[8] In other words, hope is inseparable from all the virtues, as Thomas Aquinas taught us in the thirteenth century. Hope expresses itself in just practices and it makes us virtuous leaders.

## HOPE FOR A SUSTAINABLE FUTURE

Hope is a gift, a choice, and hope springs. We might wonder, however, what practical implications there are in defining hope in such a way. Among many possible ways to test our understanding of hope in the moral life, the promotion of sustainability is challenging because, in addressing it, hopelessness seems to dominate. Scientists debate the gravity of the ongoing multifaceted environmental situation and they disagree both on the extent of the crises (for example, the lack of nonrenewable resources, pollution, global warming, droughts, and water scarcity) and on the solutions that would effectively respond to them. Moreover, as moral agents, we are torn between relying, on the one hand, on global solutions centered on expected new technological innovations and, on the other hand, on the commitments of single citizens, families, and communities to reduce their carbon footprint (for example, in containing energy consumption and waste). As Shaji George Kochuthara writes,

> We may feel helpless in the face of the ecological crisis, and especially since the political and economic structures, market interests and consumerist culture continue to aggravate the situation. However, it is important to remember that despair, fatalism and resignation are not Christian responses to sinfulness and evil. We are a people of hope. With renewed trust in God who guides the history of this universe and with renewed hope in the fulfillment of a universe where justice is ensured for all living and non-living beings—all created and loved by God—we continue our committed action as Christians for "a new earth and a new heaven."[9]

How do we foster our commitment? One concrete example allows me to illustrate how it might happen.

"In the course of history, there comes a time when humanity is called to shift to a new level of consciousness, to reach a higher moral ground. A time when we have to shed our fear and give hope to each other."[10] With these words, on December 10, 2004, the Kenyan environmental and political activist Wangari Maathai (1940–2011) received the Nobel Peace Prize. By honoring her, the first African woman on the Nobel roster, the Nobel committee endorsed and celebrated the relevance of her work aimed at creating more sustainable conditions for life on the planet. In 1977, she started to pay African women through the Green Belt Movement—"an environmental organization that empowers communities, particularly women, to conserve the environment and improve livelihoods."[11] Maathai's goal was to start tree nurseries to create stocks for replanting Kenya and, at the same time, to empower women by promoting their rights.

Her engagement in sustainable development was rooted in what she recognized as a gift in her life and also in what, around her, appeared to be lacking, even ethically problematic. On receiving the Nobel she explained:

> My inspiration partly comes from my childhood experiences and observations of nature in rural Kenya. It has been influenced and nurtured by the formal education I was privileged to receive in Kenya, the United States, and Germany. As I was growing up, I witnessed forests being cleared and replaced by commercial plantations, which destroyed local biodiversity and the capacity of the forests to conserve water.[12]

Maathai invites us to become aware that hope springs in us both from the fecund soil of an inspiring interaction with nature, where we discover creation as a glorious gift, and, at the same time, from the dry and ravaged ground that has been made such by human greed, by the unrestrained logic of the market, and through human ignorance.

In her, we recognize hope as a gift and as a series of choices that she made. Her practical actions in promoting environmental conservation were inseparable from the pursuit of democracy and peace, and were profoundly inspired by hope. For her, "The planting of trees is the planting of ideas. By starting with the simple act of planting a tree, we give hope to ourselves and to future generations."[13] Concrete actions, sometimes quite simple, have a profound impact. They generate transformative dynamics on earth and within the social fabric. They embody and generate hope.

In examining Maathai's life, we can identify moments in which the various strains of her moral character, desires, experiences, and types of hope found a synthetic and insightful expression. The hope that she discovered springing in herself gradually became embodied in the Green Belt Movement.[14] From personal and individual experience, hope emerged as communal. First, all the women belonging to the Movement shared her hope. Second, hope stands and grows beautifully in the trees that they planted. Finally, with the Nobel Prize, hope reached a global dimension.

Wangari Maathai embodied hope by leading and accompanying women and communities in discerning, deciding, and acting in concrete ways that promoted sustainable life on earth. She stands as an example and a witness that, we hope, will continue to be creatively contagious.

Hope springs in Maathai's life and actions, and, in doing this, it promotes justice, environmentally and socially. As Maureen O'Connell stresses, "justice is not only an intellectual calculation of the mind and the brain but also a desire or longing of the heart and body…justice is a vision of human relationships."[15] These relationships include the whole creation with all its living beings.

As I indicated earlier, within the Catholic Church, the call to embody and promote justice is very broad and encompassing. It reaches out to all dimensions of personal and social life, including the environment. This commitment is encouraging and inspiring. It helps our hope to spring by creating the conditions for this to happen. Catholic social teaching and theological discourse continue to remind us that justice is shaped by a resolute commitment to define and foster the common good within our world. Justice aims at achieving this good through the preferential option for the poor, effective subsidiarity, and transformative solidarity.

The Catholic commitment to social justice increasingly includes sustainability among its priorities, as the examples that follow confirm. We can begin with the Catholic Church's teaching authority, which, since the 1990s, has been forceful in calling for greater environmental justice. In his famous 1990 World Day of Peace Message, Pope John Paul II stressed the centrality of solidarity—largely present in his whole teaching on social issues—by affirming: "The ecological crisis reveals the *urgent moral need for a new solidarity*, especially in relations between the developing nations and those that are highly industrialized."[16] In 1991, the United States Catholic Conference of Bishops stated: "Only with equitable and sustainable development can poor nations curb continuing environmental degradation and avoid the destructive effects of the kind of underdevelopment that has used natural resources irresponsibly." For the American bishops, "Hope is the virtue at the heart of a Christian environmental ethic. Hope gives us the courage, direction, and energy required for this arduous common endeavor."[17] More recently, in his 2010 World Day of Peace Message, Pope Benedict XVI asked the following:

> Can we remain indifferent before the problems associated with such realities as climate change, desertification, the deterioration and loss of productivity in vast agricultural areas, the pollution of rivers and aquifers, the loss of biodiversity, the increase of natural catastrophes and the deforestation of equatorial and tropical regions? Can we disregard the growing phenomenon of "environmental refugees"…? Can we remain impassive in the face of actual and potential conflicts involving access to natural resources?…It should be evident that the ecological crisis cannot be viewed in isolation from other related questions, since it is closely linked to the notion of development itself and our understanding of man [sic] in his relationship to others and to the rest of creation.[18]

Theological reflection has also contributed to helping Christians become more aware of issues of sustainability. As an example, Cathriona Russell suggests that Christian hope fends off "the temptations of pessimism—and indeed optimism—[that] tend to paralyse and polarise responses to real concerns" about addressing specific environmental issues.[19] Finally, examples abound of religious congregations of women and men, as well as Christian communities around the globe, who are creatively engaged in practical projects that promote sustainability locally.

The virtue of hope shapes our moral lives. Hope manifests itself as a gift and in the choices that we make, just as receiving and acting are essential moral dimensions. Our experiences, however, suggest that these two moral dimensions of hope do not express sufficiently our being and doing. They both contribute and lead us to specific and unique moments in our moral journey, moments in which hope springs. This is a suggestive image that indicates how hope, besides being both gift and choice, further contributes to influence our moral life by integrating what we would discard in our moral identity, actions, and omissions. Throughout history, exemplars and leading figures, together with our own commitment, reveal how both the promotion of justice and of the common good are the remarkable fruits of hope.

Because of the difficulty of fostering sustainability in today's world, hopelessness seems to prevail. Even when this occurs, however, besides being gift and choice, hope springs in exemplary commitments that involve individuals, communities, and even the whole world. To integrate the attention given to one leader, Wangari Maathai, and to the movement that she created, I focused on the Catholic Church, listening to the prophetic voices that advocate for sustainability on behalf of humankind, particularly for today's poor and for future generations.

To affirm that hope springs suggests continuity, development, and progress—as when we think of the continuing flow of a natural spring in the midst of nature. Morally, this invites us to further education and dialogue, to learn and discuss what we still need to do to promote sustainable living conditions on earth. "Hope springs" can be a call for virtuous participation and collaboration.

## Notes

1. Pope Benedict XVI, Encyclical Letter, *Caritas in Veritate* (2009). Accessed online October 2, 2012, at http://www.vatican.va/ holy_father/benedict_xvi/encyclicals/documents/hf_ben-xvi_ enc_20090629_caritas-in-veritate_en.html, art. 48.

2. Despair is "a perverse anticipation of the nonfulfillment of hope" and presumption is "a perverse anticipation of the fulfillment of hope." Josef Pieper, *On Hope,* trans. Mary Frances McCarthy, SND (San Francisco: Ignatius Press, 1986), 47 and 48–73. On despair, see Jürgen Moltmann, *In the End, the Beginning: The Life of Hope*, trans. Margaret Kohl (Minneapolis, MN: Fortress Press, 2004), 93–95. On presumption, see James F. Keenan, *Moral Wisdom: Lessons and Texts from the Catholic*

*Tradition*, 2nd ed. (Lanham, MD: Rowman & Littlefield, 2010), 161–65; Romanus Cessario, OP, "The Theological Virtue of Hope (IIa IIae, Qq. 17–22)," in *The Ethics of Aquinas*, ed. Stephen J. Pope, Moral Traditions Series (Washington, DC: Georgetown University Press, 2002), 240; Enda McDonagh, "The Good News in Moral Theology: Of Hospitality, Healing, and Hope," in *Moral Theology for the Twenty-First Century: Essays in Celebration of Kevin Kelly*, ed. Kevin T. Kelly et al. (London/New York: T&T Clark, 2008), 85. Finally, for Moltmann, "lethargy is the real enemy of every hope....We must not surrender to lethargy of heart." Jürgen Moltmann, *Ethics of Hope* (Minneapolis: Fortress Press, 2012), 3 and 60.

3. These are the three key questions of virtue ethics, as many authors suggest. As examples, see Alasdair C. MacIntyre, *After Virtue: A Study in Moral Theory*, 3rd ed. (Notre Dame, IN: University of Notre Dame Press, 2007); Joseph J. Kotva, Jr., *The Christian Case for Virtue Ethics*, ed. James F. Keenan, Moral Traditions & Moral Arguments (Washington, DC: Georgetown University Press, 1996); James F. Keenan, *Virtues for Ordinary Christians* (Kansas City, MO: Sheed & Ward, 1996).

4. "Hope is a reaching out for anything that is perceived as good." Pieper, *On Hope*, 27. Quoted in: Patricia Lamoureux and Paul J. Wadell, *The Christian Moral Life: Faithful Discipleship for a Global Society*, Theology in Global Perspective Series (Maryknoll, NY: Orbis Books, 2010), 67.

5. See Christopher P. Vogt, *Patience, Compassion, Hope, and the Christian Art of Dying Well* (Lanham, MD: Rowman & Littlefield, 2004), 80.

6. Bryan N. Massingale, *Racial Justice and the Catholic Church* (Maryknoll, NY: Orbis Books, 2010), 104–14; Bryan N. Massingale, "The Systemic Erasure of the Black/Dark-Skinned Body in Catholic Ethics," in *Catholic Theological Ethics, Past, Present, and Future: The Trento Conference*, ed. James F. Keenan (Maryknoll, NY: Orbis Books, 2012) 121–22. See also: Maureen H. O'Connell, *If These Walls Could Talk: Community Muralism and the Beauty of Justice* (Collegeville, MN: Liturgical Press, 2012), 187–93.

7. Richard O. Randolph, "Christian Prophetic Leadership for the Environment," *Review and Expositor*, 108 (2011): 85.

8. Keenan, *Moral Wisdom*, 155–69.

9. Shaji George Kochuthara, "Re-Discovering Christian Eco-Theological Ethics," *Hekima Review*, 43 (2010), 61.

10. Wangari Maathai, "Nobel Lecture" (2004). Accessed online October 4, 2012, at http://www.nobelprize.org/nobel_prizes/peace/laureates/2004/maathai-lecture-text.html.

11. Green Belt Movement, http://www.greenbeltmovement.org.

12. Wangari Maathai, "Nobel Lecture."

13. Quoted in: Robert Pierson, "Trees and the Forest: Story and Trustori in Quaker Faith and Practice," *CrossCurrents*, 61 (2011): 150.

14. See Wangari Maathai, *Unbowed: A Memoir* (New York: Alfred A. Knopf, 2006); Anne M. Clifford, CSJ, "Trees, 'Living Symbols of Peace & Hope': Wangari Maathai & Ecofeminist Theology," in *Confronting the Climate Crisis: Catholic Theological Perspectives*, ed. Jaime Schaefer, Marquette Studies in Theology (Milwaukee, WI: Marquette University Press, 2011), 339–62.

15. O'Connell, *If These Walls Could Talk*, 122.

16. John Paul II, "Peace with God the Creator, Peace with All of Creation" (1990). Accessed online October 4, 2012, at http://www.vatican.va/holy_father/john_paul_ii/messages/peace/documents/hf_jp-ii_mes_19891208_xxiii-world-day-for-peace_en.html, art. 10.

17. United States Catholic Conference, *Renewing the Earth: An Invitation to Reflection and Action on Environment in Light of Catholic Social Teaching* (Washington, DC: United States Catholic Conference, 1992), III.D and V.D.

18. Pope Benedict XVI, "If You Want to Cultivate Peace, Protect Creation" (2010). Accessed online October 4, 2012, at http://www.vatican.va/holy_father/benedict_xvi/messages/peace/documents/hf_ben-xvi_mes_20091208_xliii-world-day-peace_en.html, art. 4 and 5.

19. Cathriona Russell, "Burden-Sharing in a Changing Climate: Which Principles and Practices Can Theologians Endorse?" *Studies in Christian Ethics*, 24 (2011): 69.

IV

---

# LIVING HOPE

# 14

# The Future Is Now: Eternal Life and Hope in John's Gospel

## *Daniel J. Harrington, SJ*

John's Gospel emphasizes that the ultimate goal of Christian hope—
eternal life with God—can be enjoyed in the present. Thus, for John,
the future is now. After defining hope and describing apocalyptic thinking, the article discusses the distinctive dimensions of Johannine hope,
various images of hope, and the role of the Paraclete in Johannine hope.

In John's theology eternal life is the object of hope, and the ground
of hope is "the hour" of Jesus—his passion, death, resurrection, and
ascension. Yet John never mentions hope. The reason is that for him, far
more than for other New Testament writers, what is the object of
hope—eternal life with God through Christ—has already begun
through Jesus as the revealer and revelation of God. In short, the future
is now.

After defining the elements of hope, this article will first show how
John has adapted the Jewish schema of *modified apocalyptic dualism* by
focusing almost entirely on the present or realized dimension of salvation brought about through the "hour" of Jesus. The apocalyptic hope
of the "new age/new world" has already begun. Through faith in Jesus
and love toward others it is possible to participate now in eternal life.
Then the article will explore some Johannine images that express the
relationship between Jesus and the believer (Word, light, water, shep-

herd, and vine) and note how they contribute to the peculiar character of hope in John's Gospel. Finally, it will focus on what is a key element in Christian life in the present: the Holy Spirit, or Paraclete.

What might the Johannine insight about hope mean for Christians today? In the Nicene Creed, we regularly profess our belief in "the resurrection of the dead and the life of the world to come." That remains the ultimate Christian hope. However, there is a life to be lived along the way. In the context of the New Testament canon, the Johannine approach to eschatology challenges believers in Jesus to act *in the present* out of their conviction that for them eternal life has already begun. That conviction entails keeping the two great commandments of Jesus: believing in Jesus as the revealer and revelation of God, and in return loving God and one another. The Johannine approach gives us the freedom to serve God as our only Master and so to refuse enslaving ourselves to lesser powers. It helps us to find joy even in times of trouble, since we trust the promises of God made through Jesus. And it gives us peace at the deepest level, since we believe that we are already participating in eternal life and that for us the future is now.

# DEFINING HOPE

At its most basic level, hope is a desire accompanied by the possibility of (or belief in) its realization. Thus, hope has an object or focus, looks toward the future, and has some ground or basis in reality.[1] The opposites of hope are despair and presumption. Despairing persons are so overwhelmed by their own inadequacies and/or by the obstacles before them that they fail to do anything that might make their hope into a reality. Presumptuous persons simply assume that they will be taken care of, and that God or someone else will do what is needed to bring about the object of their desires. By contrast, persons of genuine hope have goals, recognize what they need to do to reach those goals, and shape their lives accordingly and meet the obstacles along the way (with the help of God). Dominic Doyle's essay in this collection examines the nature of hope in more detail.

The Bible is a book of hope.[2] In the Old Testament hope is based on the person and the promises of God. Its object tends to shift or develop over the centuries: offspring and the land in the case of Abraham, Israel's greatness and goodness as a people in the case of Moses, Israel's return from exile and its renewal as the people of God, the emergence of an ideal king (messianism), and the vindication of the wise and righteous with the coming of God's kingdom (apocalypticism).

In Greek philosophical thought, the object of hope could be life after death based on the natural immortality of the soul (Socrates, Plato) or happiness in this life (Aristotle). For Jews in Jesus' time, it might be Israel's restoration as God's people, their perfect observance of the Torah, safety from attacks by its enemies, the coming of the Messiah, and/or the fullness of God's kingdom accompanied by resurrection of the dead and the last judgment. For early Christians, the ultimate object of hope was eternal life with God through Christ. The basis for their hope was the death and resurrection of Jesus (paschal mystery) and the gift of the Holy Spirit. They were convinced that for them eternal life had already begun through their faith and baptism into Christ (see Rom 6:1–4), and so they could "walk" in patience and confidence. More than any other New Testament writer, John stresses the present or *already* dimension of eternal life, to almost the total disappearance of classic Jewish eschatology. Indeed, it is possible to speak of Christian life in the present as eschatological existence.

# APOCALYPTIC THINKING

In many respects, the early Christians shared the apocalyptic language and worldview of their Jewish contemporaries. For this reason, apocalyptic has been called the mother of Christian theology. An apocalypse is a revelation about the future or the heavenly realm, often mediated by a dream or vision and interpreted by an angel. Parts of the books of Daniel and Revelation qualify as biblical apocalypses. The late-first century AD books known as *2 Baruch* and *4 Ezra* (2 Esdras 3–14) belong to the same category. The term *apocalyptic* can also refer to the kind of thinking and imagery found in these books and other writings of the time. It generally concerns the "last things" (eschatology) either directly or indirectly; that is, the resurrection of the dead, the last judgment, and rewards and punishments.[3]

The philosophical-theological foundation for much apocalyptic thinking in early Judaism and early Christianity is best articulated in the *Rule of the Community*, columns 3 and 4, one of the Dead Sea scrolls discovered in the late 1940s at Qumran.[4] That document seems to have been a rule for some kind of Jewish religious community (probably Essenes). It describes entrance into the community, lays down regulations for life within the group, and adds some hymnic material. Part of the entrance material is an instruction for the community's spiritual director that he was to impart to the new recruits. It purports to describe how the world runs, why there is evil in the world, and what will happen in the future.

The instruction maintains that at present there is a dualism between good and evil, between wisdom and folly, in the world. It presupposes the absolute sovereignty of God: "From the God of knowledge comes all that is and shall be." However, it seems that God has ceded control of human history to two spirits or powers, the Prince of Light and the Angel of Darkness. These figures are something like Michael the archangel and Satan. Those who follow the lead of the Prince of Light are the Children of Light and do the deeds of light, while those who follow the Angel of Darkness are the Children of Darkness and do the deeds of darkness. The instruction provides lists of the virtues and good deeds that mark the Children of Light and of the vices and evil deeds that mark the Children of Darkness. However, this dualism will eventually come to an end with the decisive intervention of God, the Visitation or Last Judgment. Then the Angel of Darkness and his followers will be destroyed, and the Prince of Light and his followers will be vindicated and live in eternal happiness with God (the fullness of God's kingdom).

One way to describe this almost metaphysical schema is *modified apocalyptic dualism*. There is obviously a *dualism* between the two powers, the two kinds of persons, and the two ways of behaving. Whether this dualism emerged out of the Old Testament or was imported from elsewhere (Persia is the most likely candidate) has long been debated among scholars. However, this dualism is not absolute since the instruction insists first of all on the absolute sovereignty of God ("the laws of all things are in his hand"). Thus, it can be termed *modified*. Moreover, this dualism will end with the Last Judgment, and so can be called *apocalyptic*.

The Jewish schema of modified apocalyptic dualism seems to have been the presupposition of at least two great theologians of the New Testament, Paul and John. Both further modified the schema, however, by making room for the decisive significance of Jesus' life, death, and resurrection. Paul's use of the schema can be seen most clearly in Romans 1–8. There Paul first establishes that all persons—Gentiles and Jews alike—needed the revelation of God's righteousness (or covenant fidelity) in Christ (Rom 1–3). Then he shows in Romans 4 how it is now possible through faith (after the pattern of Abraham) to enter into the new relationship with God offered by Christ (justification by faith). For Paul, the Prince of Light is Christ and the Holy Spirit, and the Angel of Darkness is the unholy trinity made up of sin, death, and the law. Christ has made it possible for persons of faith to be freed from the dominion of these three powers. Moreover, Paul was convinced that through Jesus' death and resurrection (the paschal mystery) it is now possible to enjoy some of the fruits of the divine Visitation or Last Judgment, and so to do the deeds that are appropriate to the Children of Light. Paul's principal modification of the schema of modified apocalyptic dualism is his emphasis on the partially present dimension of the Visitation without denying or neglecting its future fullness. For Paul, believers in Christ live in the "new age" and in the "new creation" brought about by Jesus' death and resurrection. They are already alive in the Spirit while awaiting the future fullness of God's kingdom, as Thomas Stegman's chapter discussing Romans 8 makes clear.

## JOHANNINE HOPE

This kind of apocalyptic thinking and its dualism seem to have been a theological presupposition for Johannine theology. However, they have been radically adapted in light of the Christ-event. In current scholarship there is something of a consensus that John's Gospel is the product of a Christian circle or school that developed a distinctive vocabulary and theology over a fairly long period.[5] The group may well have been founded by John the son of Zebedee (was he the "Beloved Disciple"?), or at least took him as its "patron saint." It appears also that the Johannine community was in the process of being excluded from the synagogue (see 9:22; 12:42; 16:2). The Gospel was put into its final form in the late first century. Its composition has been traditionally associated with Ephesus, although the earlier phases of its development may well have taken place in Palestine or its environs. The basic thesis of John's Gospel is that Jesus is the revealer and the revelation of God. Its purpose is that "you may believe [or come to believe] that Jesus is the Messiah, the Son of God, and that through believing you may have life in his name" (20:31).[6]

It is customary to divide John's Gospel into the Book of Signs (chapters 1 to 12) and the Book of Glory (chapters 13 to 21). While there are overlaps and links with the three Synoptic Gospels, this Gospel seems to represent an independent tradition within early Christianity. It features different characters (Nicodemus, the Samaritan woman, the man born blind, Lazarus, the Beloved Disciple, and so on), a different chronology and geography (Jesus visits Jerusalem at least three times), long speeches by Jesus, and a strong emphasis on the present dimensions of salvation.

The author of John's Gospel agrees with Paul and the other New Testament writers that Jesus' life, death, and resurrection inaugurated and began the "new creation" or "new age." But John is even more convinced than they are that eternal life has already begun and can be enjoyed in the present. There are some texts in John's Gospel that still look forward to the resurrection of the dead as bringing in the fullness of God's kingdom: "for the hour is coming when all who are in their graves will hear his [the Son of Man's] voice and will come out—those who have done good, to the resurrection of life, and those who have done evil, to the resurrection of condemnation" (5:28–29). This is a Christian version of the Jewish apocalyptic schema of resurrection, judgment, and rewards and punishments. This promise, however, is preceded by a discourse where Jesus reflects on his own identity as the Son of God and claims that "anyone who hears my word and believes him who sent me has eternal life, and does not come under judgment, but has passed from death to life" (5:24). In other words, God has appointed Jesus as the eschatological judge and made the criterion for the divine judgment acceptance or rejection of Jesus as the revealer and revelation of God. Consequently, eternal life begins when one comes to believe in Jesus.[7]

Likewise in the account of Lazarus' restoration to life (11:1–44), Jesus assures Martha that her brother will rise again. When Martha professes belief that he will rise in the last day, Jesus affirms that "I am the resurrection and the life. Those who believe in me, even though they die, will live, and everyone who lives and believes in me will never die" (11:25–26). Again, the Johannine Jesus modifies the schema of modified apocalyptic dualism by focusing on the present dimension of eternal life and his pivotal place within it.

The theme of faith in Jesus as the revealer and revelation of God and its role as the criterion of divine judgment appears early in the Gospel, in the aftermath of Jesus' dialogue with Nicodemus in John 3. Jesus is the point of decision (*krisis*) that determines whether one abides in the light and does the deeds of light: "And this is the judgment, that the light has come into the world" (3:19). Likewise in John 3:38 we read that "Whoever believes in the Son has eternal life; whoever disobeys the Son will not see life, but must endure God's wrath."

In John's narrative, however, the passion, death, resurrection, and exaltation of Jesus constitute one great event—the "hour" of Jesus. It is the moment toward which the whole narrative has been building ever since Jesus initially rebuffed his mother's request at Cana by explaining that "my hour has not yet come" (2:4). His passion is a victory, not a defeat. John brings this out by playing on the word *hypso*, which can mean to be lifted up on the cross and to be lifted up to glory. Recalling the bronze serpent episode in Numbers, the Johannine Jesus says, "And just as Moses lifted up the serpent in the wilderness, so must the Son of Man be lifted up, that whoever believes in him may have eternal life" (3:15). And so at the very beginning of the so-called Book of Glory, at the start of the farewell discourses (chapters 13 to 17), we are told that "Jesus knew that his hour had come to depart from this world and go to the Father" (13:1).

In this context, what does hope mean in John's Gospel? In terms of our definition of hope sketched in the beginning of this chapter, hope must have an object or focus, must look toward the future, and must have a reason or ground for its realization. For John, the object or focus is eternal life with God and his Son Jesus. The reason or ground is Jesus—the Word of God, the man from heaven, the glorious Son of Man—and especially the "hour" of Jesus—the event of his passion, death, resurrection, and exaltation/ascension. While John maintains in a few places the Jewish apocalyptic schema of modified apocalyptic dualism with its climax in the divine visitation consisting of resurrection, judgment, and rewards and punishments, he seems far more interested in the present aspects of eternal life already made possible through Jesus.

In John's Gospel, the Greek words for *hope*—the verb *elpizo* and the noun *elpis*—never appear. The primary virtues are faith and love. While the schema of modified apocalyptic dualism remains the framework for Christian life, the focus of attention for Christian life is the present. Since eternal life begins with believing in Jesus, in a sense hope is swallowed up by faith and love. For John, faith is a verb (*pisteuo*). It comes down to believing in Jesus and the one who sent him. The noun *pistis* never appears. Love (*agape*) is the proper response to, the consequence of, and the proof of believing in Jesus. Having experienced God's love in sending his Son into the world (3:16), the believer will love God and love others in return. In the great chain of love, Jesus is the link that holds everything together: "As the Father has loved me, so I have loved you; abide in my love" (15:9).

## JOHANNINE IMAGES OF HOPE

As in much of the Bible, what constitutes Johannine *hope* is best conveyed in images. The images in John's Gospel are concerned not so much with the coming fullness of God's kingdom (compare the parables in the Synoptic Gospels) as they are with the person of Jesus, believing in Jesus, and its implications for life in the present and immediate future. These images support and nourish hopeful attitudes along the way of life. Here are five such images.

# The Future Is Now: Eternal Life and Hope in John's Gospel

*The Word*: John's Gospel begins by identifying Jesus as the Word of God (see 1:1–18, the Prologue to the Gospel). The image evokes the process of speaking words as our most common mode of communicating what is on our minds. While several Old Testament backgrounds have been suggested, the most obvious one is the figure of personified Wisdom (see Prov 8, Sir 24, Wis 7). However, what John says about Jesus far outstrips what the Old Testament says about Wisdom. He states that "the Word was God" (1:1). He also insists that "the Word became flesh and lived among us" (1:14). Throughout John's Gospel, Jesus is the revealer and the revelation of God. If we want to know what God wants to say to us and what God wants us to do, attend to Jesus as the Word of God. That should be a great source of hope for the believer.

*The Light*: In John 1–12, the image of Jesus as the Light is especially prominent. In Genesis 1:3 the creation of the world begins with God's words, "Let there be light." The first lines in John's Gospel surely evoke them. Throughout the Prologue, Jesus is identified as "the light" who came into the world (1:4–5, 7–9). In the body of the Book of Signs, Jesus twice identifies himself as "the light of the world" (8:12; 9:5) and characterizes those who believe in him as "children of light" (12:36). The light imagery in John is reminiscent of the Qumran *Rule of the Community* and its instruction about the Prince of Light and the sons of light. Those who live in the light that is Jesus have good reason to be people of hope.

*Water*: Another prominent natural symbol in John's Gospel is water. Since water is essential for human life, it is among many other things a symbol of life and hope. One key "water" text comes in Jesus' dialogue with the Samaritan woman in John 4:14: "But those who drink of the water that I will give them will never be thirsty. The water that I will give will become in them a spring of water gushing up to eternal life." There are, of course, several mentions of water in John in connection with John's baptism (1:26, 31, 33). Three of Jesus' "signs" feature water: his changing water into wine (2:1–11), his healing of the paralyzed man near the pool of Bethesda (5:1–9), and Jesus walking on the water (6:16–21). Another key "water" text comes with Jesus' statement on the last day of the feast of Tabernacles (at which water symbolism was already prominent): "Let anyone who is thirsty come to me, and let the one who believes in me drink. As the scripture has said, 'Out of the believer's heart shall flow rivers of living waters'" (7:37b–38). During the Last Supper, he pours water into a basin and washes his disciples' feet (13:1–15). And at the moment of his death on the cross "blood and water" come forth from his side (19:34). As a natural symbol of life set in the story of Jesus, water gives hope.

*The Shepherd*: The most famous biblical application of this image appears in Psalm 23: "The LORD is my shepherd" (23:1). The shepherd cares for his sheep, guides them along the best paths, provides water and food, and sees to their safety. The image of "shepherd" was often applied to kings and other rulers in the ancient Near East. In John 10:1–21, Jesus identifies himself first as "the gate for the sheep" (10:7), thus suggesting a personal relationship with the sheep. He calls them by name, leads them out to pasture, and sees to their safety in the evening by opening the gate to the sheep pen and leading them back in. Then he identifies himself as "the good shepherd," in that (unlike a hired hand) he is willing to lay down his life for the sheep. The themes of mutual knowledge and divine protection make the shepherd an image of hope for those who believe in Jesus.

*The Vine*: According to John 15:1–6, Jesus is the vine, and those who believe in him are the branches. One possible Old Testament background is Psalm 80:8–18, where Israel is portrayed as a vine that God brought out of Egypt (in the exodus), cared for it, and saw to its flourishing. However, then it was crushed and burned (in the exile), and so the psalmist prays that God will once more have regard for his vine. For John, the vine is Jesus, the farmer/vine grower is God the Father, and the branches are those who follow Jesus. The vital power of Jesus courses through the whole plant and serves as its source of life. The branches either live or die depending on whether or not they bear fruit, which means abiding in Jesus and keeping his commandments to believe and to love. Recognizing the divine life within is a powerful reason for hope.

# THE PARACLETE AND HOPE

If eternal life is the object of hope according to John and it has already begun, where does hope come from in everyday life? It is from the Holy Spirit. While the believer may already participate in the ultimate goal of Christian hope, the life that the believer experiences now in the community of Jesus Christ is animated by the power of the Holy Spirit, otherwise known as the Paraclete. It is the power of the Holy Spirit that enables the Christian to be a person of hope in everyday life.

The Paraclete passages appear in Jesus' farewell discourses in John 13–17. These long discourses are set in the context of Jesus' Last Supper with his disciples. Their fundamental concern is carrying on the project begun by Jesus after his departure from this earth in his passion and death. The question is, How is the community centered around the earthly Jesus to continue in his physical absence? In the course of these discourses Jesus offers several answers: accepting salvation as a divine gift, following the example of Jesus, believing that Jesus is the revealer and the revelation of God, loving God and one another, carrying on the mission of Jesus in the world, and working for unity in the community—a unity based on that between the Father and the Son. But perhaps the most important means of continuing the work of Jesus comes in the promise that the Holy Spirit/Paraclete will guide and direct the movement begun by Jesus. This promise makes it possible for the believer in Jesus to be a person of hope in everyday existence.

The Greek word *parakletos* can be translated as helper, consoler, advocate, or counselor. It can even refer to a defense attorney who pleads the case of someone who is on trial. In John 14:15–17, Jesus states that "I will ask the Father, and he will give you another Advocate, to be with you forever." To describe the Holy Spirit as "another Advocate" means that the Spirit will take the place of the earthly Jesus and carry on his work in the community of believers: "he abides with you, and he will be in you." According to 14:26, the Spirit/Advocate will teach the community and remind them of what Jesus taught. In 15:26, the Spirit of truth will bear witness on behalf of Jesus. According to 16:7–15, the Spirit will convict "the world" in the sense of bringing to light its failure to accept Jesus as the revealer and the revelation of God and in condemning Jesus to death. Thus, the Holy Spirit/Paraclete takes Jesus' place as the abiding presence of God in the community, teaches and keeps alive the wisdom of Jesus, bears witness to Jesus, and convicts the world of sin. In short, the community of believers in Jesus is sustained and directed by the Spirit/Paraclete.

In the course of the Johannine farewell discourses, Jesus' disciples are urged to be people of hope, even in the midst of sorrow and persecution. They may be sorrowful because Jesus has told them about his imminent departure: "A little while, and you will no longer see me" (16:16a). But they can be hopeful because of what Jesus promises: "and again a little while, and you will see me" (16:16b), at least at the resurrection. Thus, the disciples are also assured of the second coming, or *parousia*, of Jesus, and so their sorrow will be only temporary. Likewise, the disciples may be frightened because of the persecution they will meet from outsiders: "In the world you will face persecution" (16:33b). Here, "the world" refers to those forces, human and superhuman, that are opposed to God and to God's Son. But they can be at peace, because "I [Jesus] have conquered the world" (16:33c). In this way Jesus prepared them to regard his passion, death, and resurrection not as a defeat, but rather as a victory over the Evil One (see John 13:27). The community of Jesus Christ is a place not only of hope but also of peace, joy, and freedom.

John's very strong emphasis on the present dimension of salvation is unique in the New Testament. While in a few passages John, along with the other New Testament writers, looks forward to the *parousia* of the risen Jesus, he also (and especially) insists that for the believer in Jesus the "Last" Judgment has already occurred and eternal life has already begun. That means that the ultimate goal of Christian hope can be enjoyed in the present. What is future (in its fullness) for most biblical writers is for John already happening. In other words, the future is now.

## Notes

1. See Daniel J. Harrington, *What Are We Hoping For? New Testament Images* (Collegeville, MN: Liturgical Press, 2006), v–x.

2. Jürgen Moltmann, *Theology of Hope: On the Ground and Implications of a Christian Eschatology* (New York: Harper & Row, 1967).

3. Frederick J. Murphy, *Apocalypticism in the Bible and Its World* (Grand Rapids, MI: Baker Academic, 2012).

4. Geza Vermes, *The Complete Dead Sea Scrolls in English* (New York: Penguin, 1997), 101–3.

5. Raymond E. Brown, *The Community of the Beloved Disciple* (New York: Paulist Press, 1979).

6. For basic information, see Daniel J. Harrington, *Meeting St. John Today* (Chicago: Loyola Press, 2011).

7. The classic formulation of the "present" eschatology of the Johannine writings remains volume 2 in Rudolf Bultmann's *Theology of the New Testament* (Waco, TX: Baylor University Press, 2007), 3–92. He simply explains away (with astonishing certitude) any elements of future eschatology.

15

# From Utopia to *Eu-topia*: Christian Hope in History

## *O. Ernesto Valiente*

This essay builds on the work of Latin American liberation theology to argue that the utopia proclaimed by Jesus is integral to the realization of God's kingdom in history. It proposes that if Christians are to offer a more credible account of their hope today, this utopia must begin to be concretized through a eu-topic project: a good and historically feasible social project that seeks to anticipate, at least in a partial manner, the fullness of the kingdom of God.

Christian faith is built on the hope that God's future will ultimately transform all of creation and bring about the fullness of God's kingdom. Christian hope is thus a mode of living with confidence in the promises of the God revealed in Jesus: that the reign of God is at hand (see Luke 10:9); that there will be "a new heaven and a new earth" (2 Pet 3:13; Rev 21:1). Such hope is grounded in the Christian proclamation of God's kingdom, which envisages a new creation and a reconciled community that enjoys a life of peace, justice, and communion with God. This promised future is a utopia—a vision of the perfected world-to-come—that orients Christian life toward God's future by shaping and nurturing Christian life in the present.

Yet in much current discourse, *utopia* is used pejoratively and utopian ideas that propose alternative visions of society often carry negative connotations. Some see utopias as illusory fantasies "with a tendency to submit reality to dreams" that encourage an escapist faith divorced from historical reality.[1] More specifically, postmodern philosophers warn that the "totalizing narratives" that constitute utopias only replace one all-encompassing ideology with another.[2] Some neo-liberal thinkers, on the other hand, simply dismiss utopian ideas as irrelevant. For the latter, the fall of the Berlin Wall put an end to all ideological contradictions, and with the advance of liberal democracy we have arrived at "the 'end point of mankind's ideological evolution'…and the 'end of history.'"[3] It is not surprising, then, when the political scientist George Kateb asks rhetorically, "Can there be anything more commonplace than the pronouncement that, in the twentieth century, utopia is dead—and dead beyond any hope of resurrection?"[4] Or when the historian Russell Jacoby laments, "A utopian spirit—a sense that the future could transcend the present—has vanished.…Someone who believes in utopias is widely considered either out to lunch or out to kill."[5]

The persistence of suffering and oppression in the world, however, belies this neo-liberal optimism that we have somehow arrived at the end of history. From a Christian standpoint, such circumstances contradict the will that God has revealed for the world and thus demand a response that is consistent with God's promise for the transformation of our present broken order. Latin American liberation theologians lend particular insight to the centrality of a utopic vision for Christian faith, as their theology has arisen in response to situations of endemic suffering and poverty. Although mindful that the fullness of God's kingdom is not coterminous with human projects, these theologians insist that God's promises already bear the seeds of this future in the here and now. They also underscore that the proclamation of the kingdom must shape both the Christian understanding of salvation and the direction of Christian praxis today.

This essay builds on the work of Latin American liberation theology to argue that the Christian utopia proclaimed by Jesus, and articulated by the Christian community, is integral to the expression of God's kingdom in history. It further proposes that if Christians are to offer a more credible account of their hope today (see 1 Pet 3:15), this utopia must begin to be concretized through a *eu*-topic project: a historically feasible social project that seeks to build a "good place" and thus anticipate, at least in a partial manner, the fullness of the kingdom. To make

199

this case, the paper explores the relationship between hope and utopia, and the proclamation of God's kingdom as the articulation of the Christian utopia. It then identifies the main features of the Christian *eu-topic* project and shows its central role in the Christian effort to construct a more just and humane world.

# HOPE, UTOPIA, AND GOD'S KINGDOM

The term *utopia* was coined by the English Christian humanist Sir Thomas More, whose famous book of that title, first published in 1516, depicted an ideal society on a remote island.[6] The name of the book is a play on words that merges the Greek *ou-topos* ("no place") and *eu-topos* ("good place"). In common usage, a utopia is an *outopos*—a place that does not exist anywhere—and the term carries the pejorative connotation associated with a dream or fantasy. But if its nature as a *eutopos* is emphasized, the term acquires the positive connotation of a *good* social project that confronts the limitations of the present world. Gustavo Gutiérrez, for example, argues that the context for More's work is the England of his time and thus More presents his utopia not just as a fantasy, but as a model of an ideal community of the future in contrast to his present historical reality.[7] In this use, utopia can express "a human aspiration toward a truly just order, a social world that is wholly human, which corresponds fully to the dreams, needs, and deepest aspirations of human life."[8]

Humanity's utopian aspirations have a long and diverse history. More's work was influenced by the rich utopian tradition of the ancient Greek world, a tradition that reaches back to the eighth century BCE.[9] Even older are some of the utopian myths found in the ancient Near Eastern cultures that influenced the biblical utopian visions.[10] However, while Greek utopias often speak of unknown people and imaginary places, such as Atlantis, the utopian visions found in the Hebrew scriptures tend to place their ideal society in the land of Israel. As John J. Collins explains:

> What we find then in the biblical tradition is not primarily a
> search for a Utopia that is no-place....The yearning is not for

the isles of the blessed, somewhere beyond the ocean.... Rather, it is the yearning for a very specific place....Much of the abiding power of the Bible surely lies in the fact that its vision of utopia is so concretely embodied in a specific land.[11]

The ancient Hebrew people lived their lives firmly rooted in history and in a hope that corresponded to the promises extended to them by Yahweh. Among the diverse utopian expressions in the Hebrew scriptures, the one that concerns us—God's kingdom—may be located within what Mary Ann Beavis defines as the Bible's dynamic-theocratic traditions.[12] As a constitutive dimension of the broader concept of God's royal sovereignty in the Old Testament, the symbol of the kingdom of God predates the Israelite monarchy and likely finds its roots in Near Eastern mythology.[13] Although it is mainly expounded by the authors of Daniel and Chronicles, both of these authors are dependent on early material from the prophets and the psalms.[14] Martin Selman explains that in early texts the kingdom "was sometimes associated with the covenant law of the kingdom, and in the later ones with the thought that whatever the opposition, God's promised purposes would be fulfilled."[15]

Accordingly, the Hebrew understanding of the kingdom developed through the vicissitudes of Israel's history. After the prophets perceived God's judgment against the people's disobedience in the fall of Israel (722 BCE) and Judah (587 BCE), they began to express the hope that their God-King would deliver the people. Thus, they saw their return from exile as "a prophetic reassertion of the reign of Israel's God" (see, for example, Isa 45:1–3; Zeph 3:14–15).[16] As a dynamic symbol that communicated the hope that God would act in history, the kingdom was neither individualistic nor otherworldly. Rather it had two basic connotations: "that God rules in his acts;" and that the kingdom "exists in order to transform a bad and unjust historical-social reality into a different good and just one."[17]

It is in continuity with this tradition of hope that Jesus must have understood the kingdom. God's kingdom occupied the center of Jesus' preaching and activity. Rejecting the possibility of an uncertain or ambiguous future, he claimed both that God's reign would come fully in the near future as the consummation of God's purpose, and also that this reign was already breaking in through his own ministry.[18] While Jesus stressed that the kingdom is solely God's initiative and something God gives completely and freely, his ministry shows that the gratuitous character of the kingdom does not rule out human activity on its behalf. Rather, as John Sachs' chapter in this book argues, God's free, loving initiative places a claim on human cooperation with God's plan for humanity.

What enables and sustains human cooperation with the kingdom is hope. Hope is the capacity that enables humans to envision a future that is not simply an extrapolation of the present. Christians confess hope as a social and theological virtue that calls them "to witness to the great transformation now afoot which promises the liberation of all human hopes to the fullest dimensions."[19] Hence, while utopias articulate the basic tension between what is and the human aspiration for what might be, hope is the capacity that drives these aspirations and orients human persons to their end in God. The counterpart to hope for the future coming of the kingdom is the utopian hope that motivates human action in the present. This dual nature of hope is especially evident in Latin American liberation theology's treatment of God's kingdom.

# GOD'S KINGDOM AND THE CHRISTIAN UTOPIA IN LIBERATION THEOLOGY

Latin American liberation theology has made the kingdom of God a central element of its project. This is the Christian symbol that best expresses that salvation is individual and social, historical and transcendent. It is the symbol that orients Christian discipleship and thus defines following Jesus as collaborating with God's plan to make the kingdom a historical reality.[20]

From its inception, Latin American liberation theology has stressed the impact that Christian eschatological hope can have in shaping the lives of Christians in the present, particularly in their social and political dimensions.[21] According to Jon Sobrino, Jesus' conception of the kingdom as "good news" to the poor also provides us with some insight into its content, since the kingdom must represent a positive alternative to the oppressive conditions under which the poor subsist. As Sobrino writes, "The Kingdom of God is a utopia that answers the age-old hope of a people in the midst of historical calamities; it is, then, what is good and wholly good. But it is something liberating, since it arrives in the midst of and in opposition to...oppression."[22]

Liberation theology's emphasis on hope responds to a concern already articulated by the Second Vatican Council. Defining the church's mission in terms of its service to God's reign (*Gaudium et Spes* [GS], 45), the council recognized that "while earthly progress must be carefully distinguished from the growth of Christ's Kingdom, to the extent that the former can contribute to the better ordering of human society, it is of vital concern to the Kingdom of God" (GS, 39). The bishops acknowledged the autonomy of the public sphere and avoided providing specific answers to sociopolitical issues, but they upheld the public role of the church. In fact, the bishops asserted that like any other religious community, the church is to "show the special value of [its] doctrine in what concerns the organization of society and the inspiration of the human activity" (*Dignitatis Humanae*, 4).

Although Christian utopian visions cannot claim to be identical to the kingdom of God, the proclamation of God's kingdom provides the foundation for a Christian understanding of salvation that begins in history and points to an eschatological future. It establishes "that which humans are to reach for and by which all progress will be judged human or inhuman....[It also] establishes the hope that humanness is possible."[23] To be sure, the utopia of the kingdom entails far more than the negation of that which impedes basic survival—hunger, violence, and injustice, for example. However, the situation in which the majority of the world's population lives has prompted liberation theologians to insist that, at a minimum, the proclamation of the kingdom should include the credible promise that all human beings will be able to satisfy their basic life necessities.

In the final analysis, the proclamation of God's kingdom articulates an overarching vision for a society that is rooted in truth, human dignity, and fraternity. This utopian vision guides a Christian praxis that seeks to anticipate and make present, even if in a provisional and imperfect manner, the eschatological promise of God's kingdom. This praxis on behalf of the kingdom entails two interrelated and continuously ongoing tasks: the prophetic denunciation of the existing order, and the annunciation and implementation of a new proposal—a *eu-topic* project.[24]

Indeed, Jesus' proclamation of the kingdom is accompanied by his prophetic denunciation of sin and anything that threatens the dignity of the human person. He contrasts current social arrangements with those of the promised future: the last will be first (Matt 19:30), leaders will become servants (Mark 9:35), the poor will be blessed (Luke 6:21), and enemies will be loved and forgiven (Matt 5:44b).[25] Likewise, the task of prophetic denunciation relates the utopian vision to present historical reality. It critically contrasts the values and promises articulated in the proclamation of God's kingdom with a specific historical situation. Such contrast not only sheds light on the limitations of the human situation, it especially exposes the evils that assail it. As Ignacio Ellacuría notes, "if the Kingdom proclaims the fullness of life and the rejection of death, and if the historical situation of human beings and of structures is the kingdom of death and the negation of life, the contrast is evident."[26]

By defining that which is to be rejected, the prophetic task opens the possibility for Christian imagination and praxis to play a central role in shaping the future of society. This is the second task of announcing and implementing a new social project. Such a project identifies priorities and outlines the direction that enables us to move, at a particular moment and in a particular context, from the abstract promises of the kingdom to their realization in history. In this collection, Thomas Massaro's essay examines this endeavor from the perspective of Catholic social teaching. As we move to delineate the basic features of what I call a Christian *eu-topic* project, it is important to keep in mind that these two tasks of denouncing and announcing are part and parcel of a continuous Christian praxis that, sustained by hope, looks to the horizon of God's kingdom yet remains firmly planted in history.

## THE CONTOURS OF CHRISTIAN *EU-TOPIC* PROJECT(S)

Driven by an active hope that anticipates the future, the Christian *eu-topic* project seeks to pursue the goodness of the kingdom through the eradication of sin. It presupposes the prophetic contrasts between the proclamation of God's kingdom and historical reality in order to propose a qualitatively different culture and society that better reflects the historical mediation of God's reign. Although one can speak of a plurality of *eu-topic* projects insofar as these may emerge from diverse historical contexts, I prefer to speak of one universal project that is enacted in different instantiations—all inspired by the values of God's kingdom and sharing as their common goal the mediation of God's promises in history. Unlike the Christian utopia, however, which explicitly points to an eschatological future, this project points to a future within history, even as it toils to mediate values that transcend history. Three interrelated features further define a *eu-topic* project: it should be partial to the needs of the poor, historically viable, and rational.

Consistent with the proclamation of God's kingdom, which is offered first to the poor, the *eu-topic* project has both a universal and preferential character. As liberation theologians have noted, this preference ensues not because the kingdom does not exist yet in its fullness, but because it is being actively denied by the presence of sin.[27] Hence, a *eu-topic* project must take up the difficult task of confronting sin. In so doing, it aims to respond to the aspirations of all human beings, but it first attends to the plight of the poor and marginalized.

From a sociological perspective, an inquiry into the situation in which the poor live cuts through layers of complex economic, social, and ideological structures that conceal vast mechanisms of oppression. It also exposes the agents that originate and perpetuate their victimization. Hence, for theological and sociological reasons, Latin American theologians argue that it is from the perspective of the poor that we can more adequately visualize a Christian *eu-topic* project: one that is not conceived in the illusionary world of abundance and self-gratification, but rather one that envisions "the existence and the guarantee of an essential core of basic life and of human family."[28]

Writing in 1989 and following this line of thought, Ellacuría insisted on the need to supplant the current *culture of wealth* that ensues from the capitalistic system of the industrialized Western nations with a *civilization of poverty* that rejects the private accumulation of wealth and ever-growing consumption as the motor of history.[29] Far from a society of "paupers," Ellacuría envisioned a civilization of work, love, and austerity structured according to Jesus' beatitudes as the Christian alternative for a more humane world. Whether or not it is labeled a civilization of poverty, what must be stressed is that the *eu-topic* project should strive to guarantee the minimum material necessities to all, uphold the values of human fraternity, and aim to create a more humane world.

In order to avoid the human tendency to escape from the world and thus reduce utopian thinking to a well-intentioned but ineffective proposal, the *eu-topic* project must be historically viable, that is, its implementation should take into account the prevailing social and political conditions and deliver a response that corresponds to the resources currently available within a given context. At the same time, one must not conflate the *eu-topic* project with the kingdom. God alone will ultimately fulfill God's kingdom, whereas this human endeavor takes shape against sin and through our continuous, ambiguous, and provisional attempts to make God's kingdom present in history, a challenge which Francine Cardman's essay in this volume helps us to appreciate. In light of human sinfulness, the *eu-topic* project can be understood as a dialectical and open-ended enterprise that strives to move progressively closer, through its different instantiations, toward what Christians discern to be the utopia of God's reign. Mindful of these challenges, Sobrino writes, "We have to take all possible steps, limited and even ambiguous though they may be, to achieve minimum but important and necessary objectives…but these have to be guided by the utopia of the shared table."[30] Grounding Christian praxis in the vision of God's gratuitous and eschatological kingdom is essential because it protects the end purpose of this praxis from being reduced to what is politically efficient and feasible at a given point in time. Christian hope is always "a hope against hope": "it begins where optimism reaches the end of its tether."[31]

Although informed by faith values that often transcend what may seem reasonable, the *eu-topic* project does not contradict the rational order and it enlists reason in order to be persuasive in a pluralistic society. This reliance on reason is indispensable in seeking the collaboration of non-Christian partners and in determining how faith claims are to be translated into political action. As Gutiérrez warns, divorced from reason, the direct imposition of faith claims onto secular society can "result in dangerous politico-religious messianism which does not sufficiently respect either the autonomy of the political arena or that which belongs to an authentic faith."[32] Hence, Christian attempts to historicize the values of God's kingdom through political programs require rational analysis of those programs. It is this appeal to reason that distinguishes a Christian *eu-topic* project from totalizing ideologies. Ideologies conceal the truth in order to preserve and legitimate a particular state of affairs. In contrast, the *eu-topic* project enlists the social sciences to confront the lies endemic to ideologies and to offer a persuasive proposal for the transformation of society.

While the proper relationship between the Christian faith and the public sphere is complex, theologians and political scientists generally agree that human reason lays the epistemological grounds for the justification of any religious claim in a pluralistic society. For political scientists like John Rawls, this reason should be understood as "public reason," that is, as something widely accessible and intelligible to most members of society.[33] In a similar vein, theologians like John de Gruchy argue that "good public theological praxis requires the development of a language that is accessible to people outside the Christian tradition, and is convincing in its own right."[34] Hence, insofar as a *eu-topic* project seeks to mediate the Christian faith in the public sphere, it needs to understand itself as a rational enterprise that is open to public scrutiny and willing to engage in a fruitful dialogue with the secular world. Indeed such dialogue requires, from all involved, an attitude of epistemological humility that makes room for a diversity of voices within civil society, chiefly those of the poor. Together they seek to create a new social paradigm that incorporates the noblest human traditions—Christian and non-Christian—around which different elements of society can come together to celebrate human dignity.[35]

To what extent a *eu-topic* project may be successful in adequately mediating the values of the kingdom is a difficult matter that perhaps can be best determined by empirically assessing the fruits of Christian praxis in the lives of those most vulnerable: "the poor have good news brought to them" (Luke 7:22). It is to them that Christians are to give an account of their hope, and this hope will only be credible if our actions generate in them additional hope. As Leonardo Boff reminds us, our efforts have a "sacramental function: they have a weight of their own, but they also point forward, and embody in anticipation what God has prepared for human beings."[36]

## Notes

1. Paul Ricoeur, "Ideology and Utopia as Cultural Imagination," in *Being Human in a Technological Age*, ed. Donald Borchert and David Stewart (Athens, OH: Ohio University Press, 1979), 121.

2. Stressing the diversity of human aspirations, Jean-François Lyotard criticizes any grand narrative that proposes the progress of history or the possibility of absolute freedom. See *The Postmodern Condition: A Report on Knowledge*, trans. Geoff Bennington and Brian Massumi (Minneapolis: University of Minnesota Press, 1993). See also Fredric Jameson, *The Seeds of Time* (New York: Columbia University Press, 1994), 53.

3. Francis Fukuyama, *The End of History and the Last Man* (Harmondsworth, England: Penguin, 1992), xi.

4. George Kateb, *Utopia and Its Enemies* (New York: Knopf, 1987), 3.

5. Russell Jacoby, *The End of Utopia: Politics in the Age of Apathy* (New York: Basic Books, 1999), xi.

6. Thomas More, *Utopia*, trans. Clarence Miller (New Haven, CT: Yale University Press, 2001).

7. Gustavo Gutiérrez, *A Theology of Liberation: History, Politics, and Salvation*, trans. Caridad Inda and John Eagleson (Maryknoll, NY: Orbis, 1973), 233.

8. Joâo Batista Libânio, "Hope, Utopia, Resurrection," in *Mysterium Liberationis: Fundamental Concepts of Liberation Theology*, ed. Ignacio Ellacuría and Jon Sobrino (Maryknoll, NY: Orbis, 1993), 718–19.

9. Mary Ann Beavis, *Jesus & Utopia: Looking for the Kingdom of God in the Roman World* (Minneapolis: Fortress Press, 2006), 10.

10. For example, the idea of paradise or Eden is often compared with the ancient Sumerian myth of Dilmun. See Beavis, *Jesus & Utopia*, 31–33.

11. John J. Collins, "Models of Utopia in the Biblical Tradition," in *"A Wise and Discerning Mind": Essays in Honor of Burke O. Long* (Providence, RI: Brown Judaic Studies, 2000), 67.

12. Beavis has classified the utopian expressions in the Hebrew Scriptures into three groups: "Mythological works," "Traditions depicting the land or nation of Israel," and the "Dynamic-theocratic traditions." Beavis, *Jesus & Utopia*, 30–31, 48–52.

13. Norman Perrin, *Jesus and the Language of the Kingdom* (Philadelphia: Fortress Press, 1976), 16–17.

14. Martin Selman, "The Kingdom of God in the Old Testament," *Tyndale Bulletin*, 40 (1989): 174.

15. Selman, "The Kingdom of God in the Old Testament," 183.

16. Beavis, *Jesus & Utopia*, 49.

17. Jon Sobrino, *Jesus the Liberator: A Historical-Theological Reading of Jesus of Nazareth*, trans. Paul Burns and Francis McDonagh (Maryknoll, NY: Orbis, 2001), 71. See also N. T. Wright, *Jesus and the Victory of God* (Minneapolis: Fortress Press, 1996), 200–209.

18. Howard Marshall, "The Hope of a New Age: The Kingdom of God in the New Testament," *Jesus the Saviour: Studies in New Testament Theology* (Downers Grove, IL: InterVarsity/London: SPCK, 1990), 212.

19. Anthony Kelly, *Eschatology and Hope* (Maryknoll, NY: Orbis, 2006), 13.

20. As Ignacio Ellacuría asserts, God's reign "is the very object of Christian dogmatic, moral, and pastoral theology: the greatest possible realization of God in history is what the authentic followers of Jesus are to pursue." "Aporte de la teologia de la liberacion a las religiones abrahámicas en la superación del individualism y del postivismo," quoted in Jon Sobrino, "Central Position of the Reign of God," in Ignacio Ellacuría and Jon Sobrino, eds., *Mysterium Liberationis*, 352.

21. See, for example, Gutiérrez's chapter "Eschatology and Politics," in Gutiérrez, *A Theology of Liberation*, 213–40.

22. Sobrino, *Jesus the Liberator*, 72.

23. Jon Sobrino, "Terrorism and Barbarity: New York and Afghanistan," in *Where is God: Earthquake, Terrorism, Barbarity, and Hope* (Maryknoll, NY: Orbis, 2006), 120.

24. In enlisting the terms "prophetic denunciation and annunciation" to describe the Christian tasks, I am drawing from the work of both Gustavo Gutiérrez and Ignacio Ellacuría. See Gutiérrez, *A Theology of Liberation*, 232–39, and Ellacuría, "Utopia and Prophecy in Latin America," in Ignacio Ellacuría and Jon Sobrino, eds., *Mysterium Liberationis*, 289–328.

25. Beavis, *Jesus & Utopia*, 101–2.

26. Ellacuría, "Utopia and Prophecy in Latin America," in Ignacio Ellacuría and Jon Sobrino, eds., *Mysterium Liberationis*, 292.

27. Sobrino, "Christianity and Reconciliation: The Way to Utopia," in Luis Carlos Sunsin and María Pilar Aquino, eds., *Reconciliation in a World of Conflicts* (London: SCM Press, 2003), 88.

28. Jon Sobrino, "Extra Pauperes Nulla Salus," in *No Salvation Outside the Poor: Prophetic-Utopian Essays* (Maryknoll, NY: Orbis, 2008), 61. See also Gutiérrez, *A Theology of Liberation*, 137.

29. Ellacuría, "Utopia and Prophecy in Latin America," in Ignacio Ellacuría and Jon Sobrino, eds., *Mysterium Liberationis*, 313–25.

30. Sobrino, "Conflicto y reconciliación," 1147 (my translation). The "shared table" is an eschatological metaphor that Sobrino borrows from Rutilio Grande. See William J. O' Malley, SJ, "El Salvador: Rutilio Grande, SJ," in *The Voice of Blood: Five Christian Martyrs of our Time* (Maryknoll, NY: Orbis, 1995), 43.

31. Kelly, *Eschatology and Hope*, 5.

32. Gutiérrez, *A Theology of Liberation*, 236.

33. Rawls distinguishes between "public reason" as the common reason of all citizens in a pluralistic society and the "non-public reason" employed by citizens as members of a religious community. See John Rawls, *Political Liberalism* (New York: Columbia University Press, 2005), 48–54.

34. John de Gruchy, "Public Theology as Christian Witness: Exploring the Genre," *International Journal of Public Theology*, 1 (2007): 39.

35. Jon Sobrino, "The Crucified People and the Civilization of Poverty: Ignacio Ellacuría's 'Taking Hold of Reality,'" in *No Salvation Outside the Poor*, 16.

36. Leonardo Boff, *Liberating Grace*, trans. John Drury (Maryknoll, NY: Orbis Books, 1979), 152.

# 16

# Hope for Creation

## John R. Sachs, SJ

> The salvation Christians hope for embraces not only human beings and all the fruits of human labor in history, but the entire cosmos. The life of the world to come is not about another world, but about this world as it will be finally redeemed and fully transformed by God to be a new creation.

The year 2012 marked the beginning of the fiftieth anniversary of the Second Vatican Council, which ended in December of 1965 with the promulgation of one of its most important documents, the Pastoral Constitution on the Church in the Modern World, officially titled *Gaudium et Spes* ("Joy and Hope") [GS].[1] Looking back now, its title seems to reflect the fact that the church found itself encouraged, even pushed by the Holy Spirit, to look at the world and at itself in a new and hopeful way. The church came to realize that to be a sacrament of salvation meant making its own "the joys and hopes, the sorrows and anxieties" (GS, 1) of the world. It realized in a profoundly new way that the salvation in Christ it preaches and mediates is salvation *for* the world, not salvation *from* the world. As Catholic theologian Edward Schillebeeckx put it, "outside the world there is no salvation."[2] Or, as Anglican bishop and New Testament scholar N. T. Wright has emphasized: Christian hope is not about going to heaven when we die, but is "hope for *God's new creation*"; not about a "salvation *away* from this world," but about God's coming to dwell in the cosmos, redeeming, transforming and making it new.[3]

We find a reciprocal dynamic of hope in *Gaudium et Spes*. It acknowledges that the church exists for the world and is committed to take the joys and hopes, the sorrows and anxieties of the world to heart. It also recognizes that salvation in Christ embraces not only every person, but all of human history and the whole cosmos. It expresses this with the biblical metaphors of a "new earth and a new heaven" (see, for example, 2 Pet 3:13; Rev 21:1) that is being brought about even now by "God's reign" present in mystery (GS, 39), appealing to believers to enter into this hope for the world fully by committing themselves, together with all women and men of good will, to its authentic development.

Almost fifty years later, this appeal has lost none of its timeliness and urgency. The world we live in seems to give little reason for hope. We have grown rightly suspicious of "progress." We have witnessed the failure, and often the brutality, of utopian political visions, as Ernesto Valiente's essay in this collection helps us to consider. For all of our great accomplishments, our whole earth suffers. Do any of our efforts really matter? Perhaps this is the very reason why the final hope of many believers seems dominated by the idea of *going to heaven* rather than by *a new heaven and a new earth or the coming of God's kingdom*, for which Jesus himself taught us to pray (see Matt 6:10).

*Gaudium et Spes* calls us to a deeper, biblical hope for the world and its salvation because it is God's beloved creation. God calls us to "a hope that loves the world" by drawing us more deeply into God's own love and hope for the world.[4] In this essay, I will reflect on the cosmic and historical dimensions of the Christian hope for salvation, a hope that manifests itself in and empowers our care for and improvement of the world.

## THE *WORLD TO COME* AS THE TRANSFORMATION OF *THIS WORLD*

Vatican II represented a profound conversion and renewal of the church, away from a fortress mentality vis-à-vis the modern world to a deeper sense of its mission in and for the world. No council document expresses this more insistently than *Gaudium et Spes*. This *turn to the world* was suspected by some to be an abandonment of the church's true nature and mission and an accommodation to secularism. Karl Rahner, however, in an essay written shortly after the close of the council, argued that such a turn to the world is demanded by Christian faith because it sees the world as God's creation.[5] According to Rahner, *Gaudium et Spes* calls believers, "on the basis of their specifically Christian faith, their eschatological hope and their love for God and [women and] men" to collaborate with all women and men of good will in working for a more humane, just, and peaceful world.[6] At the same time, he acknowledged that the document might appear ambiguous or ambivalent about the relationship between this world and the world to come, given the way it distinguishes the "earthly service of humanity" from "the heavenly kingdom," "this earth" from the "new earth," and "earthly progress" from the "growth of Christ's kingdom" (GS, 38, 39), and given that it reminds Christians that they are "on pilgrimage toward a heavenly city" and exhorts them "to seek and savor what is above" (GS, 57).

It comes as no surprise that Vatican II manifests the signs of profound change. We see this in a certain tension between traditional formulations and new perspectives. However, while *Gaudium et Spes* continued to use traditional language about this world and the world to come, it clearly moved away from a dualistic understanding of the relationship between them, speaking of the world to come, not as an *other* world but as the transformation and consummation of *this* world. This is evident in paragraph 39, a central expression of the church's eschatological vision and hope. It is not the world, but the "form of this world, deformed by sin" that "is passing away" (GS, 39). We look forward to the "the consummation of the earth and of humanity" which entails the "transformation of the universe" (GS, 39), although we do not know when or how that will happen. The "new dwelling place and new earth" God is preparing is directly linked to the reign of God proclaimed by Christ: "here on earth this kingdom is already present in mystery" and "will be consummated at the Lord's coming" (GS, 39). In speaking of the kingdom's presence on this earth as a presence in *mystery*, the council is using a concept with deep sacramental connotations. The council is professing the real presence of the kingdom that God is bringing about here, not a sign or a message about a kingdom God is preparing somewhere else. At the same time, it is a kingdom that looks toward a final fullness that exceeds anything we can experience of its real presence here and now.[7]

Instead of the cataclysmic, apocalyptic images of the Book of Revelation, *Gaudium et Spes* adopts the eschatological vision and hope of Romans 8, a vision that grows out of Israel's faith in the fidelity of the Creator to the creation. As Thomas Stegman's essay in this volume shows, hope is a central theme in Paul. In Romans, he presents the striking image of creation groaning in birth pangs, eager with longing and full of hope for a salvation embracing not only human beings but the whole of creation (GS, 39). Here as elsewhere,[8] Paul emphasizes the unity of creation in its spiritual and material dimensions. For him, the "*bodiliness*" of human beings manifests the integral unity between the human and the nonhuman creatures. He highlights the cosmic dimension of Christian hope as a "hope that the creation itself will be set free from its bondage to decay and will obtain the freedom of the glory of the children of God" (Rom 8:20–21). The future glory already revealed in the *bodily* resurrection of Christ is meant not only for humans but for all God's creation, which is in bondage to death, decay, and the consequences of human sin: "We know that the whole creation has been groaning in labor pains until now; and not only the creation, but we ourselves, who have the first fruits of the Spirit, groan inwardly as we wait for adoption, the redemption of our bodies" (Rom 8:22–23). Paul is telling us that our hope for final glory is not merely ours: through us and in us, the whole of God's creation is groaning in the very hope in which "we were saved" (Rom 8:24). Our hope is for a salvation that embraces the whole of God's creation.[9]

Paul's sensibility for the unity of God's creating and saving action has deep roots in the Old Testament. Israel's foundational experience of God is the exodus and covenant, an act of liberation from slavery and creation as God's people, with the promise of a land where it would flourish. In this event, Israel recognized the action of the one who created the heavens and the earth. The mighty arm that conquered Pharaoh is the arm that stretched out the heavens like a tent (Ps 104:2). In other words, the story of Israel's salvation and creation goes all the way back to the very beginning of God's creating, as told in the Book of Genesis, and includes the whole of creation.

The psalms portray the inherent unity of God's creating and saving action in its cosmic and historical dimensions, as is shown by Richard Clifford.[10] A good example is Psalm 136, a hymn praising God for the founding event in which Israel came to be a people in its own land. It is a story that begins with the creation of universe. Verse upon verse (3–9) gives thanks to God who made the heavens, the earth, the sun and the moon and the stars, because God's steadfast loves endures forever. This is echoed by thanks to God, who smote the firstborn of Egypt, divided the Red Sea, led the people through the wilderness into a land of their own, because God's steadfast loves endures forever (10–22). Clifford notes that "the origin of the people Israel includes the making of the physical environment and the bringing of Israel into the land."[11] Why is this significant? Because accounts of God's creating and saving action in the Hebrew scriptures are concerned with a peopled universe, about human community in relationship with God as it exists concretely in land, society, language, culture, cult, and laws.[12] This is the concrete world of God's making, the world in which God freely chooses to be in relationship with Israel and, through Israel, with all the nations. God's saving action is the fidelity of the Creator to her creation.

The cosmic scope of God's creating and saving action is foreshadowed by the covenant with Noah in which God pledges his fidelity not only to Noah and his descendants but also to all living creatures and the whole earth, which God promises never again to destroy (Gen 9:8–17). God is pictured as having learned something about the cost of creating and recreating: it will be messy, it will involve horrendous setbacks, and the work will never stop until the end. But for all that, God pledges never to start over from scratch.

In lectures given during the last years of the council, Rahner developed these biblical perspectives theologically, emphasizing the unity of matter and spirit in the cosmos: in origin, history, and goal. [13] As Creator, God is "the ground of spirit and matter in the world, the ground which has an equally immediate relationship to both."[14] Thus, matter cannot be alien and opposed to God. In Christ we see that the climax of salvation history is not the detachment of the human spirit from the world in order to go to God, "but the irreversible entrance of God into the world…the taking on of the material so that it itself becomes a permanent reality of God."[15] Finally, while the fulfillment of the world is not something that we can finally achieve ourselves in history, it is the fulfillment of the "world which we experience concretely, the world in its unity constituted of matter and spirit in one."[16] Images like *new heavens and new earth* and the *kingdom of God* express faith's conviction that human history and the material world share a common goal and "constitute a genuine unity with one another."[17] For this reason, the "final 'transformation' of the cosmos is the salvation of everything, even of matter, even of the bodily life, but it is of course a salvation into the mystery of God."[18]

# THE ESSENTIAL ROLE OF HUMAN ACTION AND THE DEVELOPMENT OF THE EARTH

Rahner's insight into the unity of the cosmic and historical dimensions of creation echoes another important emphasis of the council: the responsibility that believers have for the development of the world. Here again *Gaudium et Spes* sets a new accent. Although Christians are to "seek and savor the things which are above" while "on pilgrimage toward the heavenly city," this "increases the import of their obligation to work with all in building a more human world" (GS, 57). Christian faith gives believers greater motivation and reveals the "full meaning of this work, and gives human culture its eminent place in the integral vocation of humankind" (GS, 57). Because this "integral vocation" is finally the call to enter into God's salvation, we can see that the council moved beyond a superficial view of this world and its history. Far from regarding the world and history as a proving ground preliminary to eternal reward or punishment, the council affirmed the deeper, supernatural significance of human culture, labor, and achievement in this world and its relationship to the world to come.

While the constitution acknowledges that the Spirit "calls some to give clear witness to the desire for a heavenly home and to keep this desire alive in the human family," it recognizes that others are called "to dedicate themselves to the earthly service of humanity, making ready by this ministry the material of the heavenly kingdom" (GS, 38). Thus, the heavenly kingdom of our final hope is not a paradise already awaiting us, but a home that is yet being prepared, a home that God will fashion from the material of all our earthly labors for the development of this world. As Rahner points out, the constitution states that not only the love that motivates our actions, but the "good fruits of our nature and enterprise that we will have produced here on earth" will be transformed into the new creation (GS, 39). Indeed, Christ "now at work in the hearts of men and women through the strength of his Spirit" is the one who arouses in us a desire for the "age to come," and strengthens us in our efforts to make life more human and to "direct the whole earth to this goal" (GS, 38). Without the "material" of our labors, there would be nothing for God to transform. At the same time, the council clearly emphasizes that the world to come is not simply the work of our hands, the result of human progress, but what *God* finally makes of the works of our hands in a final act of transformation that brings our world and the whole cosmos to its consummation as a new creation.[19]

The final consummation we hope for comes about through *both* God's sovereign action *and* human labor. Such hope is neither a hope that human beings can create heaven on earth, nor an expectation that God has already prepared a heaven that somehow leaves God's creation in its concrete history behind. *Gaudium et Spes* presents a reflection on Christian hope that is both God-centered and this-worldly, directed toward God's final transformation of the cosmos in its concrete history. Moreover, "Christians ought to be convinced that the achievements of the human race are a sign of God's greatness and the fulfillment of his mysterious design" (GS, 34). God's sovereignty as Creator is not in competition with human freedom and creativity. Far from having reason to neglect the development of the world and the welfare of all peoples, Christians are "more stringently bound to do these very things" for they are "created in God's image," and by doing these things, they are "furthering the Creator's work" (GS, 34).

The constitution recalls the creation stories of Genesis, especially the Priestly account in Genesis 1:1—2:3. There, human beings stand in a unique relationship of freedom and responsibility to God and to God's creation. Created in the image and likeness of God, they are God's royal representatives, the creatures in which God can be present and active in a unique way. They are commanded to "be fruitful and multiply, and replenish the earth and subdue it" (1:28). This is not a license for exploitation, but rather a call to share in God's own creative dominion, her well-ordering of the world for the flourishing of all creatures. Human labor is seen as a participation in God's work-in-progress. Of course, this does not mean that God's action and human action are of the same order. God is not an agent like human beings, doing the kind of things we do. In Christ, we believe that God's sovereign action as Creator and Savior establishes, empowers, and transforms human action. It does not substitute for human action, but rather invites and draws human action more deeply into God's own creating and saving action.

As Rahner's student Johann Baptist Metz puts it, the "hallmark of God's divinity is that He does not cancel out other beings or destroy what they are. Instead He tones up and sharpens their innermost potentialities and capabilities."[20] This is in line with the classic maxim of Thomas Aquinas that grace does not destroy nature, but rather transforms it. We should not expect God to do the things she has made us capable of doing; we must, and we may confidently hope that she enables us to do them. Neither should we expect God to tell us exactly what we must do in every detail, for God has aptly equipped us with freedom and imagination so that we can participate creatively in the coming of the kingdom.

In making the important distinction between "earthly progress" and the "growth of Christ's kingdom" (GS, 39), the council reminds us that a "more human world" is not just an abstract ideal, but what takes concrete shape in the kingdom of God (or kingdom of heaven) that Jesus preached, actualized, and called men and women to open their lives to. Christians believe that Jesus himself is the promised coming of God's reign. In him, in his concrete words and actions, we see God bringing about that reign. In his preaching, in the images of his parables, and in his own behavior, we catch a glimpse of what Schillebeeckx calls "God's dream for the happiness of men and women and all their fellow creatures."[21] That is, how God wants his creation to be—the saving mercy, compassion, healing, justice, and peace that God's reign will finally bring about. Jesus' resurrection from the dead signals that God's dream is reality: it is the victorious beginning of the new heaven and earth.

*Lumen Gentium*, Vatican II's Dogmatic Constitution on the Church, reminds us that the very nature and mission of the church is to be a kind of sacrament, a sign and instrument of this union with God and of the unity of all humankind (LG, 1). This is precisely why *Gaudium et Spes* affirms that beyond a purely secular sense of responsibility for the common good and the improvement of the world, our faith and hope give us an even more serious obligation "to work with all in building a more human world" (GS, 57).

A related text in *Lumen Gentium* takes up this theme of hope and its obligation in a striking way:

> They show themselves to be the children of the promise, if strong in faith and in hope, they make full use of the present time (see Eph. 5:16; Col. 4:5), and with patience await the future glory (see Rom. 8:25). Let them not hide this hope in the depths of their hearts, but rather express it through the structures of secular life in continual conversion and in their struggle "against the world forces of this darkness, against the spiritual forces of wickedness" (Eph 6:12). (LG, 35)

Such a text conveys the realism of Christian faith and hope. Do we take God's creation as seriously as God does? Does our faith in the Creator express a hope for God's creation? If "faith is the assurance of things hoped for" (Heb 11:1), what we hope for is not something easily achieved. The patience that the council speaks of is certainly not a passive waiting for future glory. If, in the spirit of Romans 8, we really believe and hope in the promised fullness of glory, this faith and hope should—and will—be manifest in our lives, making us strong in our resistance against the powers that dehumanize and degrade God's creation. The patience that the council speaks of is a patience of eyes and hearts open to the world and to God, both a willingness to suffer in the struggle and a confidence in the final victory of God. As Schillebeeckx notes, the truth of Christian faith and eschatological hope will be judged according to whether Christians "show in practice in their lives that their hope is *capable* of changing the world now and of making our history a real history of salvation which brings well-being to all."[22] In his chapter in this text, my colleague Andrea Vicini highlights one important way that such hope is actualized: in serious engagement for sustainability against practices that degrade the environment.

# CHRISTIAN HOPE, IMAGINATION, AND PRAYER

*Gaudium et Spes* presented a cosmic vision of Christian hope. True Christian hope looks not to the day when one dies and goes to heaven, but to the day when Christ comes in glory, when finally God's kingdom has come and God's will is done in her creation, when God's home is finally complete and God dwells with all her creatures in glory. Creation is not merely that which happened "in the beginning" (Gen 1:1). It is a process that continues toward a final, transforming consummation, God's work-in-progress, a divine labor to which God summons us. To see the cosmos in this way and to discern how I might respond to God's call requires a faith- and hope-filled act of imagination.

Ignatius of Loyola, the founder of the Jesuits, valued an imaginative style of contemplative prayer. Using the imagination to contemplate the gospel stories about Jesus can help one develop a deeper sensibility for the reign of God and its values. In the process, one can find oneself drawn more deeply into God's hope for creation, the hope that can truly transform the world. Correlatively, one contemplates the world, paying attention to its joys and hopes, sorrows and anxieties, and especially to its suffering. In faith, one re-imagines creation more deeply as God's work-in-progress, finding new courage to say Yes to it in hope, and imagining how one might play one's own part in it. This is one way the scripture manifests the inspiring power of the Spirit, who gives us the "mind of Christ" (1 Cor 2:16) so that our work in this world is truly in tune with God's reign and contributes to its final coming. Such attunement leaves plenty of room for human freedom and creativity, much like a good jazz combo in which the players have a common theme and improvise on it, free to imagine ever-new and unique ways in which they can develop the theme and add to its richness.

Perhaps we need courage to pray like this, to pray with eyes open to the world and hearts all too aware of our fears and failings: prayer that is not only praise and thanksgiving but also protest and lament, prayer that in spite of everything can say Yes to God and therefore Yes to God's creation, prayer that lives in the hope that we do not labor in vain because God is building the house (Ps 127:1). In this spirit, we might pray in the words of Karl Rahner:

> We ask you, God of grace and eternal life, to increase and strengthen hope in us. Give us this virtue of the strong, this power of the confident, this courage of the unshakable. Make us always have a longing for you, the infinite plenitude of being. Make us always build on you and your fidelity, always hold fast without despondency to your might. Make us to be of this mind and produce this attitude in us by your Holy Spirit. Then, our Lord and God, we shall have the virtue of hope. Then we can courageously set about the task of our life again and again. Then we shall be animated by the joyful confidence that we are not working in vain. Strengthen your hope in us.[23]

## Notes

1. Paragraph references to council documents are indicated in parentheses. Translations are my own.

2. A play on the ancient phrase "outside the Church there is no salvation." See Edward Schillebeeckx, *Church: The Human Story of God* (New York: Crossroad, 1990), especially 5–15 and 132–39.

3. N. T. Wright, *Surprised by Hope: Rethinking Heaven, the Resurrection, and the Mission of the Church* (New York: HarperCollins, 2008), 5. See also *Simply Jesus: A New Vision of Who He Was, What He Did, and Why He Matters* (New York: HarperCollins, 2011).

4. "A Faith that Loves the Earth" is the title of a collection of meditations by Karl Rahner, *Glaube, der die Erde liebt* (Freiburg: Herder, 1966).

5. Karl Rahner, "The Theological Problems Entailed in the Idea of the 'New Earth,'" in *Theological Investigations*, 10 (New York: Herder and Herder), 260–72.

6. Rahner, "Idea of the 'New Earth,'" 260.

7. See also *Lumen Gentium*, 48.

8. See 1 Cor 15. It is interesting to read Paul's reflection on the different kinds of bodies (celestial and terrestrial), knowing as we do today that the carbon atoms that make up our own bodies came from stars!

9. This is consistent with Gal 6:15 and 2 Cor 5:17, the two texts in which Paul employs the term "new creation," a term which some scripture scholars insist refers beyond the individual and the church, looking toward a final fullness which includes the whole cosmos. According to Ulrich Mell, for example, "In Gal 6:15 it is not the human being that is called a 'new creation' but the world!" (compare Rom 8:22). See Ulrich Mell, *Neue Schöpfung: Eine traditionsgeschichtliche und exegetische Studie zu einem soteriologischen Grundsatz paulinischer Theologie* (Berlin: Walter de Gruyter, 1989), 317.

10. Richard J. *Clifford, Creation Accounts in the Ancient Near East and in the Bible, The Catholic Biblical Quarterly Monograph Series* 26 (Washington, DC: Catholic Biblical Association of America, 1994).

11. Ibid., 159.

12. Ibid., 153. See also Clifford's article, "The Hebrew Scriptures and the Theology of Creation," *Theological Studies* 46 (1985): 507–23.

13. First given in 1963 and 1965, later translated and published as Karl Rahner, "The Unity of Spirit and Matter in the Christian Understanding of Faith" and "The Secret of Life," in *Theological Investigations*, 6 (Baltimore: Helicon Press, 1969), 153–77 and 141–52.

14. Ibid., 156.

15. Ibid., 160.

16. Ibid., 161.

17. Ibid., 162. Elsewhere, Rahner puts this quite remarkably: "Through bodiliness the whole world belongs to me from the start, in everything that happens....In a certain sense—and I am exaggerating here, in order to make what I want to say clearer—we are all living in one and the same body—the world." See "The Body in the Order of

Salvation," in *Theological Investigations*, 17 (New York: Crossroad, 1981), 87–88.

18. Rahner, "Secret of Life," 146.

19. Rahner, "Idea of the 'New Earth,'" 265.

20. Johann Baptist Metz, *The Advent of God* (New York: Newman Press, 1970), no pagination.

21. Schillebeeckx, *Church*, 133.

22. Edward Schillebeeckx, *God, the Future of Man* (New York: Sheed & Ward, 1968), 182.

23. Karl Rahner, "Prayer for Hope," in *Prayers for a Lifetime* (New York: Crossroad, 1985), 98 (slightly abridged).

# 17

# History and Hope: Retrieving *Gaudium et Spes* for the Church and the World

## *Francine Cardman*

The essay reflects on the relationship of history and hope by considering two ways in which the history of hope has taken form in western
Christianity, and the rereading of history and hope offered by the
Second Vatican Council in *Gaudium et Spes* (GS). It concludes that re-
appropriating and refining GS for today could help resolve some current
issues regarding apostolic women religious, as well as offer renewed
hope for the world and for the church.

The fiftieth anniversary of the Second Vatican Council (1962–65)
is an appropriate time to reflect on hope and history. The council itself was a historical moment of hope, not only for many Catholics,
but for people of other Christian and religious traditions or of none, as
the Catholic Church opened itself to the world. In that surprising
moment, unexpected even five years previously, the council began a
process of renewing the church's inner life, reaffirming its faith, finding
a more modern way to proclaim its message of salvation, "reading the
signs of the times" (GS, 4), and reconnecting the "joys and hopes, the
grief and anguish of the people of our time" (GS, 1) to the faith, hope,
and love of the followers of Christ in history. Reflecting on hope and
history requires a dual focus, not only on the hope we have, as
Christians, *for* history, but also on the history *of* hope, the way in which

hope has been envisioned and embodied in different times and circumstances.

That same anniversary year of 2012 witnessed a critical moment in the history of women's apostolic religious communities in the United States that are members of the Leadership Conference of Women Religious (LCWR, representing about eighty percent of U.S. sisters). The Vatican Congregation for the Doctrine of the Faith (CDF) concluded a doctrinal assessment of the leadership organization, published its negative findings, and delegated an archbishop to oversee the conference's work for the foreseeable future. Referring to the CDF's assessment, Sister Pat Farrell, OSF, then president of LCWR, noted the approaching anniversary of Vatican II and its significance for sisters, "who so took it to heart and have been so shaped by it! It makes us recognize with poignant clarity what a very different moment this is." Among the formative influences of the council, Sister Farrell highlighted responding to the signs of the times prayerfully and prophetically, honoring conscience and freedom, developing structures of participation and collaborative leadership, and "ministering at the margins" with the poor and the vulnerable. "The experience of God from that place," she observed, "is one of absolutely gratuitous mercy and empowering love."[1]

Ministry at the margins has been especially clarifying for LCWR's member congregations as they have shaped their apostolic commitments in response to the gospel, their founding charisms, and the call of Vatican II in *Gaudium et Spes* (The Pastoral Constitution on the Church in the Modern World) to read the signs of the times. Two key points of the CDF's critique were that the leadership conference was not adequately "addressing the contemporary situation and supporting religious life in its most 'radical' sense—that is, in the faith in which it is rooted," and that it did considerable work on "promoting issues of social justice" but did not address other significant issues and teachings.[2] A central point of difference between the sisters and the CDF is precisely the question of history and hope, the faith in which Christian hope is rooted, and especially the relationship between church and world as faith and hope are lived out through love.

Efforts to reflect on the problem of history and hope in our present time are inevitably fraught with the difficulties of gaining adequate perspective while being *in medias res*—in the midst of what one is thinking about and attempting to understand. Those difficulties are amplified when it comes to thinking historically and theologically about Christian faith and life because, from the perspective of God's eternity, we humans are always *in medias res*, in an unfinished story whose end lies beyond us. We must, nevertheless, as Vatican II did, try to see and understand our part of that story with as much clarity as our limitations allow, and then *act*, that is, live faithfully *within* history and *toward* the future that we hope awaits us beyond it.

Taking the fiftieth anniversary of Vatican II as one point of reference, and the conflicting perspectives on history and hope, church and world in the difficulties between LCWR and the CDF as another, I sketch in this essay two ways in which the history of hope has taken form in western Christianity and outline their influence and limitations in subsequent centuries. I then turn to Vatican II and *Gaudium et Spes* and consider their rereading of history and hope as they sought to retrieve and revise these models for our times. In conclusion, I suggest that re-appropriating *Gaudium et Spes* fifty years after the council and refining it for today would not only help to resolve some of the issues between the CDF and LCWR, but also would offer renewed hope for the world and for the church.

# CHURCH AND WORLD: TWO MODELS FROM LATE ANTIQUITY

The fourth century is often referred to as a turning point in Christian history, the beginning of the "Constantinian era," a period which Karl Rahner saw as ending only with Vatican II.[3] That fateful century might better be understood as having two focal or turning points: at one end, the emperor Constantine's growing involvement with the church and his deathbed baptism; at the other, the sack of Rome in 410 by Alaric's Visigothic army. At each endpoint stands a figure who attempted to understand, evaluate, and persuade his fellow

Christians about the meaning of the events they were witnessing. One is Eusebius of Caesarea (c. 260–339), a bishop in the Roman province of Palestine during Constantine's reign (305–37), who is remembered as the first church historian and the biographer of Constantine. The other is Augustine of Hippo (354–430), a bishop in the Roman province of Africa, remembered for his prolific theological and pastoral writings and their enduring influence on western Christianity; among his works is *City of God*, his response to the fall of Rome. Eusebius and Augustine serve as chronological markers of this eventful century and also represent two rather different views of church and world, history and hope. The perspectives they take on the events of their day became paradigmatic ways of imagining and embodying these relationships in the history of the church. Their influence reaches into the twenty-first century.

## The Eusebian Model

In writing his *History of the Church* (311–24), Eusebius had to deal with pressing questions about history, hope, and divine providence. The worst persecution in the church's history had just ended, its shock value multiplied by the forty-plus years of relative peace that had preceded it. The memory of persecution was fresh in Eusebius' mind and his evaluation of Constantine was colored by relief at its end and the new imperial policy of religious toleration for all. Now Christians had to come to grips with understanding what had happened and why. First, there were the persecuted: why had God allowed Christians to suffer so? Eusebius attributed their suffering to divine judgment on their behavior: "Increasing freedom had transformed our character." Christians had grown lax, as if they had lost the fear of God; the persecution was God's merciful way of leading them back to true practice of their faith.[4] Then there were the persecutors: what became of them? Here, too, divine judgment was at work, not to correct the perpetrators, but to exact retribution. The rise of Constantine and his defeat of his foes to become sole emperor in 324 was, in the end, the work of God's providence.[5]

Eusebius places his historical narrative within the larger framework of the history of salvation. It moves from the incarnation and "the kind and gracious deliverance" worked by Jesus Christ and sweeps to its triumphant conclusion in his day with the end of persecution and the destruction of God's enemies. In his estimation, Constantine is a servant and a "friend of God," "our divinely favored emperor" who was vested with "a semblance of heavenly sovereignty."[6] His governance is patterned on God's rule and conformed to the divine monarchy. By the time Eusebius writes a life of Constantine and an effusive oration in his praise near the end of his reign, he views the empire as a reflection of God's kingdom manifest in history. From Eusebius' perspective, the divine preference is for monarchical government under a Christian emperor who protects the church and ensures its well-being. The Eusebian model of church and world historicizes the eschatological or final reign of God and in large measure equates it with a Christian empire. There is little room for ambiguity. Deviation from the model or prescribed roles and performance in it results in divine punishment; adherence to its standards draws all closer to the fulfillment of God's providential plan for history. It would become a potent vision for later Christian polities, both secular and ecclesiastical.

## The Augustinian Model

Over the last two decades of his life Augustine wrote his monumental opus, *The City of God* (413–24). His intent in writing it was both polemical and pastoral. The first ten books were meant to counter "pagan" claims that Christians were in large measure responsible for the sack of Rome in 410 and to refute the mystique of Rome's history, culture, philosophy, and religion. The following twelve books set forth the origin, progress, and final ends of the city of God, with the intent of calming Christian anxieties and redirecting Christian hope from the history of empire to the history of the heavenly city.[7] That Rome, by then so old it seemed eternal, should fall before barbarians came as a shock to pagans and Christians alike: the former because their gods had apparently failed to protect them; the latter because divine providence, which had brought church and world together in an increasingly Christian empire, now seemed to have abandoned them to the tumult of history.

Leaving aside his arguments against the pagans and the display of his vast store of cultural knowledge, it is Augustine's story of the two cities that is most pertinent here. He writes as a theologian, not a philosopher or historian. The story he tells begins before time and ends beyond it. In between there is the history of the world and of humankind which, at least for some, is also the history of salvation. Within human history and outside it, there exist two cities formed by two loves: "the earthly [city] by love of self, extending even to contempt of God; the heavenly [city] by love of God extending to contempt of self."[8] Each is a community of angels and humans, united by their loves and their rational natures. The citizens of each city abide in eternity and a portion of each city also dwells for a time as pilgrims in history. The two cities cannot be understood simply as heaven and earth or as spiritual and secular realms within earthly history. Nor can the members of each city who sojourn on earth be known by any but God, who has known them from eternity. Not all in the church are members of the heavenly city, not all outside belong to the earthly. The city of God cannot be identified with any empire or human institution, not even the church.

The distinction of the two cities, explicated at length in book 19, allows Augustine to disentangle the church and Christian hope from the fate of Rome and its empire. Empires come and go; God uses them for God's purposes, which are not frustrated. The church's relationship to the Roman Empire is utilitarian and contingent. The empire is a relative good—a means, not an end; it is a means that itself will end. Because evil and the lust for domination were consequences of the fall, there will always be need of political states to govern the unruly relations of human beings in this world. Augustine's picture of political life is not pretty. Governments are bands of brigands, lacking true justice though enforcing a rough measure of it. They seek peace, even when waging war; they impose order, but with a certain violence endemic to the fallen state of humankind. Their authority comes from God and must be obeyed, except when it threatens true religion. The portions of each city that live in human history benefit from the temporal goods and the ordering functions of government. For the pilgrim city of God, Augustine memorably describes this symbiosis with the state as "mak[ing] use of the peace of Babylon."[9]

Augustine is ambivalent about political life and government, pessimistic or perhaps darkly realistic about human nature and social relations in a fallen world. Yet, well before he wrote book 19 of *City of God*, he had already made a pragmatic decision as bishop to employ the coercive power of the state to end the century-long schism of the Donatist churches in North Africa and compel them to become Catholic Christians. Augustine believed that history's hope and meaning lie beyond itself, outside of time and necessity, hidden in the mysterious purposes of God. Within history, however, he was willing at one crucial juncture to use compromised means to obtain an end he thought consistent with God's providence: correcting errant Christians and unifying the church in North Africa. It would prove to be a fateful precedent.

For later interpreters and historical actors, Augustine's narrative of the two cities would lead to divergent tendencies regarding what might be hoped for or achieved within history. Some concluded that disengagement from, even disdain for the *polis* or the world was the prudent path. Others set out on the way of engagement, even over-engagement, attempting to construct the heavenly city among the kingdoms of earth. Each approach could be cynical in its intent and execution; each could be earnest and in good faith; both could prove dangerous for the social and political life of the human community.

## TRANSITIONS AND TRANSFORMATIONS

As Augustine lay dying in 430, the world he knew was dying with him. The transition from the Roman Empire and late antiquity to the Middle Ages, a period and geography often referred to as "western Christendom," led to new kingdoms and patterns of relationship between church and world. These kingdoms tended to operate on a blend of Eusebian eschatology, in which Christian kings had a religious and political responsibility for the welfare of the church, and a reinterpreted political Augustinianism, which sought to build the city of God in history with the tools of Babylon and Christian faith. Charlemagne built one such empire in the late eighth century. Conflicts between sacral and secular power became regular features of this hybrid model of church and world in the high Middle Ages. As the European nation-states evolved, their interests increasingly conflicted with those of the church and the papacy. The Reformations of the sixteenth century sundered the apparent unity of the churches in the West, and the rise of western democracies in an age of revolution undermined the once-privileged position of religion in a rapidly changing world.

In the face of such disturbing developments, the Catholic Church maintained a continuing preference for monarchy, both among nations and in its institutional life. As the culture of Christendom and the politics of monarchy began to give way before the pressures of modernity, the Catholic Church became, by the middle of the nineteenth century, increasingly defensive in its institutional posture, negative in its evaluation of social and political change, and deeply pessimistic about the prospect that lay before it.[10] Hope for history receded to a distant horizon.

# VATICAN II AND *GAUDIUM ET SPES*

When Pope John XXIII announced in January of 1959 that he would convene an ecumenical council, the Catholic Church was flourishing in most of its historic centers and in so-called mission lands, Europe had made amazing progress rebuilding after the war, and the United States was experiencing a period of unparalleled prosperity, with most of its immigrant Catholic communities on the way toward becoming middle-class and "American." At the same time, political discontent was growing within colonial empires, the poor and disenfranchised were demanding their human dignity and rights, the nuclear arms race was on, the Cold War between communism and democracy was heating up, and the frontiers of space were beginning to open with the launching of the Soviet Union's Sputnik satellite. In the first set of conditions, all seemed right with the world and the church. In the second, the world seemed to be in peril, the church itself overshadowed. What could an ecumenical council of the Catholic Church have to say to either set of realities?

Beginning with John XXIII's opening address at Vatican II and the council's unprecedented *Message to Humanity* that followed shortly thereafter in October of 1962, and culminating in its last and largest document, *Gaudium et Spes*, near the council's close in December of 1965, there was, in truth, much to say.

# Living Hope

In his opening address, Pope John sounded themes that would resonate throughout the council's work. The council was to be pastoral, faithful to tradition while finding a language of faith appropriate to modern thought; in dialogue with the world and attentive to its needs and hopes. In contrast to the "prophets of doom" in his own house, the pope read the signs of the times as a moment of grace, "a new order of human relations" that had within it potential for moving history toward the fulfillment of God's purposes in creation. The council would help the church look to the future without fear. Pope John identified promoting human dignity and pursuing the unity of both the Christian and the human family as central concerns for the church and the council, "in order that the earthly city be brought to the resemblance of the heavenly city."[11] Similar chords were struck in the bishops' message to the world: the council seeks to manifest the face of Christ to the world by attending to the poor and powerless and "fix[ing] a steady gaze on those who still lack the opportunity to achieve a life worthy of human being." The bishops invited all persons to join them "in building up a more just and brotherly city in this world," and they identified two issues of special urgency: peace and social justice. Their hope in Jesus Christ was the source of their desire that "God's kingdom may already shine out on earth in some fashion as a preview of God's eternal kingdom."[12]

These early themes expressed key elements of Vatican II's outlook and intention, and they provided the structure and approach of *Gaudium et Spes*. They stand in sharp contrast to the defensive posture and rejection of modernity so characteristic of nineteenth and early-twentieth-century Catholicism. The Augustinian overtones in the two messages are unmistakable, but their openness to the world signals a new orientation toward history and hope.

The opening words of *Gaudium et Spes* boldly set out the council's stance on the relationship of the church's salvific mission, the profound needs of humanity, and the hope Christians have within and for history: "The joys and hopes, the grief and anguish of the people of our time, especially of those who are poor or afflicted, are the joys and hopes, the grief and anguish of the followers of Christ as well" (1). As it reads the signs of the times, GS connects the needs and aspirations of the human family to the vocation of all women and men to solidarity with each other and ultimately to fullness of life with God. A deep conviction runs throughout: that Christians on pilgrimage to God's kingdom bear a message of salvation for all humanity and are in "solidarity with the human race and its history" (1). Rather than drawing them away from the world and its sorrows, faith immerses them more fully in the world's pain and urgently calls them to serve humankind.

The common humanity and essential equality of all persons made in the image of God are the basis of human dignity. That shared dignity is the foundational reality that orients all relationships and must be respected by, and within, all institutions of human life. Christians share responsibility for making history more human by fashioning a "dwelling place fit for humanity," a world better suited to human dignity (57). GS grounds the church's responsibility to the world in a key insight of *Lumen Gentium* (LG, the Dogmatic Constitution on the Church): the church is the sacrament of unity of the entire human race and a sign of salvation (GS, 42, 45; LG, 1). Without being bound to any human institution, the church makes appropriate use of "temporal realities" (GS, 76) in its service to the world. But it also critiques those realities, as when GS insists that the measure of economic and social life must be the dignity and vocation of the human person (63), that the fundamental equality of all women and men must be respected (29), and that all persons have a right of access to and participation in culture, education, and economic, social, and political life (68). The church also critiques itself, as when GS acknowledges that the church must overcome its own disunity and create within itself "mutual esteem, reverence, and harmony" and "acknowledge all legitimate diversity" if it is to be a sign of unity and a facilitator of dialogue in the world (92).

At times the language of GS seems to equate the earthly city with life on earth, the heavenly city with eternal life, for example, when it refers to Christians as residents of both cities. But in the same section it acknowledges that Christians have a responsibility to history and to their neighbors; neglecting either is to "neglect God himself, and endanger their salvation" (43). Elsewhere it rightly points out that "the earthly and the heavenly city penetrate one another," a mystery that will per-

233

dure until history and time come to an end (40). The continuing reality of sin does not excuse but rather requires Christians to take action for making the world, humankind, and themselves more fully human.

*Gaudium et Spes* is not a perfect document. It was, as the bishops at the council recognized, a new kind of conciliar document—a *pastoral constitution*—and a new way of speaking about the church and the world.[13] In this sense it was the beginning rather than the culmination of a development in the church's life and teaching. That in its final form GS was promulgated as a constitution tied it to the three dogmatic constitutions (on the church, revelation, and liturgy), which, together with GS, were the foundational achievement of Vatican II. The intersecting themes of these four constitutions articulate the council's central vision. Their presence in GS underlines the doctrinal significance of its teaching on the church in the modern world and the principles from which it addresses the urgent issues of the day.

Aspects of GS are dated now simply by its age and era. Its use of the two cities metaphor would benefit from further refinement. Its engagement with the world could be deepened both theologically and practically. There is, nevertheless, much yet to be learned from its efforts to negotiate the relationship of the two cities in the twentieth century and to clarify the church's mission in the world.[14] GS connects the gospel message of eternal life with the human realities of historical life. Furthermore, it always grounds the church's mission of social justice and human solidarity in God's mission to the world through Jesus Christ's life, death, and resurrection, the foundation of Christian faith, hope, and, love.

## HISTORY AND HOPE

Retrieving and re-appropriating *Gaudium et Spes* for today offers hope for church and world. To accomplish this task requires that we look with realism and generosity on the needs and urgent issues of our day, as both Hosffman Ospino's and Andrea Vicini's chapters in this book suggest to us. It especially requires that we focus, with clarity and compassion, on all those who, fifty years after Vatican II, still seek basic human dignity and the means of active participation in making the world "a dwelling place fit for humanity." Taking up this challenge would turn our eyes and hearts outward, to mission rather than maintenance, to hope rather than fear for the future—both of the church and of the world. A faithful and critical retrieval of *Gaudium et Spes* would help us break out of the bleak choices presented by so much religious and political discourse today: a revived political Augustinianism, a new kind of Eusebian theocracy, or a retreat from history. Geopolitically and demographically speaking, neither religious coercion nor return to Christendom is an option. Choosing the mission of God in and for the world, however, *is* an option—for life and for hope. As a sacrament of unity, the church makes the face of Christ known by spreading the fullness of charity everywhere, so the world becomes a humane and peaceful home for the human family, and a sign of its eternal home. The mission of God in Jesus Christ reveals both hope for history and hope for fullness of life and love beyond history.

Retrieving and re-appropriating *Gaudium et Spes* would also illuminate and help renew the church's internal life. By taking steps to embody in its own structures and practices the values of equality, mutuality, and participation that are so essential to human dignity and community, the church would become a more effective sign of the unity and human solidarity it preaches. By valuing and supporting many and diverse forms of discipleship, ministry, service, and mission, it would become a more effective witness to the message of salvation that is its gift to the world.

Returning to the place where this essay began, I would suggest that the vision of *Gaudium et Spes* is clearly evident in the religious life and ministries of the Leadership Conference of Women Religious and the communities of apostolic religious women they represent. Their practice of discipleship and ministry at the margins is an expression of religious life radically rooted in the Christian faith so clearly articulated in GS. Theirs is not the only possible expression of religious life rooted in faith, but it is an authentic one that overcomes the extremes of disengagement or over-engagement with the world. Theirs is a choice for hope: for the mission of God, for the church, and for the life of the world.

Joined with the voices of countless other women and men during these past fifty years, the sisters' hope for history echoes Pope John

# Living Hope

XXIII at the beginning of Vatican II: "The council now beginning rises in the Church like daybreak, a forerunner of most splendid light. It is now only dawn." The fullness of day is yet to come.

## Notes

1. See https://lcwr.org/sites/default/files/news/files/pat_farrell _osf_-_lcwr_presidential_address_2012-_final.pdf. Accessed on September 7, 2012.

2. See http://www.usccb.org/upload/Doctrinal_Assessment_ Leadership_Conference_Women_Religious.pdf. Accessed on September 7, 2012.

3. Karl Rahner, "Toward a Fundamental Theological Interpretation of Vatican II," *Theological Investigations*, vol. 20, trans. E. Quinn (New York: Crossroad, 1986), 83–6.

4. Eusebius, *The History of the Church: From Christ to Constantine*, trans. G. A. Williamson, ed. Andrew Louth, revised edition (London: Penguin, 1989), 8.1. All quotations come from this translation.

5. Books 8–10.

6. Eusebius, *Oration in Praise of Constantine*, trans. Ernest Cushing Richardson, *Nicene and Post-Nicene Fathers*, 2nd series, vol. 1, ed. Philip Schaff and Henry Wace (Buffalo, NY: Christian Literature Publishing Company, 1890). Constantine's attributes, in sequence: 2.4; 1.6, 5.1; 3.5. Available online, revised and edited for New Advent by Kevin Knight, at http://www.newadvent.org/fathers/2504.htm. Accessed on November 6, 2012.

7. Augustine, *The City of God against the Pagans*, ed. and trans. R. W. Dyson (Cambridge: Cambridge University Press, 1998). See Dyson's introduction, p. xiii, for Augustine's description of the contents. All quotations come from this translation.

8. See 14.28.

9. See 19.26.

10. See John O'Malley's lucid discussion of "the long nineteenth century" that, in its influence, extended until the mid-twentieth century: John W. O'Malley, *What Happened at Vatican II* (Cambridge, MA: The Belknap Press of Harvard University Press, 2008), 53–92. Pius IX's *Syllabus of Errors* (1864) is an emblematic text of the time.

11. Pope John XXIII, "Opening Address at Vatican II," *Council Daybook, Vatican II*, sessions 1–4, ed. Floyd Anderson (Washington, DC: National Catholic Welfare Conference, 1965–66), 25–9.

12. "'Message to Humanity' Issued at the Beginning of the Second Vatican Council by its Fathers, with the Endorsement of the Supreme Pontiff" (October 20, 1962), in *The Documents of Vatican II*, ed. Walter M. Abbott, SJ, and Joseph Gallagher (New York: The America Press, 1966), 3–7. It is also available in a Kindle edition.

13. For the development of GS and debates about it at the council, see O'Malley, *What Happened at Vatican II*, at various points in chapters 6 and 7.

14. For a thoughtful assessment see Christine Firer Hinze, "Straining toward Solidarity in a Suffering World: *Gaudium et Spes* 'After Forty Years,'" in *Vatican II: Forty Years Later*, ed. William Madges, Annual Publication of the College Theology Society, 2005, vol. 51 (Maryknoll, NY: Orbis, 2006), 165–95.

# 18

# Epilogue

O ur purpose in writing this book has been to take us all on a journey toward a greater appreciation of God's presence in our experience of hope. This book's journey has been made up of four movements: Grounding, Nurturing, Sustaining, and Living Hope. Each chapter has reflected one of these various movements as an expression of the one invitation that comes to us from the Holy Spirit: to receive hope's gift and choose hope's path; to journey trusting in Jesus' promise of life; to draw confidence from what sustains our hope, even as we must respond to what challenges it; and finally to live on confident in the ways that our hoped-for-future is present now, even though its fullness is still to come.

The movement of hope, as the chapters have portrayed it, not only draws us beyond ourselves, uniting us with the universal hope in the coming fullness of God's reign, it also draws us to recognize that there is hope for those we love and for ourselves. The movement of hope in our lives invites us further: it asks how will we engage in the practice of Christian hope, how will we make hope present in the world we share? Will we be open to the Spirit's call to conversion at the heart of hope? Will we choose to reflect and act on our hopes, so that what is waiting to be born within us can emerge, so that what is yet dormant within our society can begin to bloom? And will we strive to be faithful to the practice of hope when we find ourselves in the midst of experiences that discourage hope?

The seventeenth-century English essayist Francis Bacon described hope as a good breakfast, but a poor dinner, implying that hope could not sustain us, that it could not affect life in the real world. The authors of this book, however, contend that we come to know hope deeply when we practice its movement deliberately, when we accept that change in life—the re-imagining, reframing, and re-conceiving of our lives and our world—is not only possible but necessary. As Daniel Harrington proclaims, "the future is now." Practice hope.

# Select Bibliography

Anderson, Gary. A Time to Mourn, a Time to Dance: The Expression of Grief and Joy in *Israelite Religion*. University Park, PA: Pennsylvania State University Press, 1991.

Aquinas, Thomas. *Summa theologica*, 5 vols. (Allen, TX: Christian Classics, 1981), II–II, qq. 17–22.

Augustine, *City of God*, ed. David Knowles. New York: Penguin Books, 1972.

Barré, Michael. "'Fear of God' and the World View of Wisdom," *Biblical Theology Bulletin* 11 (1981): 41–43.

Beavis, Mary Ann. *Jesus & Utopia: Looking for the Kingdom of God in the Roman World* Minneapolis: Fortress Press, 2006.

Benedict XVI, Pope. *Caritas in veritate*. Papal encyclical of June 29, 2009. http://www.vatican.va/holy_father/benedict_xvi/encyclicals/documents/hf_ben-xvi_enc_20090629_caritas-in-veritate_en.html.

————. *Spe salvi*. Papal encyclical of November 30, 2007. http://www.vatican.va/holy_father/benedict_xvi/encyclicals/documents/hf_ben-xvi_enc_20071130_spesalvi_en.html.

Brueggemann, Walter. *Hope within History*. Atlanta: John Knox Press, 1987.

Bultmann, Rudolf. *Theology of the New Testament*. Vol. 2. Waco, TX: Baylor University Press, 2007.

Byrnes, Michael. *Conformation to the Death of Christ and the Hope of Resurrection: An Exegetico-Theological Study of 2 Corinthians 4, 7–15 and Philippians 3, 7–11*. Tesi Gregoriana Serie Teologia 99. Rome: Gregorian Pontifical University Press, 2003.

Capps, Donald. *Agents of Hope: A Pastoral Psychology*. Eugene, OR: Wipf and Stock, 1995.

Crowley, Paul. *Unwanted Wisdom: Suffering, the Cross, and Hope.* New York: Continuum, 2005.

Daley, Brian. *The Hope of the Early Church: A Handbook of Patristic Eschatology.* Cambridge: Cambridge University Press, 1991.

de Shazer, Steve and Yvonne Dolan, *More than Miracles: The State of the Art of Solution-Focused-Brief-Therapy.* Binghampton, NY: Haworth Press, 2007.

Doyle, Dominic. *The Promise of Christian Humanism: Thomas Aquinas on Hope* (New York: Crossroad, 2012).

Dykstra, Robert C. *Counseling Troubled Youth.* Louisville: Westminster/John Knox Press, 1997.

Ellacuría, Ignacio and Sobrino, Jon, eds., *Mysterium Liberationis: Fundamental Concepts of Liberation Theology*, Maryknoll, NY: Orbis, 1993.

Farley, Wendy. *Tragic Vision and Divine Compassion: A Contemporary Theodicy.* Louisville: Westminster John Knox, 1990.

Greer, Rowan. *Christian Life and Christian Hope: Raids on the Inarticulate.* New York: Crossroad, 2001.

Gutiérrez, Gustavo. *A Theology of Liberation: History, Politics, and Salvation*, trans. Caridad Inda and John Eagleson. Maryknoll, NY: Orbis, 1973.

Hagan, Jacqueline Maria, *Migration Miracle: Faith, Hope, and Meaning on the Undocumented Journey.* Cambridge, MA: Harvard University Press, 2008.

Harrington, Daniel J. *What Are We Hoping For? New Testament Images.* Collegeville, MN: Liturgical Press, 2006.

————. *Why Do We Hope? Images in the Psalms.* Collegeville, MN: Liturgical Press, 2008.

Harrington, Wilfrid J. "Paul's Word of Hope." *Scripture in Church* 31 (2001): 249–56.

Hayes, Zachary. *A Vision of the Future: A Study of Christian Eschatology.* Collegeville, MN: Liturgical Press, 1990.

Heil, John Paul. *Romans: Paul's Letter of Hope.* Analecta Biblica 112. Rome: Pontifical Biblical Institute, 1987.

John Paul II, Pope. *Sollicitudo rei socialis*, papal encyclical of December 30, 1987. http://www.vatican.va/holy_father/john_paul_ii/encyclicals/documents/hf_jp-ii_enc_30121987_sollicitudo-rei-socialis_en.html.

Keenan, James F. *Moral Wisdom: Lessons and Texts from the Catholic Tradition.* 2nd ed. Lanham, MD: Rowman & Littlefield, 2010.

Kelly, Anthony. *Eschatology and Hope.* Maryknoll, NY: Orbis Books, 2006.

Kerwin, Donald and Jill Marie Gerschutz, eds., *And You Welcomed Me: Migration and Catholic Social Teaching.* Lanham, MD: Lexington Books, 2009.

Keshgegian, Flora. *Time for Hope: Practices for Living in Today's World.* New York: Continuum, 2006.

Kim Berg, Insoo and Yvonne Dolan, *Tales of Solutions: A Collection of Hope-Inspiring Stories* New York: W. W. Norton, 2001.

Kotva, Joseph J., Jr. *The Christian Case for Virtue Ethics.* Moral Traditions & Moral Arguments. ed. James F. Keenan. Washington, DC: Georgetown University Press, 1996.

Lamoureux, Patricia, and Paul J. Wadell. *The Christian Moral Life: Faithful Discipleship for a Global Society.* Theology in Global Perspective Series. Maryknoll, NY: Orbis Books, 2010.

Lennan, Richard. "The Church as a Sacrament of Hope," *Theological Studies* 72 (2011): 247–74.

Levenson, Jon D. *Creation and the Persistence of Evil: The Jewish Drama of Divine Omnipotence.* Princeton, NJ: Princeton University Press, 1994.

Lynch, William. *Images of Hope: Imagination as Healer of the Hopeless.* Baltimore: Helicon, 1965. Republished Notre Dame, IN: University of Notre Dame Press, 1974.

May, Gerald G. *Addiction and Grace: Love and Spirituality in the Healing of Addictions.* San Francisco: Harper & Row, 1988.

Metz, Johann Baptist. *Poverty of Spirit.* New York: Paulist Press, 1998.

Moltmann, Jürgen. *The Coming of God: Christian Eschatology.* Minneapolis: MN: Fortress, 1996.

————. *Ethics of Hope.* Minneapolis: Fortress Press, 2012.

————. *Theology of Hope: On the Ground and the Implications of a Christian Eschatology.* Translated by James W. Leitch. Minneapolis: Fortress Press, 1967.

Niebuhr, Reinhold. *Moral Man and Immoral Society.* New York: Charles Scribner's Sons, 1932.

O'Malley, John W. *What Happened at Vatican II.* Cambridge, MA: The Belknap Press of Harvard University Press, 2008.

Ospino, Hosffman, ed., *Hispanic Ministry in the Twenty-First Century: Present and Future.* Miami, FL: Convivium Press, 2010.

Pieper, Josef. *On Hope*. San Francisco: Ignatius, 1986.

Pineda-Madrid, Nancy. *Suffering and Salvation in Ciudad Juárez*. Minneapolis, MN: Fortress Press, 2011.

Pontifical Council for the Pastoral Care of Migrants and Itinerant People, *Erga Migrantes Caritas Christi*. Vatican City, 2004.

Rahner, Karl. "On the Theology of Hope," *Theological Investigations* (vol. 10), trans. David Bourke (New York: Crossroad, 1977), 242–59.

Ratzinger, Joseph. *Eschatology, Death, and Eternal Life*. Washington, DC: Catholic University of America Press, 1988.

————. *The Yes of Jesus Christ: Spiritual Exercises in Faith, Hope, and Love* (New York: Crossroad, 2005).

Rausch, Thomas P. *Eschatology, Liturgy, and Christology: Toward Recovering an Eschatological Imagination*, Collegeville, MN: Liturgical Press, 2012.

Sachs, John R. *The Christian Vision of Humanity: Basic Christian Anthropology*. Collegeville, MN: Liturgical Press, 1991.

Sobrino, Jon. *No Salvation Outside the Poor: Prophetic-Utopian Essays*. Maryknoll, NY: Orbis, 2008.

————. *The Principle of Mercy: Taking the Crucified People from the Cross*, 1992, trans. Various (Maryknoll, NY: Orbis Books, 1994).

Stuhlmacher, Peter. "Eschatology and Hope in Paul." *Evangelical Quarterly* 72 (2000): 315–33.

Teilhard de Chardin, Pierre. *The Divine Milieu*. New York: Harper and Row, 1960.

Townes, Emilie M. ed., *Embracing the Spirit: Womanist Perspectives on Hope, Salvation, and Transformation*. Maryknoll, NY: Orbis, 1997.

Tracy, David. *Plurality and Ambiguity: Hermeneutics, Religion, Hope*. San Francisco, CA: Harper & Row, 1987.

Underhill, Evelyn. *Practical Mysticism*. Guildford, Surrey: Eagle, 1991.

Vogt, Christopher P. Patience, *Compassion, Hope, and the Christian Art of Dying Well*. Lanham, MD: Rowman & Littlefield, 2004.

Volf, Miroslav and William Katerberg, eds. *The Future of Hope: Christian Tradition Amid Modernity and Postmodernity*. Grand Rapids, MI: Eerdmans, 2004.

von Balthasar, Hans Urs. *Dare We Hope "That All Men Be Saved"? With a Short Discourse on Hell*. San Francisco, CA: Ignatius Press, 1988.

Wainwright, Geoffrey. *Eucharist and Eschatology*, London: Epworth, 1971.

# Contributors

The authors are members of the faculty of the School of Theology and Ministry at Boston College.

**John F. Baldovin, SJ,** is a member of the New York Province of the Society of Jesus. He has taught at Fordham, Notre Dame, and the Jesuit School of Theology at Berkeley. He has also served as president of the North American Academy of Liturgy and the international ecumenical *Societas Liturgica*. He was a member of the advisory committee and translations committee of ICEL from 1994–2003. His latest book is *Reforming the Liturgy: A Response to the Critics* (Liturgical Press, 2008).

**Dominic Doyle** studied theology at Cambridge University, then, after two years of teaching literature and history at an international school in Sri Lanka, he moved to Boston for graduate studies at Harvard University and Boston College. His research interests include theological anthropology and philosophical theology, with a particular interest in Thomas Aquinas. Having just completed his first book, *The Promise of Christian Humanism: Thomas Aquinas on Hope* (Crossroad, 2011), he is working on a book on the theological virtues and positive psychology.

**Francine Cardman** teaches historical theology and church history, with a focus on Christianity in late antiquity. She is particularly interested in the relationship of faith and praxis in the development of early Christian ethics. She has published essays and articles on early Christian theology, the ministry and leadership of women in early Christianity, Augustine's praxis of ecclesiology, ecumenical theology, and the Second Vatican Council. She has also translated Augustine's commentary on the Sermon on the Mount.

**Christopher Frechette, SJ,** is assistant professor of Old Testament. He holds a Licentiate in Sacred Theology from the Weston Jesuit School of Theology and a doctorate from Harvard University. He conducts research in biblical interpretation and in the cultural and historical background of the Bible. He is especially interested in ideas and practices that address divine-human relationships in light of suffering, loss, and trauma.

**Colleen M. Griffith,** Associate Professor of the Practice of Theology, works at the intersection of theology and spirituality. Her writing and research interests lie in the areas of theological anthropology, historical and contemporary spirituality, and method in practical theology. Her most recent publication is *Catholic Spiritual Practices: A Treasury Old and New*, co-edited with her husband Thomas H. Groome. Griffith's *Prophetic Witness: Catholic Women's Strategies for Reform* received a 2010 first place award from the Catholic Press Association.

**Thomas H. Groome** teaches and writes on the history, theory, and practice of religious education and practical theology. His principal publications are *Christian Religious Education* (Harper and Row, 1980), *Sharing Faith* (HarperCollins, 1991), *Educating for Life* (Crossroad, 1998), *What Makes Us Catholic?* (HarperCollins, 2002). His most recent book is *Will There Be Faith?* (HarperCollins, 2011). His writings have appeared in many languages including Mandarin and Korean. He has been teaching at Boston College for thirty-seven years.

**Daniel J. Harrington, SJ,** has been editor of New Testament Abstracts since 1972. He is a past president of the Catholic Biblical Association of America (1985–86), and is the author of more than fifty books, the most recent of which is *Witnesses to the Word: New Testament Studies Since Vatican II* (Paulist Press, 2012). His academic specializations include early Jewish writings (including the Dead Sea scrolls) and New Testament interpretation and application.

**Philip Browning Helsel** is an ordained minister of Word and Sacrament in the Presbyterian Church (USA). He earned a doctorate in pastoral theology and a master of divinity degree from Princeton Theological Seminary. His work has centered on care of the dying, grief and care-giving, and the sociology of family. He has served as a chaplain in psychiatric hospitals, general hospitals, and hospice settings. He has been published in numerous journals.

**Richard Lennan,** a priest of the diocese of Maitland–Newcastle (Australia), focuses his research and teaching on ecclesiology. He is the author of *The Ecclesiology of Karl Rahner* (Oxford University Press, 1995) and *Risking the Church: The Challenges of Catholic Faith* (Oxford University Press, 2004). He has also edited three books and published articles on ecclesiology and the theology of ministry. From 2005–07, he served as president of the Australian Catholic Theological Association.

**Thomas Massaro, SJ,** is a Jesuit of the New England Province. He received his doctorate in 1997 from Emory University and taught at Weston Jesuit School of Theology in Cambridge, Massachusetts, and the School of Theology and Ministry at Boston College. In 2012, he became dean of the Jesuit School of Theology (Berkeley) of Santa Clara University. His teaching and research interests include Catholic social thought, church and state issues, and economic justice and public policy.

**Christopher R. Matthews,** editor of New Testament Abstracts and Research Professor of New Testament, received his doctoral degree from Harvard in 1993. The author of *Philip: Apostle and Evangelist: Configurations of a Tradition* (2002), he recently collaborated with François Bovon on a translation of the early Christian apocryphal text the *Acts of Philip* (Baylor University Press, 2012). He also serves as Editor-in-Chief of the online resource Oxford Bibliographies: Biblical Studies.

**Hosffman Ospino,** Ph.D., is an Assistant Professor of Hispanic Ministry and Religious Education. His research and writings explore the relationship between faith and culture and the impact of this relationship on Christian ministerial and educational practices. Dr. Ospino is the Principal Investigator for the 2011–13 National Study of Catholic Parishes with Hispanic Ministry. He is the editor of *Hispanic Ministry in the 21st Century: Present and Future* (Convivium Press, 2010).

**Nancy Pineda-Madrid,** Associate Professor of Theology and Latino/a Ministry, holds a Ph.D. in Systematic and Philosophical Theology from the Graduate Theological Union. Her recent book, *Suffering and Salvation in Ciudad Juárez* (Fortress Press, 2011), addresses the tragic killing of women, the resistance to this evil, and its theological lessons. She has authored more than twenty articles and is writing a book on La Virgen de Guadalupe. In 2012, she received the Loretto Legacy Award for Religion and Theology.

**John R. Sachs, SJ,** received his doctorate from the University of Tübingen and has been teaching systematic theology since 1984. The author of *The Christian Vision of Humanity: Basic Christian Anthropology* (Liturgical Press, 1991), his articles on theology and spirituality have appeared in *Theological Studies, Gregorianum, Concilium, The Month, and Supplement to the Way.* He has been a retreat and spiritual director for over thirty-five years and is active in pastoral ministry in the Boston area.

**Thomas D. Stegman, SJ,** is a Jesuit from the Wisconsin Province. His research and writing focus on Paul's letters and Pauline theology. He is author of *The Character of Jesus: The Linchpin to Paul's Argument in 2 Corinthians* (Pontifical Biblical Institute, 2005) and *Second Corinthians* (Baker Academic, 2009). He is currently working on *Holy Ones, Called to Be Holy,* a book on Pauline spirituality to be published by Paulist Press.

**O. Ernesto Valiente** is a native of El Salvador. His theological concentrations include Christology, soteriology, political theology, and Latin American liberation theology. He is currently working on a monograph titled "Following Jesus from Conflict to Communion: A Liberationist Approach to Reconciliation," which explores the contribution of contemporary liberation theology to the quest for social reconciliation. He lives in Watertown, Massachusetts, with his wife, Kari, and his daughter, Hannah.

**Andrea Vicini, SJ, MD,** has a Ph.D. in theological ethics from Boston College and an S.T.D. from the Faculty of Theology of Southern Italy. His research focuses on fundamental moral theology, bioethics, sexuality, medical ethics, and environmental issues. Among his recent publications are *Genetica umana e bene comune* (2008); "Bioethics: Basic Questions and Extraordinary Developments," in *Theological Studies* (2012); and "New Insights in Environmental and Sustainable Ethics," in *Asian Horizons* (2012).

# Scripture Index

# Hope

# Subject and Author Index